D0859983

SIX MEMOS FROM THE LAST MILLENNIUM

EXPLORING JEWISH ARTS AND CULTURE
Robert H. Abzug, Series Editor
Director of the Schusterman Center for Jewish Studies

Jews in the realms of the arts and culture have imagined extraordinary worlds and shaped dominant cultures in ways that are only now being fully recognized and studied. The books in this series, produced by established scholars and artists, will further this revelation and make substantive contributions to both scholarly and public understandings of art, drama, literature, photography, film, dance, music, foodways, cultural studies, and other expressions of humanity as filtered through the Jewish experience, both secular and religious.

Six Memos FROM THE Last Millennium

A NOVELIST READS THE TALMUD

By Joseph Skibell

University of Texas Press
Austin

Copyright © 2016 by Joseph Skibell
All rights reserved
Printed in the United States of America
First edition, 2016

Requests for permission to reproduce material from this work should be
sent to:
    Permissions
    University of Texas Press
    P.O. Box 7819
    Austin, TX 78713-7819
    http://utpress.utexas.edu/index.php/rp-form

⊗ The paper used in this book meets the minimum requirements of
ANSI/NISO Z39.48-1992 (R1997) (Permanence of Paper).

LIBRARY OF CONGRESS CATALOGUING-IN-PUBLICATION DATA

Skibell, Joseph, author.
    Six memos from the last millennium : a novelist reads the Talmud / by
Joseph Skibell. — First edition.
        pages   cm — (Exploring Jewish arts and culture)
    ISBN 978-1-4773-0734-2 (cloth : alk. paper)
    ISBN 978-1-4773-0735-9 (library e-book)
    ISBN 978-1-4773-0736-6 (non-library e-book)
1. Talmud—Biography.   2. Tannaim—Biography.   3. Amoraim—
Biography.   I. Title.   II. Series : Exploring Jewish arts and culture.
    BM501.15.S55   2016
    296.1′20092—dc23
    [B]   2015020373

doi: 10.7560/307342

For my uncle
Richard Skibell
and in memory of my uncles
Leslie Lezan
Bernard Skibell
and
David Skibell

לכה דודי נצא השדה.
שיר השירים -- ז:יב

CONTENTS

A NOTE ON THE TITLE

ITALO CALVINO SPENT THE BETTER PART OF 1985 PRE-paring to deliver the Charles Eliot Norton Lectures at Harvard. The great Italian novelist died before he could present his talks, and though he'd completed only five of the six lectures he had planned, the work was published the following year under its intended title, *Six Memos for the Next Millennium*.

According to the Hebrew calendar—which, unlike its Gregorian counterpart, moves in only one direction—the current year is 5776. In other words: we're deep into the sixth millennium.

The Talmud was closed, by its editors, around 4235 (475 CE), and with Calvino in mind—his playful erudition has long been a beacon for me—I've come to think of the stories I discuss in this book as memos from an unnamed writer working in the hinge-time between the fourth and fifth millennia.

Hence: *Six Memos from the Last Millennium*.

And in deference to the tradition created unintentionally by Calvino—a cosmicomic baker's half-dozen in reverse: five pieces for the price of six—I've included only five chapters here.

ACKNOWLEDGMENTS

AS I WAS FINISHING THIS BOOK, I WAS STRUCK BY how many friends said to me, "Yeah, you were working on that when I met you." It has been over a decade since I made the commitment to live with these stories. I'm grateful for the friends, relatives, students, and colleagues with whom I've studied and explored these tales, in conversation, in a private study group, and in classes at Emory University, the Michener Center for Writers at the University of Texas, Congregation Agudas Achim in Austin, and the Young Israel of Toco Hills. Their insights have deepened my appreciation and understanding of these texts. Arthur Kurzweil gave me the right words of encouragement at exactly the right time, and Andrea Cohen-Kiener, the book's first reader, buoyed the project up with her enthusiasm, as did Reuven Travis. Karmi Ingber generously offered a comprehensive critique. (All errors in the texts, of course, are mine.) I'm grateful also to Robert H. Abzug, its second reader and its guardian angel, and to Jim Burr and Dave Hamrick at UT Press for taking a chance on a book that doesn't easily fit into any publishing category. The Bill and Carol Fox Center for Humanistic Inquiry provided me with the time and the quiet in which to prepare the final drafts. Arianna Skibell, a generous and talented editor, is a constant source of inspiration for me, and I'm especially grateful to Barbara Freer Skibell, who has spent as many years living with these stories as I have. Her fine mind, her open heart, and her questing spirit inform every page.

xiii

A NOVELIST READS THE TALMUD
AN INTRODUCTION

ONE EVENING, I WENT TO MY TALMUD CLASS. IT WASN'T
a large class, maybe four or five men, but that night, for whatever
reason, I was the only student there. I'd come to the study of Talmud relatively late in life, beginning in my mid-thirties. The Judaism I'd been served up as a kid had been a pretty thin gruel, and I
spent most of my young adult life looking for wisdom elsewhere:
in literature and art, in rock 'n' roll, in Eastern and Western phi-
losophy, in mythology, in depth psychology.

Despite the richness I found in each of these, my hunger for
meaning persisted, and—naïvely perhaps—I approached the Talmud, the repository of thousands of years of ancient wisdom, as
a seeker might, crossing into its sacred precincts with the hope
of finding a kind of livable transcendence there, a way of fusing
the mundane hours of earthly life with a cosmic sense of holiness
and wonder.

I was particularly interested in the stories—the anecdotes,
allegories, fables, legends, and tall tales—in the Talmud's five
thousand–plus pages. As a novelist, I spend my days steeped in
stories. Stories are the doorway into meaning for me, the royal
road into consciousness. Sacred stories even more so, I thought.
My teachers, however, either skipped over these tales or sprinted
past them quickly, and certainly they received none of the time
and attention, the almost scientific dissection, we gave, as a class,
to the Talmud's legal arguments.

I didn't share my teachers' reluctance to linger in these parts
of the text, and I devised my own plan to study them. I decided to
move through *Ein Ya'akov (The Well of Jacob)*, the volume in which
these stories are collected, starting with the section of the Talmud
we were then studying in class. (The Talmud's 517 chapters are
collected in 30-some sections usually called tractates in English.)
The tractate was *Bava Kamma (The First Gate)*, and the first story
that piqued my interest there concerned a figure named Ulla.

According to the story, when the daughter of a Babylonian rabbi dies, his colleagues decide to pay him a condolence call. They invite Ulla along, but Ulla will have none of it.

"What does your Babylonian method of consolation have to do with me?" he says to them. "It's completely blasphemous! When you all make a condolence call, you say, 'What can be done?'—meaning 'What can be done against the will of the Holy One?'—suggesting that if something *could* be done, you'd do it; and what is more blasphemous than that?"

Instead Ulla visits Rav Samuel on his own. Offering words of consolation, he quotes an oddly chosen passage from the Torah, reminding the bereaved father that "The Holy One said to Moses: 'Do not oppress Moab and do not wage war against them.'"

Now, if these words seem far from the point to the grieving father, it doesn't matter. Ulla is happy to elaborate upon them, and he sketches out a complicated argument involving the ancient Hebrew wars and the messianic future, and conversations between the Holy One and his prophet Moses, before arriving at his conclusion: "Were your daughter righteous and worthy of righteous descendants, she would have been spared."

I turned the page to read the conclusion of the story, but it ended there.

A STRANGE STORY by any stretch of the imagination.

Ulla, whoever he is—and all we know about him at this point is that he is not living, with his rabbinical colleagues, in Babylonia—refuses to join the local rabbis in paying a condolence call. Rejecting as blasphemous what we might understand as an expression of helpless compassion—*What can be done?*—Ulla visits Rav Samuel alone and essentially tells the poor man to look on the bright side: in the light of true piety, the death of this daughter is no great tragedy, and here is the sacred verse to prove it.

In the original Aramaic, with its Hebrew quotations from the Bible, the story is barely 150 words long. Still, it paints an evocative scene, its power deriving principally, I thought, from the extreme states of its protagonists: grief in the case of Rav Samuel, unyielding theological principle in Ulla's. Beyond this, though, the story supplies the reader with little help in its own decipherment.

In what at first blush appears to be a grand failure of imagination, our anonymous author doesn't even sketch in Rav Samuel's response. Though Rav Samuel's silence and Ulla's unchecked speech create in the reader an expectation of a dramatic reversal, that reversal never comes, and we're left on our own to imagine Rav Samuel's reaction, one that might fall anywhere along a broad spectrum of possibilities.

Missing, too, is the rabbis' response to Ulla's snub, a detail that might otherwise orient us within the moral geography of the story, although we can assume that no religious leader—certainly not one acting in accordance with the behavior of his peers—enjoys being charged with blasphemy.

On the other hand, great spiritual teachings are often counterintuitive and difficult to appreciate. Strip the story of its rabbinic inflections, substitute for Ulla the name Coyote or that of any other trickster figure, and it's not hard to read it as a mind-stopping parable of nonattachment or Zen-like acceptance of life on its own terms.

Is Ulla a theological clown—in other words, are we meant to laugh at his antics? Or an unfeeling boor—should his treatment of Rav Samuel fill us with indignation? Or is he, perhaps, an enlightened master?

THESE QUESTIONS WERE very much on my mind when I arrived at my class and found myself the only student there. I mentioned the story of Ulla to my teacher. I told him that I'd begun reading the Talmudic tales, and that this story had me stymied right at the start.

"So you want to know what the story's about?" he said. "Well, since you're the only one here tonight, why don't we spend our class time looking into it?"

I followed him to the bookshelf, where he took down an exceedingly large volume of *Bava Kamma*. "This has all the notes in the bottom margin," he told me. "That's how we rabbis pretend to know everything." He opened the book and searched for the correct page. "Okay, here we go."

He sat at the table, the enormous book open before him, skimming through the story, while I sat expectantly at his elbow. He turned the page, twisting his beard in his fist. He turned back to the page before. He read the notes in the bottom margin. Finally, he slammed the book shut.

"Yeah, I have no idea," he said.

I TURNED NEXT to the classical commentators. Perhaps they might shed some light on this curious tale, but their commentaries, concerned principally with the application of sacred law, seem little interested in the character dynamics and the possible comic or tragic implications of Ulla's boorishness. Instead, they argue over the appropriate way of consoling a mourner.

Maybe reading the story in context, I thought, would help me understand it.

Along with the Bible, the Talmud is one of the foundation texts of Rabbinic Judaism. An ancient code of philosophical jurisprudence, it comprises two essential parts, the Mishnah and the Gemara. According to tradition, the Mishnah was revealed by the Holy One to Moses at Mount Sinai as an oral law accompanying and clarifying the written law, the Torah. One rabbinic legend asserts that the Holy One dictated the Torah to Moses by day and explained it to him by night.

This explanation is the Mishnah.

Passed down orally from generation to generation, the Mishnah was put into writing only around the year 3960 (200 CE) when, in the wake of persecution and exile, it was feared the oral teachings might be lost.

The Gemara, the other half of the Talmud, is a multigenerational metacommentary on the Mishnah dating from between 3960 and 4260 (200 and 500 CE).

I'm oversimplifying—a dangerous thing to do with a text as polymorphously diverse as the Talmud—but it seems to me that the Talmud weaves together three braided strands: the legal, the philosophical, and the legendary. The wide-ranging legal discussions of the rabbinic sages—known, in Hebrew, as the *Halakhah* (or the *Way*)—fill about three-fourths of the Talmud's five thousand–plus pages, and the *Aggadah* (literally, the *Telling*, the philosophical and legendary parts) the remaining fourth.

Among that fourth, salt-and-peppered into the text, sometimes in the Mishnah, sometimes in the Gemara, are stories about the lives of the sages, the holy men and mystics, who take part in the Talmud's theo-legal discussions.

(Imagine if, sprinkled within their legal decisions and dissenting opinions, the Justices of the US Supreme Court included anecdotes about their sex lives, allegorical fables about their travels, tall tales about their encounters with figures from American history—Abe Lincoln, Thomas Edison, Ethel and Julius Rosenberg—and even their conversations with God, and you'll have some idea of the warp and weave of the Talmud.)

Though modern scholars may argue vehemently over the precise literary structures of the Talmud, there's a working assumption, although it might not always be clear how, that a piece of the Gemara is related thematically to the part of the Mishnah it intends to illuminate.

One might therefore assume that reading the story of Ulla and Rav Samuel in the context of its placement in the Talmud might reveal something about the story's deeper meaning. Doing so, though, only raised more questions than it answered.

Ulla's story appears in a part of the Talmud concerned with cases of damages, specifically with goring oxen across social classes (i.e., what happens when an ordinary Israelite's ox gores an ox belonging to the Temple or when an Israelite's ox gores the ox of a Canaanite).

NOW I WAS more confused than ever.

Are the Talmud's editors hinting, subtly or unsubtly, that Ulla is the social equivalent of a goring ox? Is his story an example of violent speech? Or is his refraining from blasphemy the opposite of violent speech? Will he be rewarded by Heaven for how he speaks to Rav Samuel or rather denied a reward for it?

In either case, I was no closer to answering the fundamental questions the story presents, not as part of a legal discussion, but as a *meaningful fiction*: Who is Ulla? Is he a hero or a villain? Should we, his audience, applaud his refraining from blasphemies, or is his worldview, when the rubber meets the road, as absurd and as cruel as it, at first blush, seems?

And finally: what do we learn about the world and ourselves from this sacred fiction?

FOLLOWING ULLA DOWN the rabbit hole, I began pulling together as many stories as I could find concerning him, and I discovered a curious thing. As a literary figure—as a figure made out of words (who can vouch for the historical man?)—Ulla seems to possess a small number of traits and a distinct personality, and he appears to be involved in a single story, a single drama concerning his trip from the Land of Israel to Babylonia, a drama that ends with his tragicomic death.

And drama is the correct word.

These tales—though often anecdotal and fragmentary—are unvaryingly dramatic in form. Like a stage play, they're written as scenes, playing out in an eternal present tense; the characters, lacking almost all interiority, must speak their rare private thoughts aloud in soliloquies; the narrator, employing the simplest of voices and vocabularies, restricts himself almost always, as a playwright does in his stage directions, to things that can be seen or heard; the scenes adhere to the classical unities of time, place, and action, as well.

As I plunged into these tales, I began to wonder, what mosaics would appear if the various scenes—scattered in so many pieces across the Talmud and the midrashic literature—were brought together? Would they form a larger drama, a greater narrative with consistent characters, a sustained storyline, and a coherent system of imagery?

This seemed to be the case, and I seemed at last to have found the key to unlocking the door into these tales, at least for me. In the years I've spent studying and teaching these stories, I've discovered that obscure elements in one fragmentary scene often illuminate elements in another, revealing a veritable rabbinical *comédie humaine*, replete with every recognizable type and variation of *Homo spiritus*.

Sometimes wild, sometimes rude, sometimes bawdy, though employing simple means, these are not simple stories. Like much ancient sacred literature, they often fly in the face of our conventional notions of piety. The holy men depicted in the Talmudic tales are clearly holy. No one is disputing that. According to tradition, to even be mentioned in the Talmud, one had to be able to raise the dead. Still, the saints and sages in these stories are often depicted as flawed and tragic figures, only-too-human, after all, despite their high attainments in the sacred spheres. This is only right, I think, and honest. In the rabbinic imagination, the creation of holiness is a human, and not a superhuman, endeavor. As the poet Wallace Stevens reminds us, the way through the world is more difficult to find than the way beyond it. And one can learn as much if not more, I suspect, from a great person's flaws than from his accomplishments.

RABBINIC COMMENTATORS FROM the Middle Ages to the present hour, reading these stories primarily as history, have tended to explain away the miracles, the unrealism, the fantastical elements, while bowdlerizing the morally difficult and bawdy parts. Modern academic scholars, on the other end of the spectrum, though unafraid to take the unvarnished measure of these tales, are seldom concerned—professionally at least—with the question of how these stories speak to the reader's most pressing human needs.

A novelist, however, is able to live in the vale between these two opposing and imposing camps. An imaginative writer's concerns are different. A storyteller is interested in the arresting, the stirring, the provocative; with what lifts the heart, quickens the pulse, and stirs the soul. Literature, after all, is meant to transform us, sacred literature even more, and so why not analyze and interpret these stories as a novelist would? They're fictions, after all, though fictions in the most profound sense of the word. They work the same way profound fiction works: while delighting us through our childlike love of stories, they attempt to express something essential about human life.

The chapters that follow are an imaginative and personal response to this sacred literature. My readings of these tales are, I know, wildly subjective, idiosyncratic, and far from definitive. These stories seem inexhaustible to me, and I know my interpretations, no matter how full, can only be partial.

Still, I've done my best to explore these stories as deeply as possible, to shine some light on this brilliant, beautiful, and strange body of literature, and to contribute whatever I can to the discovery and recovery of the beauty and depth they offer us as meaningful fictions.

ONE FINAL NOTE: As I said earlier, I've come to think of these stories, as an imaginative conceit, as memos from an unnamed writer, an Aggadist, a master of *Aggadah*, a teller of tales, working in the hinge-time between the fourth and fifth millennia on the Hebrew calendar. Each of the following chapters is preceded by the memo, the story under discussion, unadorned by commentary, so that the reader may encounter it in its original state.

TIMELINE OF RELEVANT EVENTS,
ACCORDING TO RABBINIC TRADITION

Hebrew Calendar	Event	Common Era
1	Creation of the World	-3760
930	Death of Adam	-2831
1056	Birth of Noah	-2705
1656	Great Flood Covers the Earth	-2105
1948	Birth of Abraham	-1813
2048	Birth of Isaac	-1713
2084	Akedah: "Sacrifice" of Isaac	-1677
2108	Birth of Jacob and Esau	-1653
2238	Jacob and Family Go to Egypt	-1523
2332	Egyptian Enslavement Begins	-1429
2448	Exodus from Egypt Revelation at Mt. Sinai	-1313
2488	Death of Moses Children of Israel Enter Canaan	-1273
2892	David Becomes King	-869
2924	Solomon Becomes King	-837
2935	First Temple Completed	-826
3338	First Temple Destroyed	-423
3339	Babylonian Exile	-423
3412	Second Temple Completed	-349
3413	Ezra Leads the Return from Exile	-348
3622	Second Temple Rededicated	-139
3700	Romans Gain Control of Judea	-61
3829	Second Temple Destroyed	69
3949	Mishnah Compiled	189
c. 4160	Jerusalem Talmud Complete	c. 400
4235	Babylonian Talmud Complete	475

SIX MEMOS FROM THE LAST MILLENNIUM

Rabbi Yohanan (died c. 4040/279 CE) and Rabbi Shimon ben Lakish (c. 4010–4060/ second half of second century CE)

LET ONE WHO WISHES TO SEE THE BEAUTY OF RABBI Yohanan take a silver chalice as it emerges from the silversmith's furnace. Let him fill it with red pomegranate seeds and encircle its brim with a garland of red roses. Let him place it half in sun and half in shade. Its lustrous glow will be an approximation of Rabbi Yohanan's beauty.

One day, Rabbi Yohanan was bathing in the Jordan. Resh Lakish saw him and jumped into the Jordan after him. Rabbi Yohanan said to him, "Your strength belongs to Torah!" Resh Lakish said to him, "Your beauty belongs to women!" He said to him, "If you repent, I will wed you to my sister who is even more beautiful than I." He accepted these conditions upon himself, but when he tried to jump back and collect his clothes, he could not do so, because his strength was depleted. Afterwards, Rabbi Yohanan taught him Scripture and Mishnah and made him into a great man.

One day, the sages in the House of Study were divided over the following question: at what point in their manufacture are a sword, a knife, a dagger, a spear, a handsaw, and a scythe susceptible to ritual uncleanness? The answer first suggested was: when their manufacture is finished. But when is their manufacture finished? Rabbi Yohanan said, "After they have been tempered in a furnace." Resh Lakish said, "Only after they've been quenched in water." Rabbi Yohanan said, "A robber knows well the tools of his trade." Resh Lakish said, "What benefit have you bestowed upon me? There, they called me Master; and here, they call me Master." Rabbi Yohanan said, "I brought you under the wings of the Shekinah." Rabbi Yohanan was mortified by the sharpness of the exchange, and Resh Lakish fell ill.

His sister came and wept before Rabbi Yohanan, pleading: "Forgive him for the sake of my children." Rabbi Yohanan replied, "Leave your fatherless children with me, and I shall rear them." "For the sake of my widowhood then!" He said to her, "Let your widows rely on me." After that Rabbi Shimon ben Lakish died, and Rabbi Yohanan grieved for him considerably.

The sages said, "Who will go and ease his mind? Let Rabbi Elazar ben Pedat go, for his scholarship is brilliant." Rabbi Elazar ben Pedat went and sat before Rabbi Yohanan, and to everything Rabbi Yohanan said, Rabbi Elazar observed, "There is a statement that supports your position." "You're supposed to be like bar Lakisha? With bar Lakisha, when I stated a matter, he would raise twenty-four objections, which I responded to with twenty-four rebuttals, and as a result of this give-and-take, the matter became clear, and *you* say, 'There's a statement that supports your position' as if I didn't know on my own that what I said is right?" Rabbi Yohanan stood and tore his clothes in mourning. Dissolving into tears, he cried out, "Where are you, bar Lakisha? Where are you, bar Lakisha?" screaming until his sanity wore away.

The sages prayed for mercy on his behalf and he died.

BABYLONIAN TALMUD, TRACTATE *BAVA METZIA* 84A.

Chapter 1

Eros and Alchemy in the Waters of the Jordan

RABBI YOHANAN IS, BY HIS OWN ADMISSION, ONE OF the beautiful people of Jerusalem, perhaps even the last surviving remnant of that beauty. Descended from Joseph (in the Book of Genesis), he is, like Joseph, an extraordinarily handsome man, so handsome, in fact, he makes a practice of sitting outside the women's bath, and when the daughters of Israel emerge, cleansed in preparation for joining with their husbands, his beauty is so striking, they're unable to erase the image of his radiant face from their minds that, even while making love to their spouses, and as a consequence their children are as beautiful—and some say as beautiful and as learned—as Rabbi Yohanan.

This phenomenon occurs, I hasten to add, not through sympathetic magic—a pagan concept anathema to the rabbinic mind—but through the power of the imagination to create what it imagines. This is Rabbi Yohanan's stock-in-trade.

Still, how is this practice not prohibited?

Sacred law, aware of the combustibility of the imagination, forbids a man from making love with one woman while thinking of another. Surely this prohibition applies to women as well. And also how appropriate is it for the head of the rabbinic academy in the Land of Israel to be loitering outside the women's bath?

Not inappropriate at all, it seems. For one thing, though the women see Rabbi Yohanan, it's highly probable that he doesn't see them. His eyebrows (at least when he is a very old man) have grown so long, they actually cover his eyes, and whenever he wishes to see a thing, he must say, "Raise up my eyebrows" to two of his students who gently part the curtain of his hair with delicate silver sticks.

Still: "Does the master not fear the evil eye?" his colleagues ask him. And by this, they mean: *With your great beauty on display for all to see, are you not afraid of the destructive power of envy?*

But the answer is no.

As a descendant of Joseph, Rabbi Yohanan is immune to the evil eye: just as Joseph was unmoved by the seductions of Potiphar's wife, so his descendants do not yearn for what does not belong to them, including, in this case, the newly baptized lovers of other men.

And if this were not sufficient to quell the waft of impropriety clinging to the scene, the Talmud next brings forth the case of Rav Gidel. Rav Gidel not only sits *within* the gates of the women's bath, he actually advises the women on their immersions: "Immerse like this, immerse like that," he tells them.

When questioned by his colleagues—"*Is the master not afraid of the evil inclination?*"—thanks either to his wretched eyesight or to his astonishing self-restraint, Rav Gidel responds, "They seem like white geese to me."

AND JUST HOW BEAUTIFUL *is* Rabbi Yohanan?

The Talmud addresses this question with one of its most visually articulate images:

> Let one who wishes to see the beauty of Rabbi Yohanan take a silver chalice as it emerges from the silversmith's furnace. Let him fill it with red pomegranate seeds and encircle its brim with a garland of red roses. Let him place it half in sun and half in shade. Its lustrous glow will be an approximation of Rabbi Yohanan's beauty.

Now, imagine that newly minted chalice, brimming with plump pomegranate seeds, ringed by a rosy corona, glinting, now in shade, now in sunlight, in the sparkling waters of the Jordan as the river wends its way through the dry yellow hills of the Judean desert, and the image in your mind might be an approximation of the lustrous glow that captures the eye of Shimon ben Lakish, a thief, a brigand, a killer, up to no good on that bright and ringing day.

The Aggadist, the teller of our tale, paints this scene, which follows the description of Rabbi Yohanan's beauty, with his usual terseness:

One day, Rabbi Yohanan was bathing in the Jordan. Resh Lakish saw him and jumped into the Jordan after him. Rabbi Yohanan said to him, "Your strength belongs to Torah!" Resh Lakish said to him, "Your beauty belongs to women!"

Though our story does not mention it, a beat or two earlier in the Talmud we've learned that, uncharacteristically for a man of his station, Rabbi Yohanan has no beard. This detail helps to fill in the missing colors of our scene. As we saw with the women at the bath, Rabbi Yohanan's beauty tends to stir the fires of the imagination. *Resh Lakish saw him and jumped into the Jordan after him.* Is it any wonder really that Resh Lakish, spying from a distance those smooth blushing cheeks and that long luscious red hair and that burnished coppery skin dripping with water, mistakes the bather in the river that day for a rubicund maid?

Imagination igniting his lust, he rips off his clothing and plunges into the water for what we can only presume are base and immoral purposes.

Now, at this tense moment, I should probably mention that, in addition to the information concerning his beardlessness, we're also told, again a beat or two ahead of our story, that Rabbi Yohanan's *membrum virile* is as large as a three—or even—some say—a five-*kav* flask. (A Talmudic unit of measurement, a *kav* equals in volume roughly two dozen eggs.)

So although Rabbi Yohanan's smooth cheeks may have beguiled Resh Lakish into imagining a ruby-skinned girl, the 72-to 120-eggs-sized pendulum hanging below his waist and breaking the surface of the water as Rabbi Yohanan turns and rises to face his assailant surely disabuses Resh Lakish of any such notion and perhaps even stuns him into silence, since, as the two men size each other up, Rabbi Yohanan is the first to speak.

"Your strength belongs to Torah!" he says.

"Your beauty belongs to women!" Resh Lakish fires back.

A curious shorthand: on the surface of things, Rabbi Yohanan, understanding everything in an instant, it seems, appears merely to be exhorting Resh Lakish to turn away from his life of crime and dedicate himself to a life of holiness instead. And we can perhaps hear in Resh Lakish's retort—*Your beauty belongs to women!*—a flustered, protesting explanation: *It was all a mistake, sir! I thought you were a woman! I hope you don't imagine I'm a homosexual!* Or a sneering taunt: *I'll tear you limb from limb, you little queer!*

In either case, having pushed and been pushed back, Rabbi Yohanan pushes again, and surely his counterthrust is as surprising to Resh Lakish as it is to the reader:

> He said to him, "If you repent [of your errant ways], I will wed you to my sister who is even more beautiful than I."

As we will see, Rabbi Yohanan has made a lifelong habit of perhaps too easily disposing of the people nearest him. Here, he offers his sister in marriage, it seems, to a brutal rapist, and against all expectation, the moment is decisive:

> [Resh Lakish] accepted these conditions upon himself, but when he tried to jump back and collect his clothes, he could not do so, because his strength was depleted. Afterwards, Rabbi Yohanan taught him Scripture and Mishnah and made him into a great man.

Though the comedy of this first scene—there are four in our story—does much to distract us from its violence, still, we mustn't forget that Resh Lakish's intention, when he jumps into the river, is to rape a stranger, to penetrate her against her will, subjugating her to his own violent uses. Part of the comic reversal, of course, is that Rabbi Yohanan, the girl-faced scholar, rises from the water and, revealing his superior masculine armature, disarms the aggressor, subjecting him to his greater will instead: *Your strength belongs to Torah!*

Despite its comedic flair, I think we can agree this is not the sort of scene you imagine finding in the authorized biography of a holy man or, in this case, of two holy men. Nor does a future rabbi attempting to rape his future teacher seem like Hollywood's idea of "meeting cute."

And yet, for all its questionable violence, the scene ends on a ringing note of happiness: brotherly love, a newly forged friendship, marriage, redemption, rebirth are all present here as themes. Resh Lakish may enter the river a brutish thug, but he leaves it, reborn, as the meekest of scholars, lacking sufficient strength to even lift up his clothing.

(According to Rashi, a medieval scholar and the father of all biblical and Talmudic commentators, Torah undoes the physical strength of its adherents. By merely accepting the yoke of Torah upon himself—he has yet to study a single word—Resh Lakish loses his animal aggression.)

THE POWER OF THE IMAGINATION *to create what it imagines.*

Water, ritual immersion, the arresting gaze, imaginary and erotic penetrations giving birth to beauty and to knowledge: curiously the scene at the river presents us with a recalibration of all the images we find in the story of Rabbi Yohanan at the women's bath.

At the bath, Rabbi Yohanan insinuates himself—noetically—into the sex lives of the women there; and at the river, he does the same with Resh Lakish, thrusting himself with rapier-like precision not to the *physical* core, but to the *psychological* core, of the advancing stranger—*Your strength belongs to Torah!* —touching him in his most hidden and fruitful place. The children born of these women are miniature reflections of Rabbi Yohanan, each bearing the stamp of his beauty; and by turning him into a scholar, Rabbi Yohanan makes Resh Lakish over in his own image as well.

In both scenes, Rabbi Yohanan's beauty functions as an erotic enticement that he does not physically fulfill. The women return to their husbands. Resh Lakish is given Rabbi Yohanan's sister to wed, and he departs the river affianced to both, a husband to one and a *haver*—a sacred companion—to the other.

The river and the bath are both *mikvot*, ritual baths, bodies of natural water imbued, according to rabbinic law, with the ability to purify and make holy. A convert immerses in a *mikveh*, as does a woman each month at the end of her menses. Although Resh Lakish undergoes a kind of conversion, the encounter with Rabbi Yohanan is erotic in all senses but the physical, and it leaves Resh Lakish ravished: *When he tried to jump back and collect his clothes, he could not do so, because his strength was depleted.*

The imagery is wonderfully confused here. Resh Lakish emerges from the river in a postcoital-seeming swoon, naked and depleted like a sated lover, but also—the image morphing as in a dream—like the newborn conceived in this violent coupling, emerging naked and helpless from the river's womb.

In either case, the experience has utterly transformed him: he is unable to reclothe himself in the cumbrous garments of his former identity.

NOW, IN A stroke of storytelling genius, our anonymous Aggadist—whoever he is, whoever he was—presents the entirety of Rabbi Yohanan and Resh Lakish's life together in two small book-ended scenes, two twin narratives, the first—which we've seen—describing the moment of their meeting, the second the moment of their departing from each other forever; and raising a subtle flag to draw our attention to this symmetry, the Aggadist introduces both scenes with the same phrase: *One day.*

One day—"*yoma had*" in the Aramaic of the text—is, on the one hand, merely a storyteller's stock phrase like *Once upon a time*, but it's also an aural twin for the Hebrew expression *yom ehad*, meaning "day one" or "a first day."

On the first day of Creation, as you'll perhaps recall from the opening verses of the Bible:

The Holy One separated light and darkness, calling the light Day, and the darkness Night. And there was evening and there was morning: one day (*yom ehad*).

Yom ehad . . . *yoma had* . . . Whisper these two phrases to yourself and soon, though you're speaking two different languages, they'll sound identical.

A remarkable literary feat: with this seemingly insignificant phrase, the Aggadist has planted us firmly within the world of primary oppositions: light and darkness, Heaven and earth, male and female, even hello and goodbye.

All the themes of our story, it turns out, are contained in this sly bilingual Joycean pun.

OUR SECOND SCENE begins as follows:

One day, the sages in the House of Study were divided over the following question: at what point in their manufacture are a sword, a knife, a dagger, a spear, a handsaw, and a scythe susceptible to ritual uncleanness?

The sages, charged with deciphering and adjudicating the sacred law, are hard at work in the House of Study, when another pair of primary oppositions enters our tale: ritual purity and its opposite. The laws of ritual cleanliness are Byzantine in their complexities. Suffice it to say, for our purposes: an object becomes impure when it comes into contact with a corpse or another source of defilement, and it must be made pure by immersion, lest it become a source of defilement itself.

Metal utensils—the swords, knives, daggers, and spears under discussion in the House of Study—fall into a category of their own, however, remaining insusceptible to impurity until their manufacture is complete.

But when is their manufacture complete?

This is the question the sages have been circling around, and their opinions are divided:

Rabbi Yohanan said, "After they have been tempered in a furnace."
Resh Lakish said, "Only after they've been quenched in water."

According to a simple reading of the scene, the two are merely disputing the niceties of a metallurgical process called annealing. Rabbi Yohanan maintains that, in the making of a sword or a knife or the like, the manufacture is complete after the material has been heated in a furnace; Resh Lakish disagrees, insisting that the object must be cooled as well, quenched in water.

In response to Resh Lakish's assertion, things seem to take a nasty turn.

"A robber knows well the tools of his trade," Rabbi Yohanan says.

Now, Rabbi Yohanan may simply be bowing, either reluctantly or admiringly, to Resh Lakish's greater practical expertise here. Of the two men, Resh Lakish, with his former days as a brigand, is probably the only one who has ever handled a sword. Whatever his intention, by reminding a penitent of his disreputable past, Rabbi Yohanan has once again, it seems, penetrated Resh Lakish to the core.

We've been here before or someplace very much like it. The two men "traded eights" in a similar way at the river, and though the stakes seem smaller here, the effect of Rabbi Yohanan's riposte on Resh Lakish appears even more devastating.

The barbed, pointed, cutting remark pierces him to the quick, and the bitterness of Resh Lakish's response is unmistakable.

"What benefit have you bestowed upon me?" Resh Lakish says. "There"—among the robbers, he means—"they called me Master; and here"—among the rabbis—"they call me Master."

"I brought you under the wings of the Shekinah," Rabbi Yohanan tells him, meaning under the wings of the Divine Presence, out of his immoral world of banditry and into the precincts of holiness.

These are the last words the two men ever speak to each other, and the second scene concludes, as does the first, with a narrative summation:

Rabbi Yohanan was mortified by the sharpness of the exchange, and Resh Lakish fell ill.

Something has gone terribly wrong.

On the first *yoma had* at the river, a new life is created; and on the second *yoma had* in the House of Study, that new life loses its pulse and begins to die.

THOUGH, ACCORDING TO SCHOLARS, except for a single passage of doubtful authenticity, there are no overt references to alchemy in the entire body of Talmudic literature, it's hard not to read our story as an alchemical romance.

Alchemists trace their intellectual ancestry back to the smiths and their forges, and as we've seen, the uses of metallurgy, in all its metaphorical brilliance, are present here: heating, smelting, forging, annealing. Metallurgy announces itself immediately in the story's opening aperçu: Rabbi Yohanan's Birth of Venus–like appearance out of the fires of a furnace. (*Let one who wishes to see the beauty of Rabbi Yohanan take a silver chalice as it emerges from the silversmith's furnace.*) The image takes on even more resonance when we realize that Rabbi Yohanan's (atypically depersonalized) patronymic, *bar Nappaha*, means *son of the blacksmith*.

Fire is Rabbi Yohanan's motivic element as well. Born of a fiery furnace, he literally radiates light, and everything about him—his character, his style of consciousness, his understanding of the Torah—has a fiery, solar inflection.

(Even the reference to Rabbi Yohanan's three-to-five-*kav* flask begins to make a kind of sense if we think of him as an alchemist.)

Refinement, the freeing of essence from dross, and *transmutation*, the elevation of a metal from its lowest to its highest grade, are an alchemist's stock-in-trade, and these, of course, are the metaphorical concerns of our drama. Fire, according to the alchemists, is the master of the work, the agent of transformation, and we've seen how Resh Lakish, ignited by the desire of his imagination, hurls himself into the bubbling alembic of Rabbi Yohanan's river where Rabbi Yohanan turns up the heat, beginning the process of refinement, taking a rapist-thief, a man of the lowest mettle, and transmuting him into a holy scholar.

In this way, the Holy One on his *yom ehad* and Rabbi Yohanan on his *yoma had* seem to be going about the same alchemical business, teasing light out of darkness, gold out of lead. And like the Holy One in his splendid isolation during the Six Days of Creation, Rabbi Yohanan also makes man: *RABBI YOHANAN (taught him Scripture and Mishnah and) MADE (Resh Lakish into a great) MAN.*

IN SCENE TWO, in the House of Study, the subject under discussion is the "completion of the work." The second *yoma had* is still, it seems, the First Day of Creation, and on it, Rabbi Yohanan intends to finish the work he began at the river, the refinement and elevation of Resh Lakish.

So while, on the one hand, the two scholars are dueling over the smithing of swords, on the other, they're speaking to each other in an alchemical code.

Fire is sufficient, Rabbi Yohanan says, in finishing the work.

But Resh Lakish demurs. Though the work may begin in fire, it must end in water.

Now as fire is Rabbi Yohanan's motivic element, water, as we will soon see, belongs to Resh Lakish, and this makes sense. The two friends are contrapuntally connected.

Through the process of annealing—the topic of the hour—a metal is softened and prepared for the further work of stamping, shaping, and forming. Gold, as any alchemist worth his salt knows, is both *ductile* and *malleable*, able to deform under tensile stress (while being heated, for example) *and* compressive stress (while being cooled). The same is true of silver, whereas lead is only malleable. It can only be pushed.

As it turns out, our two friends are very much like the weapons they're discussing. Having been pulled towards each other in the river, they are now, in the House of Study, pushed apart. This separation is what alchemists call the *opus contra naturam*, a deliberate breaking down of the primary matter into its constituent parts, before it's recombined in a new and nobler way.

Though fiercer, the heat during the *opus contra naturam* is meant, thanks to the protective waters of the *bain marie*, to remain safe to the touch. The *balneum Mariae*, or *le bain Marie*, is one of the oldest vessels in alchemy, its invention attributed to Mary the Jewess, the first nonfictitious alchemist in history. A double boiler essentially, the *bain marie* separates and contains fire and water, so that both may serve the work equally, the fire heating the water, the water moderating the heat.

And that's part of the problem here. The erotic waters of the first *yoma had*—that wet, sensual river of lust and desire—have evaporated and been replaced by the overheated intercourse of scholars; and the swordlike phalluses of Scene One have morphed into the phallic blades under discussion in Scene Two.

Remember all those blades illustrating Rabbi Yohanan's point: *a sword, a knife, a dagger, a spear, a handsaw, a scythe?* Children of smiths, the alchemists also considered themselves the children of Mars, the emblems of whose fiery red heat were—in alchemical shorthand—these very blades.

Red and hot like the planet Mars, on the second *yoma had*, Rabbi Yohanan is, as he was on the first, armed and ready for battle.

Resh Lakish tries to warn him: *The vessels must be quenched in water.* But Rabbi Yohanan, thrusting aside Resh Lakish's gentle warning, turns up the heat with an insult that scalds: *A robber knows well the tools of his trade.*

The remark seems to pierce Resh Lakish's fragile sense of self. Feeling burnt, he burns back— *What benefit have you bestowed upon me?*—and despite Rabbi Yohanan's calming response— *I brought you under the wings of the Shekinah*—Resh Lakish is unmade and unmanned. The hand is scorched, the substance burnt, and the two friends are torn apart, both mortified over the exchange.

I BROUGHT YOU under the wings of the Shekinah.

No sooner has the Shekinah, a figure of feminine compassion, been evoked than a compassionate woman takes the stage. Introduced in the first scene, Rabbi Yohanan's sister, the sister "more beautiful than I," appears at last in the third.

Still twinned with her brother, she has been undergoing a parallel experience of love and loss. Just as the erotic wrestling of the first *yoma had* created a family for her—her brother brings her home a husband—so the sharp-edged altercation of the second *yoma had* is tearing that family apart. And with her husband mortally wounded by the exchange, she has come to her brother to plead with him to forgive his errant friend.

Yes, forgive.

Although, according to the sacred law, it is forbidden to remind a penitent of his past, and though, as moderns, our sympathies more probably lie with Resh Lakish, according to a more ancient calculus, he is the offending party, having dressed down his teacher in public.

Each of the four scenes in our drama has only two characters. Perhaps because he finds himself in a defensive posture or perhaps because his sister is the elder of the two, in this third scene, unlike in the previous two, Rabbi Yohanan is not the first to speak.

His sister enters weeping, and she pleads with him, begging him to forgive Resh Lakish.

If not for Resh Lakish's sake, she says, "Forgive him for the sake of my children!"

Stonewalling her, Rabbi Yohanan replies, "Leave your fatherless children with me, and I shall rear them."

"For the sake of my widowhood then!" she cries.

But he answers in the same vein, "Let your widows rely on me."

They are stalemated, and as in the scenes that precede it, this scene too concludes with a narrative summation: "After that Rabbi Shimon ben Lakish died, and Rabbi Yohanan grieved for him considerably."

LIKE ALL SIBLINGS, Rabbi Yohanan and his sister share a common, though not an identical, history.

Their parents, it appears, had no greater task to accomplish than bringing Rabbi Yohanan into the world. In line with our alchemical themes, their father is depicted as a kind of chemical reactant, an element consumed in the course of the chemical change he brings about. As soon as Rabbi Yohanan is conceived, he dies. Rabbi Yohanan's mother survives only nine months longer. Upon giving birth to Yohanan, she dies as well, and his parents' earthly work is complete.

Though we hear little of his sister, Rabbi Yohanan enters the Talmudic discourse while still in utero:

> A pregnant woman inhaled the scent of food on the Day of Atonement, when it is forbidden to eat, and was seized with a craving for food. People came to Rebbi, the leader of the generation, and asked him if she might be permitted to eat. "Go and whisper in her ear that it's the Day of Atonement," he replied. When they did this, her cravings instantly ceased.

This unborn child, controlling his hunger in his mother's womb on the Day of Atonement, is none other than our Rabbi Yohanan, of course, and his extraordinary piety persists throughout his life. The true north of his personal compass always points towards Heaven. The earth and the fullness thereof hold no interest for him. Part of his beauty—how far we've come from the ancient world and its aesthetic!—is his great corpulence. And though he's capable of walking on his own, he typically leans on his students as a way of conserving his strength so he may employ it exclusively for the study of Torah.

This is how we find him when, one day, leaning on the shoulder of Rabbi Hiyya bar Abba, the two are walking from Tiberias to Sepphoris.

Coming upon a farm, Rabbi Yohanan says to Rabbi Hiyya, "You see this farm? It had been mine, and I sold it, because I wanted to devote myself entirely to the study of Torah." They come upon an olive orchard next, and Rabbi Yohanan says, "You see this olive orchard? It had been mine, and I sold it, because I wanted to devote myself entirely to the study of Torah." They come upon a vineyard, and he says, "You see this vineyard? It had been mine, and I sold it, because I wanted to devote myself entirely to the study of Torah."

At that, Rabbi Hiyya begins to weep.

"Why are you weeping?" Rabbi Yohanan asks him.

Rabbi Hiyya: "I weep because you did not put anything aside for your old age."

Not a farm, not an orchard, not even a vineyard.

"Hiyya, my son, is what I did really as foolish as you seem to think? I gave up something that took no more than six days to be created and acquired something that took forty days and forty nights to be revealed." Rabbi Yohanan explains: "For it took the Holy One no more than six days to create the entire world, but to reveal the Torah took him forty days and forty nights."

BECAUSE HE INITIATES and concludes this conversation—and also because his closing remarks coincide with the story's end—we may hear Rabbi Yohanan's final statement as definitive or inarguable. If we only had the discipline, the will, the strength of character, the story seems to be telling us, we'd all make the same high-minded renunciations of the material world and its comforts.

In this slanted light, Rabbi Hiyya's tears—which I read initially as tears of compassion—become part of an entirely different emotional spectrum, signifying awe, admiration, a trembling sense of reverence. Or worse, they're the "womanly" tears cried over trivial and unheroic things: a farm, an orchard, a vineyard.

To read the story in this way, though, is to understand the incident it describes only from Rabbi Yohanan's point of view. Many voices, central to the rabbinic tradition, certainly argue against this kind of asceticism. "He who says he has only Torah doesn't even have Torah," a Rabbi Yossi says elsewhere in the Talmud, casting a cold eye on Rabbi Yohanan's earthly renunciations. Rabbi Yossi means that the Torah's precepts must be embodied and lived. Study is not sufficient in itself. The Five Books of Moses are, among many other things, not least a guide to sacred agriculture.

(Between the laws of forbidden mixtures, of obligatory gifts to the poor, of obligatory gifts to the priests, of tithes, of secondary tithes, of first fruit offerings, of the sabbatical year, the Torah's agricultural concerns are extensive.) In addition to providing for one's old age, a farm, an orchard, and a vineyard are opportunities for living the kind of fully embodied spiritual life Rabbi Yohanan seems to have denied himself.

WHY ARE YOU WEEPING?

The Aggadist offers no guide to the emotional subtext of his dialogue, and the ambiguity this creates allows the stories to be turned and turned again. Held up like a prism to the interpretive light, the same story will refract many different colors, depending upon the angle of our perception, the angle of our concerns.

Tears—we might say, though I know not everyone is inclined to think in these terms—are the body's response to the agonies of the soul. In washing clean our eyes, tears clarify our perceptions. As far as Rabbi Yohanan is concerned, Rabbi Hiyya's tears have been proven mathematically unnecessary. Since the Holy One took forty days to dictate the Torah to Moses and only six to fashion the Heavens and the earth, the Torah must be 6.6666667 times more valuable than the rest of Creation.

These same tears, though, look quite different through Rabbi Hiyya's eyes. Especially when one realizes that Rabbi Hiyya lives in extreme poverty, and that unlike Rabbi Yohanan, he has no choice about it.

A nice irony: though the statement in the Talmud that forbids a scholar to go about in patched shoes is attributed to Rabbi Hiyya, he himself goes about in patched shoes!

(Reconciling opinions are presented in short order to quell the frisson of this seeming contradiction: the prohibition obtains only when a patch is on top of another patch, and only when *that* patch is on the top part of the shoe, and even when it's on the top part of the shoe, only when a scholar is walking on the road and, on the road, only in the dry months of summer.)

I feel compelled to point out nevertheless: that his patched shoes are no longer a violation of the sacred law does nothing to alleviate Rabbi Hiyya's poverty. And here, the student seems to know something his teacher does not. Having little to sustain him in his youth, Rabbi Hiyya can only imagine, based on bitterest experience, how much harder a life without wealth would be—*will be*—in old age.

Without the benefit of Rabbi Hiyya's experience, Rabbi Yohanan approaches the issue of poverty in old age with a blithe sense of unconcern. *Do you see this orchard . . . do you see this vineyard?* he keeps asking the younger man, blind himself to the spiritual as well as the physical benefits of all he has renounced.

Do you see . . . do you see? He's blind as well to the earthbound structures in the story that *do* support him. In the diminishing hierarchy of material things—*not a farm, not an orchard, not a vineyard*—there are two even smaller supports the self-blinding, self-laming Yohanan cannot see. He is, of course, leaning on Rabbi Hiyya's shoulder. Rabbi Hiyya serves him as a kind of wife, cleaving to his side, propping him up as a rib might, holding his carriage erect. And Rabbi Hiyya, of course, is standing upright, bearing this burden, in his patched shoes.

Shoes that are, only by the Talmud's barest of hairsplitting definitions, shoes.

And beneath those shoes, shoring Rabbi Hiyya up, I might add, is the earth itself, which Rabbi Yohanan has renounced as 6.6 times less valuable than the Torah, which he imagines is all that sustains him.

He's blind as well to the extra weight—physical in the concrete details of the story; emotional in terms of its characters—that his self-laming renunciations have placed upon those who care for him, those who love him, those who, as in the case of Rabbi Hiyya, even worry over his future for him.

WHY ARE YOU WEEPING?

This question—curiously enough—appears in another story featuring Rabbi Yohanan.

Rabbi Elazar ben Pedat, another of his students, has fallen ill.

Like Rabbi Hiyya, Rabbi Elazar is poor, and when Rabbi Yohanan comes to visit him, he finds him lying in a darkened hovel. Pulling back his sleeve, Rabbi Yohanan bares his own arm, and the glow of his radiant body fills the miserable room with a glorious light.

By this light, Rabbi Yohanan notices that Rabbi Elazar is weeping.

"Why are you weeping?" he says. "Is it because you did not study enough Torah? Surely we have learnt: 'The one who does much and the one who does little have the same merit, provided their hearts are directed towards Heaven.'" Probing further: "Is it perhaps because of your meager livelihood?" He is quick to reassure him: "Not everyone has the privilege of enjoying two tables—Torah *and* wealth."

Is it this, is it that? he continues. "Is it because of your lack of children? Here is the bone of my tenth son!"

As a grisly reminder of his ten sons who all have died, Rabbi Yohanan keeps the bone—some say the tooth—of his tenth son, and whenever anyone complains to him of their troubles, he produces the bone, and his fellow's woes are instantly recontextualized.

"No, I am weeping on account of this beauty of yours," Rabbi Elazar tells him, "which in the end will waste away in the earth."

"On that account," Rabbi Yohanan responds, "you surely have good reason to weep."

And the two of them weep together.

NOW, IF WE RECALL that Rabbi Yohanan's beauty is conflated with the beauty of Jerusalem, lying, at the time of our story, in ruins, his weeping will perhaps seem less egomaniacally comical. Still, the scene speaks to the limits of his empathy. Once again, the student must teach the teacher. Literally glowing with ruddy health, Rabbi Yohanan expresses his sympathy for the ailing Elazar with a certain philosophical detachment—*Everyone must die, and few of us achieve all he wishes*—while Rabbi Elazar, in contrast, though facing his own death, is able to empathize with Rabbi Yohanan over the eventuality of his.

The distant prospect of his own death touches Rabbi Yohanan

in a way that the seemingly imminent death of Rabbi Elazar does not.

(I say *seemingly imminent* because, at the end of the story, Rabbi Elazar has been healed by Rabbi Yohanan's touch. Rabbi Elazar will not only survive Rabbi Yohanan, he will, in fact, be present at his teacher's death.)

WHY ARE YOU WEEPING?

I suggest we do no interpretive violence to the story if we hear Rabbi Yohanan's question not as a rhetorical question, but as a sincere inquiry; if, by *Why are you weeping?*, we imagine he's saying not *Relate to me the conditions that are causing you to weep and I will demonstrate how baseless they are*, but rather *Explain to me, if you will, why human beings weep. Why are you weeping?*

Let's be honest: his life has been one of extraordinary loss. Perhaps this is what has numbed his heart. As we've seen, his father, having done his part, burns up in the conflagration of his conception, his mother does not survive the fiery ordeal of his birth, and he enters the world an orphan, not even linked to his father by name. Though he's mentioned countless times in both Talmuds, his wife or wives, the mother or mothers of those ten lost sons, appear only by inference. He marries his sister off to a man who attempted to rape him, and later, as we'll see, he very nearly murders his nephew, his only male heir.

As it turns out, Resh Lakish isn't even the first study partner Rabbi Yohanan has consigned to death. The first is a man named Ilfa:

> Ilfa and Rabbi Yohanan studied Torah together, but when they found themselves greatly distressed by poverty, one said to the other, "Let us go into business and make true in our own lives the words 'There shall be no needy among you.'"

He's quoting from the Book of Deuteronomy, chapter 15, verse 4, to be exact.

On their first day out of the House of Study, the two men sit against the foot of a deteriorating wall to eat.

A deteriorating wall is, of course, neither a good portent in a story nor a safe place to sit and eat:

> While they were eating, two angels came by. Rabbi Yohanan overheard one angel saying to the other, "Let us bring down the wall upon them and kill them, for they are about to neglect eternal life and occupy themselves with temporal concerns." However, the second angel replied, "Let them be. The time is not yet up for one of them."
>
> Rabbi Yohanan said to Ilfa, "Did you hear anything?" Ilfa said, "No." Rabbi Yohanan then said to himself, Since I heard and Ilfa did not, *I* must be the one whose time is not yet up.

Though, at least according to Rabbi Yohanan's thinking, his companionship is the only thing standing between Ilfa and death, Rabbi Yohanan returns to the House of Study alone, saying nothing of the angels to his friend, telling him only, "I will go back to my studies and make true in my own life the words 'The poor shall never cease out of the land.'"

Another quotation from Deuteronomy, chapter 15, verse 11 this time. Rabbi Yohanan seems to have skipped over the six verses in between these two quotations, verses that are an exhortation to neither harden one's heart nor close one's hand against one's brother, but to give him whatever he is lacking.

Though Rabbi Yohanan adheres to his plan, returning to the House of Study, Ilfa survives, and his survival seems to cast Rabbi Yohanan's assumptions into doubt. Surely, if one of them were fated to die, it wasn't Ilfa, who survives, despite abandoning his studies and thereby, one assumes, forfeiting some measure of divine protection.

Still, we see how easily Rabbi Yohanan seems to abandon a *haver* to his fate.

PERHAPS IT'S HERE, picnicking in the shadow of this crumbling wall, that Rabbi Yohanan begins to conflate earthly pursuits with death. He's not the only one. Within many strains of rabbinic thought, there's a tendency to deemphasize the importance of the physical, even to disparage it as ephemeral, trivial, debased. Not a little effort is expended by commentators, for instance, asking us to understand Rabbi Yohanan's beauty not as physical beauty, but as a symbol of his radiant wisdom.

This is all well and good—especially for the ascetic (who often conflates the feminine with the physical)—until we recall that Rabbi Yohanan's sister is, by his own admission, the "more beautiful" of the two. By this measure, Resh Lakish has married and fathered children with the *wiser* of the two siblings. Nevertheless, despite his sister's greater wisdom, in Scene Three of our story, Rabbi Yohanan refuses to heed it.

We can imagine these two glorious beauties, these two fiery redheads, confronting each other like the two cherubim in the Holy Temple, their faces aflame with passion and anger. His heart as dry as boiling sand, Rabbi Yohanan responds to his sister's pleas to save their family with what appears to be a bitter lack of compassion. Wiser and more beautiful than he, she advocates for another kind of alchemical fire: the fire of the hearth. The word *ach* in Hebrew means both *brother* and *hearth*, and here, Rabbi Yohanan's sister asks him to redirect his gaze towards home, to remember that he is the center of a family. Offstage, after all, away from their lives as scholars in the House of Study, Rabbi Yohanan and Resh Lakish are brothers-in-law. Together, the three of them form a family that includes the sister's children and presumably Rabbi Yohanan's wife, the mother of his lost sons, and his late-life daughters as well.

But the hearth holds no fascination for him. He desires no farm, no orchard, no vineyard, no farmhouse, no hearth, no home. In fact, he has no practical concerns. As a scholar, he cares only about the Torah. As an alchemist, he is dedicated exclusively to the *opus*, to the work. His patronymic tells the entire story: he is the son of a nameless blacksmith. There was no father present to teach him the practical uses of the forge. (One has no need to quench a sword in water if it never has to be cool enough to touch.) Indifferent to earthly life, unlike his sister, who, in her wisdom, loves the man body and soul, Rabbi Yohanan cares only for the state of Resh Lakish's soul. This is the alchemical *opus*, as far as he is concerned: having refined the base fellow into a scholar, he's here now to complete the work, to transmute Resh Lakish to his highest grade, his golden self.

Gold, ductile and malleable we recall, can be pulled and pushed. Having pulled Resh Lakish to him, now, as a further refinement, Rabbi Yohanan pushes him away.

But what is this further refinement required of Resh Lakish?

SURELY SINCE that first day at the river, Resh Lakish has continued to refine and elevate his character under Rabbi Yohanan's tutelage. He's turned his back on his former life and his former companions. He's now so circumspect, we're told, that anyone he speaks with in the marketplace can get a loan without witnesses. He and Rabbi Yohanan in fact have become inseparable, interdependent, over the years. Asked at one point to lecture without Resh Lakish present, Rabbi Yohanan refuses. "Can one hand clap by itself?" he says. And even when he and Resh Lakish disagree, Rabbi Yohanan says, "What can I do when one who is my equal differs from me?"

Still, despite Rabbi Yohanan's Henry Higgins–like attempts to refine the former bandit, a certain brutality remains stamped into his character. Resh Lakish is no less rough and muscular than he's always been, and many of his teachings, in fact, have a violent, even murderous cast to them: "The words of Torah abide only in one who kills himself for them," he says, or "A man's impulse for evil grows from day to day and seeks to slay him."

Poring over the Holy Scriptures, he is far from a mild-mannered bookworm: "One who saw Resh Lakish in the House of Study would think he was uprooting mountains and grinding them one against the other."

He works for a time as a night watchman, catching thieves, and the sages are not averse to calling on the old brigand whenever they need his daring, his cunning, and his muscle. Though they despair that a kidnapped colleague may have already been slain by his captors, Resh Lakish is not so easily cowed.

"Before I say that Rabbi Imi is slain," he proclaims, "I will run the risk of being slain myself!"

He not only rescues Rabbi Imi, he tricks the kidnappers into destroying themselves.

"Come with me to a certain elder who will pray on your behalf," he tells them, and he takes them to Rabbi Yohanan, who offers up this prayer: "May what you intended to do to Rabbi Imi be done to you; and may it befall all people like you."

Before they even reach the next town, they've all been slain.

Even with his scholarly colleagues, Resh Lakish can be rough. Once, for example, as a rebuke for speaking ill of others, he stuffs sand into Rabbi Abbahu's mouth. Another time, he informs a Babylonian colleague, "God hates you!"

Alchemy—we have to bear this in mind—is not about creation. The alchemist creates no new elements. He merely rearranges existent elements into new combinations. Resh Lakish may be technically correct when he laments that *There, they called me Master, and here, they call me Master.* On an elemental level at least, it's true: he is unchanged. His outsized appetites, his ferocity, his natural strength, his wildness—characteristics belonging equally to Rabbi Yohanan, I might add—are all still present in his character. The only difference is that now they've been harnessed to a sacred purpose. Now, as Rabbi Yohanan points out, he dwells beneath the wings of the Shekinah.

Still, the questions remain: if their disagreement concerning the manufacture of metal vessels isn't what distresses Rabbi Yohanan (*What can I do when one who is my equal differs from me?*), and if Resh Lakish's roughness and natural brutality aren't what concern him, then what was he after on that second *yoma had*, how was the work to be completed, and what exactly went wrong between the two on that day when swords and knives and daggers and spears divided them so sharply, cutting each man to the quick?

THE VESSELS *must be quenched in water.*

The fiery Yohanan seems drawn to watery partners. After they part company at the deteriorating wall, Ilfa, for instance, earns his living as a merchant at sea. He returns to town years later to discover that Rabbi Yohanan has become the head of the rabbinic academy. When the townspeople jeer at him—"Had you only devoted yourself to study, you too could have become head of the academy!"—he answers them by climbing to the top of a ship mast and threatening to throw himself into the water if he's unable to answer any of the rabbinic questions they put to him.

This is a bit like Brer Rabbit asking not to be thrown into the briar patch. Water is Ilfa's home, the source of his income, the source of his life, and the same is true for Resh Lakish. His Torah is a Torah of water. Once, for example, when he was walking on a road, we're told:

> Resh Lakish reached a pond. A man came along, hoisted him onto his shoulders, and began ferrying him across. Resh Lakish asked, "Have you learned Scripture?" The man said, "Yes, I have learned Scripture." Resh Lakish said, "Have you learned Mishnah?" The man: "Yes, I have learned four orders of the Mishnah."

There are six.

> Resh Lakish said to him, "You've hewn for yourself four mountains of Torah! Yet you carry ben Lakish on your shoulders? Throw ben Lakish into the water!"

Into water is where one goes, it seems, to prepare for more wisdom, for more knowledge. Into water is where one goes to become a greater man. And at least once before, water has saved Resh Lakish's life.

IN HIS ROUGHER DAYS, Resh Lakish sold himself—for a good price, naturally—to cannibals. On the last day of his life, the cannibals grant each of their prisoners whatever he wishes so that happiness might sweeten his blood. Resh Lakish has brought along a water skin inside of which he's hidden a stone:

> When they asked him, "What would you like?" Resh Lakish replied, "I want you to let me tie your arms, set you down, and give each of you a blow and a half with this water skin."

Imagining they have the upper hand, the cannibals allow Resh Lakish to bind and seat them. Stunned, as each of them receives a blow, each gnashes his teeth. They almost appear to be smiling.

> Resh Lakish said, "Are you laughing at me? Remember, you still have half a blow coming." And he killed them all.

THOUGH FIRE is a traditional metaphor for divine knowledge— according to Resh Lakish himself, "The Torah given to Moses was written with black fire upon white fire, sealed with fire, and swathed with bands of fire"—water is a common metaphor for divine knowledge as well. "There is no water except Torah," the Talmud states. "Just as a person cannot go three days without water, neither can he go three days without the Torah."

Water and Torah are inextricably mixed in Resh Lakish's thinking. Elsewhere, we read:

> Rabbi Shimon ben Lakish used to study Torah with great intensity in a cave outside Tiberias. Every day a water carrier would have a pitcher of water ready for him, so that when he entered the cave feeling very tired, he would take the pitcher and drink.

Even as a scholar, Resh Lakish maintains a kind of bandit's hideout in the hills.

> Once, when the water carrier came by and sat down next to him to rest a bit, he said, "Master, do you remember that you and I used

to go to school together? But you were deemed worthy of higher study of Torah, while I was not deemed worthy."

An alternative history for Resh Lakish perhaps—ancient writers are not as fanatical as we moderns are about what constitutes historical fact—but here again, we have a pair of matched opposites: schooled together, one student excelled, the other didn't. And now, the water carrier has a request: "Pray for me that in the World to Come, my portion may be next to yours."

This is not an unreasonable request. The water carrier is Resh Lakish's servant, after all, and the effort he expends each day toting that heavy pitcher of water through the desert and up into the cave is responsible—in small part, true, but responsible nonetheless—for bringing more wisdom into the world each day. And why shouldn't he merit a place at the scholar's table in Heaven?

True, the water carrier might not have the same passion, the same heat, the same fiery temperament as Resh Lakish. He might not be willing to kill himself, as Resh Lakish has done, that the words of Torah might abide in him. Still, Resh Lakish might have said to him: *Midway through my life's journey, I dedicated myself to the holy path of Torah. It's never too late. You can do the same.* Quoting Rabbi Tarfon's famous maxim, he might have told him: "*It's not incumbent upon you to complete the work, but neither are you free to desist from it altogether.*" At the very least, he might have quoted Rabbi Yohanan's words to Rabbi Elazar ben Pedat and said: *The one who does much and the one who does little have the same merit, provided their hearts are directed towards Heaven.*

But instead:

Resh Lakish replied, "What can I pray for on your behalf other than that your portion may be with your fellow craftsmen, since each and every man will be made to dwell only with the fellows of his craft?"

Now, I suppose you could argue that daily we're all making our place in the World to Come, that with our every good deed and our every destructive act, we create our circumstances in the true world that follows this world of illusion. Though this train is bound for glory, as Woody Guthrie reminds us, it don't pull no gamblers, liars, thieves, nor big-shot ramblers. There'll be no line-jumping in the World to Come, it seems. There, everyone will dwell in the place he has made for himself, each man will sit with his fellows, and a simple water carrier would be out of his depths at a table of learned men.

Let's assume, for a moment, that what Resh Lakish tells the water carrier is true. Still, mightn't we argue that if a marauding, murdering rapist-thief can become a great man of learning, a man of holiness, the *haver* of the most illustrious sage of the era, a lowly water carrier might, with a little encouragement, improve his spiritual lot? After all, when Moses delivers his farewell speech to the people of Israel in the Book of Deuteronomy, he addresses not only the tribal chiefs and the elders, but also the wood-choppers and the *water carriers*.

But instead, Resh Lakish essentially tells the water carrier: *Once a water carrier, always a water carrier.* And though eloquently refuted by his own spiritual rags-to-riches story, this disturbing dismissal echoes his own self-pitying cry: *There, they called me Master, and here, they call me Master. What benefit have you bestowed upon me?*

As his *haver*, as his holy twin, as, in a sense, his creator (*Rabbi Yohanan made Resh Lakish a great man*), Rabbi Yohanan is well aware of the spiritual blocks within Resh Lakish's soul. He knows Resh Lakish's spiritual wounds. For all his spiritual upward mobility, Resh Lakish cannot credit, cannot believe in, the alchemical refinement and transmutation of his own base nature: *There, before the* opus, *and here, after the* opus, *I am the same. Once a water carrier, always a water carrier. A robber is a robber is a robber, and he knows well the tools of his trade.*

Worse, this unbelief in his own essential holiness is a profound failure of the principle Rabbi Yohanan lives by: the power of the imagination to create what it imagines. Gazing upon Resh Lakish's face should have had the same effect on the water carrier that gazing upon Rabbi Yohanan had upon Resh Lakish and the women at the bath.

NOW, WE CAN READ the second scene in the House of Study psychologically as well as alchemically. There, Rabbi Yohanan's intention is to confront Resh Lakish with his self-imposed sense of limitation, to reflect it back to him in a shocking way, to pierce him with this knowledge in order to challenge it and, by these means, to free his friend from its psychic constrictions. Rabbi Yohanan understands that unconsciously Resh Lakish feels he has never transcended his own dark past, and he confronts him with this belief by embodying it fully and throwing it in his face: *A robber knows well the tools of his trade.* This is the *opus contra naturam*, a working against nature, an intentional tearing apart.

In the white heat of this work, however, the fire gets too hot. Rabbi Yohanan has ignored Resh Lakish's warning that *the work must end in water*—and Resh Lakish gets burned.

The outcome shouldn't be surprising.

While Resh Lakish may in fact be blind to the perfect purity of his soul—a purity beyond the defilements of his earthly experiences—how can Rabbi Yohanan imagine he will cure Resh Lakish of this blindness when he, too, is blind, self-blinded to his earthly need for love, for companionship, for family? He's burned through all these relationships, and now, telling himself he cares only for the fiery Torah of Heaven, he's been blind as well to the effects of Resh Lakish's watery presence in his life.

All these long years, a second *opus* has been underway. While it's true that immediately upon clapping eyes on him, Rabbi Yohanan saw a reflection of himself lying dormant in Resh Lakish—*Your strength belongs to Torah*—Resh Lakish also sees something of his own watery, earthy, sensual self in Rabbi Yohanan's unlived but authentic life: *Your beauty belongs to women.*

Bedazzled perhaps by that beauty, we've allowed this statement to fall between the cracks. However, in the world of our story, a world of mirrored correspondences, Resh Lakish's statement is offered, like Rabbi Yohanan's, as a corrective. And it's every bit a diagnosis of one-sidedness—as well as a prescription for its cure—as Rabbi Yohanan's matching proclamation.

Though Rabbi Yohanan may have succeeded by the end of Scene One in the godlike work of making a man of Resh Lakish, Resh Lakish's work of making a woman out of Rabbi Yohanan— bringing out of him a kind of inner feminine—proves a longer and more arduous task.

But of course it does.

Rabbi Yohanan is a respectable man, a sage, a scholar. He is, arguably, the central figure in the ancient rabbinic world, and he has less ostensible reason than a marginal fellow like Resh Lakish to repent, to rethink his life, to submit to the ego-death their fraught encounter at the river requires of both of them.

He is too identified with his own solar consciousness—Heaven, fire, the soul are his concerns, not earth, water, the body—and too focused on the refinement of Resh Lakish, to see that he, too, is in need of transformation and refinement, of having the famous *silver* of his character spun into *gold*.

Fire in the ancient world is celestial, of course, descending from the sun and the stars, but it's also terrestrial, arising out of the earth as springs and geysers, gases and volcanoes. Resh Lakish is an alchemist as well, perhaps the greater of the two, and from his point of view, fire is still the master of the work, the agent of transformation, but it's not necessarily the bright yellow flame of the sun, the fierce, flashing fire of Heaven, but the low blue flame of the body, the wet, sensual heat of the earth that does the cooking as well.

As water is Resh Lakish's element, he brings his own Jordan River with him, in him; and from the moment they meet, though Rabbi Yohanan doesn't quite realize this, he has been immersing in Resh Lakish's *mikvah*, in the purifying water that *is* Resh Lakish.

(And there's a stone, of course, a hidden agent of change in the water Resh Lakish carries with him, but as with the cannibals Resh Lakish sold himself to, Rabbi Yohanan won't know it's there until it hits him.)

Resh Lakish tries to warn Rabbi Yohanan—*heated by fire, the vessels must be cooled in water*—but, intent on his own agendas, Rabbi Yohanan pays him no heed. It's as though Resh Lakish were insisting: *I, too, am part of this work. I, too, am having an effect on you.* But his appeal to Rabbi Yohanan—to cool his fiery character in the watery, earthy, feminine world of form and experience—cannot be heard over the roar of Rabbi Yohanan's blazing furnace.

Rabbi Yohanan ignores his statement in the House of Study, just as he ignores his statement at the river.

ODDLY ENOUGH, everything that touches this story seems to come in bookended pairs. The Aggadist knows his Bible inside and out, and so perhaps it's not too strange to discover that in the Book of Genesis, as in our story, there are two accounts of the creation of human beings.

The first account embodies a theme we're familiar with—that of twins, mirroring, enmeshment:

> And the Holy One said, "Let us make man in our image, after our likeness." . . .
>
> And the Holy One created man in his image, in the image of the Holy One, he created him, male and female he created them.

But nine or so verses later, we read:

> . . . the Holy One formed man of dust from the ground, and blew into his nostrils the soul of life, and man became a living being.

But: "It's not good for man to be alone," the Holy One says to himself.

And so:

> The Holy One cast a deep sleep upon the man. . . . He took one of his sides and filled in flesh in its place. Then the Holy One fashioned the side that he had taken from the man into a woman, and he brought her to the man . . .

Separation and conjunction are the order of the second creation, and the story ends:

> . . . and they were both naked, the man and his woman, and they were not ashamed.

They were both naked, and they were not ashamed.
This verse returns us or it should—with a thump and a bump—to our scene in the Jordan where Rabbi Yohanan and Resh Lakish confront each other for the first time, both naked and unashamed. Like the Holy One creating man in the first account, Rabbi Yohanan makes Resh Lakish *in his own image, after his likeness*, while Resh Lakish follows the second model, attempting to draw Rabbi Yohanan's feminine half out of his male body.

(Like Adam, Rabbi Yohanan, as we'll see, more or less sleeps through the process, waking up only at its end.)

An astonishing thought that flies in the face of hundreds of years of theology: Though the medievalists believed, based on a reading of the Book of Genesis, that woman, taken from the side of man, was therefore existentially dependent upon him, a consistent reading of the chain of being, which places man *above* everything created *before* him, actually makes woman, not man, the apex, the zenith, the crown of creation. And this is true in alchemy as well. The marriage of the White Queen with the Red King, the union of *albedo* and *rubedo*, silver and gold, the integration of male and female consciousness, is the end of the work.

This is something that Resh Lakish seems to understand. His fire may be wetter, and therefore slower, than Rabbi Yohanan's, but it's cooking nonetheless, and the aim of *his* alchemical *opus* is the refinement and transmutation of the silver Rabbi Yohanan into his higher golden self, a self, in the language of our story, that belongs to women and is therefore *more* beautiful and *more* wise.

For three scenes, Rabbi Yohanan stubbornly resists submerging into these unseen depths, into the waters of the dark feminine (with all its classical associations: emotions, physicality, earth, sexuality). Slowly, despite himself, however, experiences have their way with him, and he begins to transform.

We can chart his movement imagistically. At the end of the first scene, while Resh Lakish dithers in a swoon, Rabbi Yohanan remains in the water, stalwart, unmoved, for all appearances unchanged. By the end of the second scene, he has begun to be *moved*, to be *acted upon* (*Rabbi Yohanan was mortified*). This intellectual mortification deepens into grief by the end of Scene Three, and at the end of Scene Four, the *opus* is complete.

Resh Lakish the alchemist has fully transformed Rabbi Yohanan, and the God-reared orphan, who needed no father, no mother, no study partner, no wife, no sons, no farm, no orchard, no vineyard, no earthly life at all, cannot live, it turns out, without a friend.

Unable to voluntarily enter the waters, the waters come to him, involuntarily, as tears.

IN FACT, by the fourth scene of our story, Rabbi Yohanan is grieving so much he no longer comes down to the House of Study:

> The sages said, "Who will go and ease his mind? Let Rabbi Elazar ben Pedat go, for his scholarship is brilliant."

Having dispensed with the first two, Rabbi Yohanan is now in need of a third *haver*. The sages recommend Rabbi Elazar ben Pedat—whom you will remember from the story in which he and Rabbi Yohanan weep over the then-distant prospect of Rabbi Yohanan's death.

Now in the House of Study:

> Rabbi Elazar ben Pedat went and sat before Rabbi Yohanan, and to everything Rabbi Yohanan said, Rabbi Elazar observed, "There is a statement that supports your position."

This is a curious turn. Having argued with and been challenged by equals—by Resh Lakish and his sister—in our three previous scenes, Rabbi Yohanan seems unprepared for Rabbi Elazar's too-gentle obsequiousness here. Rabbi Elazar has come, of course, to console the grieving Rabbi Yohanan, and it doesn't occur to him that the best consolation might be a barbed intellectual brawl. The unforgivable brusqueness of Resh Lakish—rudely calling out his teacher in public—now becomes precious in Rabbi Yohanan's eyes. Using the Aramaic form of Resh Lakish's name, Rabbi Yohanan says to Rabbi Elazar:

> "You're supposed to be like bar Lakisha? With bar Lakisha, when I stated a matter, he would raise twenty-four objections, which I responded to with twenty-four rebuttals, and as a result of this give-and-take, the matter became clear, and *you* say, 'There's a statement that supports your position' as if I didn't know on my own that what I said is right?" Rabbi Yohanan stood and tore his clothes in mourning. Dissolving into tears, he cried out, "Where are you, bar Lakisha? Where are you, bar Lakisha?" screaming until his sanity wore away.

The story's final coda: "The sages prayed for mercy on his behalf and he died."

LEAVE YOUR ORPHANS *to me and I shall rear them.*

As long as we've got our Bibles open, let's move a little deeper into the Book of Genesis, to the story of Jacob and Esau.

Now, from a simple reading of the Bible, Esau doesn't seem so bad. A little thick maybe, a little slow, certainly not up to the trickery his mother Rebecca and his brother Jacob cook up to rob him, first of his birthright and then of the paternal blessing, both of which belong properly to him, as the elder of twins.

(Yes, another pair of twins.)

As you'll perhaps recall from the Book of Genesis, Abraham, having discovered the existence of the Holy One, is granted a late-life child with his aged wife Sarah. The child is named Isaac, and eventually the Holy One commands Abraham to sacrifice him, accepting, at the last moment, a ram instead. Isaac lives and goes on to marry Rebecca, and together they have two sons, the twins Jacob and Esau.

The rabbinic tradition gives Esau a pretty bum rap, willfully overlooking the deceptions Rebecca and Jacob run on everyone around them, while tar-and-feathering Esau as a murderer, a marauder, a libertine, a thief.

(If this is starting to sound a little familiar, it should. The story of Jacob and Esau is the quiet subtext of our tale.)

And as far as the traditional reading goes, there's probably no darker, more unredeemable figure in the entire rabbinic *comédie humaine* than Esau. He is the opposite of everything the rabbinic tradition holds dear. Coarse, vulgar, physical, violent, profane, he is contemptuous of his parents, of the sacred, of the sanctity of life.

Unlike the pious Rabbi Yohanan, who, while still in the waters of his mother's womb, refrains from nourishment on the Day of Atonement, Esau, according to rabbinic legend, tries to kick his way out of Rebecca's womb whenever she passes an idolatrous altar so that he may worship there.

Another legend: out of kindness, the Holy One takes five years from Abraham's life so that the saintly patriarch needn't live to see his grandson becoming the worst of sinners—an idolater, a murderer, a rapist of betrothed maidens, all on the day of Abraham's funeral.

Why is Esau the firstborn, the Midrash asks? The answer: he emerges from the womb first so that he may come out with all the birth muck, sparing his brother Jacob's dignity. The day he spurns his birthright for a bowl of red lentils, unable to control his hunger, is, according to the commentators, the day on which he kills his first man.

And yet, from a reading of the text in the Book of Genesis, unadorned by these commentaries, Esau might seem sympathetic.

"Bless me too, Father!" he says to Isaac, upon discovering that his brother and mother have conspired to trick him out of the paternal blessing:

"First he took away my birthright and now he has taken away my blessing! . . . Have you not reserved a blessing for me? . . . Have you but one blessing, Father? Bless me, too, Father!" And Esau wept aloud.

Who can hear such a lament and remain coldhearted?

The answer to that question may be surprising. It's not only the traditional biblical commentators who see Esau in such a poor light, but the Holy One—from whom the commentators, I'm certain, have taken their cue—sees him in this way as well.

Here is what we find in the Book of Jeremiah:

> Concerning Edom, the descendants of Esau, thus says the Lord of Hosts: "I am bringing Esau's doom upon him. . . . It is I who have bared Esau. . . . He cannot hide. His offspring is ravaged, his kin and his neighbors—he is no more. Leave your orphans to me. I will rear them. Let your widows rely on me."

These last are, of course, the words Rabbi Yohanan speaks to his sister when she begs him to forgive Resh Lakish, if not for his sake, then for hers, and if not for her sake, then for the sake of her children.

The moment, as it expands intertextually, is chilling.

By comparing Resh Lakish to Esau, Rabbi Yohanan seems to be telling his sister, *I took a coarse, violent, rapacious, lusty criminal, thinking I could refine him, but I was wrong. Esau will always be Esau. There is no redemption for your husband. His doom is sealed. As for your fatherless children, I shall rear them, and, as a widow, you can rely on me.*

BUT HERE'S A CURIOUS THING.

Once again, if we imagine this scene between Rabbi Yohanan and his sister onstage, the predominant color would be red: red pomegranate seeds, red rose petals, a heated forge, a glowing chalice, the fire of the sun. These are the images to which Rabbi Yohanan and his sister are compared; and that is odd, because red, as a color, belongs to Esau.

"He was red," the commentaries state, "his food red, his land red, his warriors red, their garments red."

On the surface, at least, Rabbi Yohanan seems to share with

Esau a number of other traits as well: his ruthless strength, his warrior-like brutality, a coarsened indifference to the suffering of others. Though Jacob, in the Book of Genesis, upon reuniting with his brother, hopes that the sight of his children will mollify what he fears is Esau's long-simmering rage against him, Rabbi Yohanan's fratricidal anger towards Resh Lakish seems to extend beyond his own generation.

After Resh Lakish's death, Rabbi Yohanan twice encounters his nephew, and the second time, attempts to kill him:

> Rabbi Yohanan lifted his eyes and gazed at the young son of Resh Lakish. At that, his mother rushed in and took him away, saying to her son, "Get away from him, lest he do to you what he did to your father."

HALF IN SUN, HALF IN SHADE.

In that lush description of Rabbi Yohanan's beauty, the newly minted chalice is placed half in sun and half in shade. Like all of us, it seems, Rabbi Yohanan has a dark and a light side. There's a part of him—a dark twin, let's say—that he can't bring himself to face. (The revelation of this murderous brute in Rabbi Yohanan destroys Resh Lakish.) The encounter with the dark self, however—this is the caustic red sulfur of alchemy—seems to be an essential part of the refining process.

After years of separation from his twin, the night before meeting up again with Esau, Jacob wrestles with a stranger at the Jabbok River. The Aggadist, as I've said, knows his Bible: the Jabbok is a tributary of the Jordan, the river where our two twins wrestle and meet. The stranger is often identified as Esau's guardian angel. In other words, Jacob seems to be wrestling with the dark half of the equation—the soul wrestling with the body, Heaven wrestling with earth, fire wrestling with water. Jacob and the stranger are evenly matched, and neither can prevail. At daybreak, at a stalemate, Jacob agrees to let the stranger go in exchange for a blessing. The stranger gives him a new name.

Rabbi Yohanan also wrestles with a dark man at the River Jordan, and he, too, is blessed with a new identity: *Your beauty belongs to women.*

THE AGONIES OF THE SOUL.

Now, we can say that these two companions failed in their alchemical romance to bring into being what their imaginations saw in each other, but in truth they were successful, or at least partially successful for a time.

Lead, as the alchemists tell us, is the basest of metals. Ductile but not malleable, it can be heated and pulled, but not pushed or cooled. Resh Lakish *is* elevated and refined, transmuted into a great man, by the pull of Rabbi Yohanan's heat. He breaks, however, when Rabbi Yohanan pushes him away, treating him coolly in the House of Study and freezing him out in the scene that follows.

Silver, however, the element associated with Rabbi Yohanan, is both ductile and malleable. It can be pulled *and* pushed. Though made of baser stuff, Resh Lakish appears to be the finer alchemist, his imagination more perfectly creating what it imagines. As much as his wet, sensual heat pulls Rabbi Yohanan towards him, it's Resh Lakish's death that finally *pushes* Rabbi Yohanan over the edge, finishing him in all senses of the word.

A sword, a knife, a dagger, *a silver chalice*: when is their manufacture complete? Though the work begins in fire, it must end, as Resh Lakish teaches us in the House of Study, in water: *Rabbi Yohanan stood, tore his clothes, and dissolved into tears.*

In this final scene, in the final moments of his life, before insanity robs him of his identity, Rabbi Yohanan opens at last to the earthly things he has forsworn his entire life: principally the physical agonies of love and loss. Tears clarify his perception, and at last, he feels the all-too-human, all-too-earthly, all-too-watery pain of being orphaned, of being abandoned, of being alive and alone in the world.

And the question he has asked again and again in these stories— *Why are you weeping? Why are you weeping?*—is at last answered by a responding question: *Where are you, bar Lakisha? Where are you, bar Lakisha?*

AND WITH THESE TEARS, our old friends, the body and the soul, enter the scene again, as though they were Beckett's clowns Vladimir and Estragon, always together, always threatening to part.

On one level of our discourse, I think it's safe to say, Resh Lakish and Rabbi Yohanan stand in for these two imaginal aspects of human life, Resh Lakish standing in for the body, Rabbi Yohanan for the soul. According to rabbinic thought, while the body may be elevated by the soul for a time, its earthly compass directed towards Heaven's true north, in the end, like lead, it resists complete sublimation and returns as dust to the earth. The silvery soul, however, pulled down—against her will, by the way—to the earthly field, can only be refined—made golden—through the experience of earthly life. This is, in fact, how the whole system is said to work: the soul descends so that she may ascend, and the refinements the soul gains in her earthly sojourn are all she takes with her when, trailing clouds of glory, she returns to her source in the Heavens.

THE HEBREW ROOT of the word *Lakish* refers to late things: late crops, late rains, the growth that follows a harvest. Though the *opus* is finished before the end of our story, its completion, and the knowledge it brings, come too late for our tragic protagonists. Like the body and the soul, Resh Lakish and Rabbi Yohanan have lived fitfully, imperfectly together. Nevertheless, they've needed each other. The body perishes without the soul; the soul loses its grounding without the body.

And perhaps it's only when life is over, when our body and soul have gone their separate ways, that we can begin to understand—though too late—what each has made of the other.

Rabbi Shimon bar Yohai (flourished c. 3890–3920/130–160 CE)

WHY DID THEY CALL RABBI JUDAH THE CHIEF SPOKES-man on every occasion?

For once Rabbi Judah and Rabbi Yossi and Rabbi Shimon sat, and Judah opened by saying, "How pleasant are the works of this nation! They've established markets, they've established bridges, they've established bathhouses." Rabbi Yossi was silent. Rabbi Shimon responded, "Everything they established, they established only for their own needs. They established markets to seat prostitutes there, baths for their own enjoyment, and bridges to collect from them tolls."

Judah ben Gerim went and related the conversation and it was heard by the government. They said, "Judah, who praised, shall be elevated; Yossi, who was silent, shall be exiled to Sepphoris; Shimon, who deplored, shall be executed."

He and his son hid in the House of Study. Every day his wife would bring them bread and a pitcher of water, and they would eat. When the degree intensified, he said to his son: "Women are light-headed. Maybe they will torture her and she will reveal us."

They went and hid in a cave. A miracle occurred. There was created for them a carob tree and a spring of water. They would take off their clothes and sit up to their necks in sand. All day they studied. At the time of prayer, they put on their clothes and prayed and again took off their clothes so that they should not wear out. They sat in the cave twelve years. Elijah came and stood at the entrance of the cave. He said, "Who will inform bar Yohai that Caesar has died and his decree is nullified?"

They went out. They saw people plowing and sowing. They said, "They are abandoning eternal life for temporal life!" Every place they gazed upon was immediately consumed by fire. A heavenly voice rang out and said to them, "Did you go out to destroy my world? Return to your cave!"

They went back. They sat there twelve months. They said, "Even the judgment of the wicked in Gehenna is for only twelve months." A heavenly voice rang out, saying, "Come out of your cave."

They went out. Every place that Rabbi Elazar struck, Rabbi Shimon healed. He said to him: "My son, you and I are enough for the world."

Friday afternoon at the approach of the Sabbath, they saw an old man holding two twigs of myrtle running at twilight. They asked him, "Why do you have these?" He answered, "In honor of the Sabbath." "Wouldn't one be enough for you?" "One for 'remember' and one for 'keep.'" Rabbi Shimon said to his son, "See how the commandments are beloved by Israel!" And their minds were put at ease.

Rabbi Pinhas ben Yair, Rabbi Shimon's son-in-law, heard and he went out to greet him. He took him to the bathhouse. Rabbi Shimon was smoothing his skin. Rabbi Pinhas ben Yair saw that there were cracks in Rabbi Shimon's skin. Rabbi Pinhas ben Yair began to cry. The tears flowing from his eyes caused Rabbi Shimon to cry out. Rabbi Pinhas said, "Woe to me that I have seen you in such a state!" Rabbi Shimon answered him, "Fortunate are you to have seen me in such a state. Were it not for this state, you would not have seen me at all!"

Originally, when Rabbi Shimon would pose a problem, Rabbi Pinhas ben Yair would solve it with twelve solutions. In the end, when Rabbi Pinhas ben Yair would pose a problem, Rabbi Shimon bar Yohai would solve it with twenty-four solutions. Rabbi Shimon said, "Since a miracle has occurred, I will go and repair something."

As it says, "And Jacob arrived whole . . ."

Rav says, "Whole in his body, whole in his money, and whole in his Torah."

". . . and he found favor in the city."

Rav says, "He established coins for them."

Samuel says, "He established markets for them."

Rabbi Yohanan says, "He established bathhouses for them."

Rabbi Shimon asked them if there is something that needs repairing. They replied that there are places that may be impure, and it is uncomfortable for the priests to detour around them. Rabbi Shimon asked if there was someone who could vouch for the purity of the place in question. An old grandfather testified that in this place ben Zakkai planted and later picked lupines which were the priest's portion of *terumah*. Rabbi Shimon did as ben Zakkai. He cut lupines and threw them. Wherever it was hard, he purified it; wherever it was soft, he marked it.

According to Rashi: A miracle occurred. Wherever there was a dead body, it floated to the surface and Rabbi Shimon marked the grave.

The old grandfather said, "Bar Yohai has declared a cemetery ritually pure!" Rabbi Shimon said to the old man, "If you had not been together with us, or even if you had been together with us and were not counted amongst us, you would be correct speaking this way, but now that you were together with us and were counted amongst us, people will say, 'Even prostitutes fix each other's hair.' Doesn't it stand to reason that scholars would enhance one another?" Rabbi Shimon gazed at the old man and his soul departed.

Rabbi Shimon went out to the marketplace. He saw Judah ben Gerim. Rabbi Shimon remarked, "This one is still alive!" He gazed upon him and turned him into a stack of bones.

BABYLONIAN TALMUD, TRACTATE *SHABBAT* 33B–34A.

Chapter 2

Turning the Hearts of Fathers

"HOW PLEASANT ARE THE WORKS OF THIS NATION!" Rabbi Judah says. "They've established markets, they've established bridges, they've established bathhouses."

Though Rabbi Judah is not the hero of our tale—in fact, almost immediately after this statement, he falls out of the story completely—it's appropriate that we begin with him. Opening statements are Rabbi Judah's métier, it seems. No matter the occasion, he is always the first to speak.

Even so, it's an astonishing statement. The nation in question is the Roman occupiers who, in the year 3700 (63 BCE), conquer Jerusalem, turning the autonomous kingdom into a Roman client state and ultimately, a few years later, destroying the Holy Temple.

Imagine a Sandinista praising American culture during the years the Reagan administration was arming the Contras—*They brought us Coca-Cola, Mickey Mouse, and the free market!*—and you'll have some idea how extreme Rabbi Judah's statement actually is.

The Aggadist doesn't go to much trouble setting up his scene. The story begins: "Once Rabbi Judah and Rabbi Yossi and Rabbi Shimon bar Yohai sat," and Judah ben Gerim happened to be near them.

He doesn't tell us who these people are, or whether they're in a public or a private space. Are they inside or outside? We don't know. The Aggadist doesn't tell us. Nor does he tell us what prompts Rabbi Judah's strange panegyric to Roman culture. Apropos of nothing, it seems—although perhaps they're sitting in a public square, after all, taking in the changes that have come to their city—Rabbi Judah opens the conversation with his admiring observation.

We might ask: Why would he say such a thing? Is it a moment of Stockholm syndrome perhaps, an overidentification with his captors? Is he engaging in some sort of spiritual calisthenics, an attempt to isometrically tone the muscles of his saintliness against the heaviness of political catastrophe? Perhaps he's acting upon a rabbinic precept, a precept grounded in a sense of radical monotheism: If everything comes from a single source—the Holy One—and the Holy One is good, everything therefore must *be* good, and we must learn to see the good in everything.

Rabbi Judah is certainly a proponent of this view. Elsewhere in the Talmud, he's depicted as a poor man, content with his meager lot, blessing the Holy One's magnanimity for every crumb and scrap. Though, for instance, he and his wife must share a wrap made out of wool ends—she using it as a shawl when she markets, he as a *tallit* when he prays—he never covers himself with this ragtag garment without intoning the benediction: *Blessed is he who has provided me with a robe.*

An admirable worldview—one not likely to foment an underground resistance movement—although perhaps extolling the cultural virtues of a brutal, repressive occupier is taking an excellent spiritual discipline a step too far. It's hard to say, and the story itself offers no commentary on the matter.

Though Rabbi Judah's statement will change all their lives, all we really know is how his colleagues react to it.

"RABBI YOSSI WAS SILENT."

Rabbi Yossi has come neither to praise Caesar nor to bury him in scorn. He neither affirms nor contradicts Rabbi Judah's civic encomium, though it's not hard to imagine his silence as discomfort. There's no telling who may be listening to them. Surely anti-Roman zealots number among the rabbis' friends. They can be as lethally oppressive as the Romans. A comment in either direction might be dangerous. Best, under those circumstances, to remain silent.

Rabbi Shimon admits to no such caution.

"Everything they established," Rabbi Shimon tells his peers, "they established only for their own needs. They established markets to seat prostitutes there, baths for their own enjoyment, and bridges to collect from them tolls."

Don't be fooled by the glories of Western civilization, he seems to be saying. *These cultural achievements are nothing more than man's lust, his egotism, and his greed, asserting themselves through cutting-edge technologies.*

The three speech-acts, made before a witness, are the action of the story's opening scene, and they cover the full spectrum of possible responses to the Roman occupation: praise, silence, condemnation. Naturally enough, word gets out about this potentially subversive conversation. Judah ben Gerim, Rabbi Shimon's student, has been indiscreet, it seems. Whether he goes directly to the government as an informer or simply repeats the story without malice, permitting it to spread—this is the reading I prefer—it isn't long before the authorities hear about it.

Their response is swift and draconian: "Judah, who praised, shall be elevated; Yossi, who was silent, shall be exiled to Sepphoris; Shimon, who deplored, shall be executed."

A TEXT BASED UPON an oral tradition is a bricolage of sorts, a collage assembled out of sundry pieces. This is an early Hebraic tradition: No sooner had Moses received the tablets containing the Ten Commandments than he hurls them to the ground, shattering them into pieces, pieces he has to fit back together, one imagines, as he constructs a second set.

(Oddly enough, at least according to my dictionary, *mosaic*, in this sense of the word, has nothing to do with Moses.)

In any case, our story of these three rabbis has been shoehorned into the Talmud at this point as a way of answering the question: "Why did they call Rabbi Judah the first speaker on every occasion?" Though our story serves, in its place, as an answer to this question—*Judah, who praised, shall be elevated*: by government decree Rabbi Judah was given the honor of speaking first at all public occasions—the story itself has no interest in this question and never addresses it explicitly.

Given the political situation, it's a dubious honor, and the question of how Rabbi Judah is afterwards treated by his fellows—as a quisling or an Uncle Tom or a pious fellow simply trying to discern the Holy One's hand in difficult straits—is a question left, as well, for another day. After his star turn, Rabbi Judah simply drops out of the story, as does Rabbi Yossi, hotfooting it, presumably, to the Galilee before the Romans change their mind about him.

We're left to follow Rabbi Shimon. Sentenced to death and abandoned by his friends, what does he do?

RABBI SHIMON HID with his son in the House of Study.

Now, this may not strike you—it does not strike me—as the most devious of hideouts. Not finding them at home, where else would you look for a rabbi and his son but in the House of Study? While the rabbis know enough about Roman culture to have strong opinions about its markets and its roads and its baths, the Romans don't seem to possess a comparable knowledge of the Judean culture they're repressing. Houses of Study don't seem to appear on the Roman maps of the city, and Rabbi Shimon and his son are safe enough. For the time being, anyway.

We read:

Every day his wife would bring them bread and a pitcher of water, and they would eat. When the decree intensified, he said to his son, "Women are light-headed. Maybe they will torture her and she will reveal us."

They went and hid in a cave.

In abandoning his wife, Rabbi Shimon has turned his back on the traditionally feminine attributes the women in these stories generally (but not always) embody: compassion, tenderness, mercy, flexibility, a concern for relationships. Filing these under the pejorative heading *light-headed*, he lights out for the territories with his son instead.

A miracle occurs for the two men at the cave: "There was created for them a carob tree and a spring of water," and they adjust to their new life:

> They would take off their clothes and sit up to their necks in sand. All day they studied. At the time of prayer, they put on their clothes and prayed and again took off their clothes so that they should not wear out.

They have no idea how long they will have to remain hidden, and they attempt to coherently re-create their lives in the wild. Rabbi Shimon's flesh-and-blood wife, who formerly brought them bread, is transformed, Daphne-like, into a blooming carob tree. Her pitcher of water becomes a living stream. The House of Study becomes a cave. Through their prayers, Rabbi Shimon and his son maintain a connection to human life—forbidden by sacred law from praying nude, they don their clothes thrice daily—but in almost every other way, they themselves are transformed, as though mythically, into natural elements in this wild, desolate landscape, their heads human, but their bodies two pillars of sand.

(This is not the only time the Talmud anticipates the work of Samuel Beckett.)

An Eden of sorts is regained, with a tree and a river running through it, but there are differences as well. Rabbi Shimon's helpmate in this desert garden is not a wife, but a son; and whereas Eve, the mother of all life, is formed from the side of Adam's body—from near his heart—a son is created by the seed of his father's phallus.

In this masculine Eden, the male organ has replaced the womanly heart.

(Or as James Joyce might say: the womb-manly hurt.)

Perhaps Rabbi Shimon felt that the House of Study, a male preserve, was threatened less by the Roman police than by the sentimental disposition of a mother and a wife. ("*Women are light-headed.*") In any case, her loaf of bread and her pitcher of water, emblems of the very foundation of civilization—cooking and tools—have no place in the dry, desolate world Rabbi Shimon and his son now call home.

In this wild place, they become wild themselves, their bodies merging with the earth in a kind of mortification of their senses—half man, half stalagmite—and though their minds are filled with Torah, it's a disembodied Torah, a Torah of wild and howling expanses, freed from gross materiality, far from the civilized world with its bridges and its bathhouses and its markets.

According to tradition, in this cave Rabbi Shimon authors (or receives) the *Zohar*, the principal book of Kabbalistic mysticism, and this is fitting. The mystic sees *through* the material world, after all, to the luminous essences shining beneath it.

How long do Rabbi Shimon and his son live like this?

"They sat in the cave twelve years," we're told.

THE PROPHET ELIJAH who shows up in these stories from time to time *is* and *is not* the Elijah in the Bible's Book of Kings, the Elijah who defended the worship of the Holy One on Mount Carmel against the priests of Baal, and who survived the schemings of Ahab and Jezebel, and who raised the dead and brought fire down from the sky, and who ultimately ascended to Heaven in a whirlwind.

The Elijah who appears in our stories, more often than not in disguise, is the Elijah the Holy One mentions in the Book of Malachi.

There, the Holy One makes this promise:

Lo, I will send the prophet Elijah to you before the coming of the great and awesome day of the Lord. He will turn the hearts of fathers towards their sons, and the hearts of sons towards their fathers, so that, when I come, I do not strike the earth with utter destruction.

A harbinger of the Messiah, this Elijah has a sweetening influence on everyone he meets. He's a benevolent trickster, somewhat magical, neither living nor dead.

During his life as a biblical prophet, Elijah spent a considerable amount of time in a cave himself, attended to by miracles, communing with the Holy One, and so it's only appropriate that he shows up now to inform Rabbi Shimon and his son that Caesar has died, that, as a consequence, the decree against Rabbi Shimon has been annulled, that they no longer need to hide.

He's mindful of the inhuman wear and tear of their ordeal—for twelve years, Rabbi Shimon and his son have lived without sunlight, without walking, without hearing a human voice other than their own, subsisting on carobs and water, concentrating exclusively on prayer and the study of Torah—and he breaks the news of their liberation to them as gently as possible.

Standing at the mouth of the cave, he says, "Who will inform bar Yohai that Caesar has died and his decree is nullified?"

Let us linger for a moment to admire Elijah's extraordinary tact: He does not address the two men directly. That would be too shocking, too brusque, for them in their delicate states. Instead, he delivers the information disguised as a question directed to someone other than our two outlaws, referring to Rabbi Shimon not only in the third person but by his patronymic, evoking in this way a sense of identity that is deeper historically than his own small self—a self which, by this time, is almost certainly in tatters. Elijah softens the blow, gentling its effect, relegating Rabbi Shimon and his son to the periphery of the moment. They stand on the sidelines, it seems, imagining that they have accidentally overheard someone else's conversation. This gives them the time and the space to assimilate this astonishing news, to absorb the shock of it, and to emerge from the cave at their own enfeebled pace.

Birth, death, rebirth, these are soulful translations: it's difficult to cross from one world to another. Every threshold has its peril. Elijah may have been protecting himself from danger as well, for, as it turns out, Rabbi Shimon and his son have trouble adjusting to their new liberated state:

They went out. They saw people plowing and sowing. They said, "[These people] are abandoning eternal life for temporal life!" Every place they gazed upon was immediately consumed by fire.

For twelve years, fed and succored by the hand of Heaven, Rabbi Shimon and his son have devoted themselves single-mindedly to spiritual pursuits. Subsisting on carobs and water, for twelve years, they have done nothing but study and pray. They've lost, it seems, all comprehension of the civilized world, and after twelve years of renunciation, Rabbi Shimon's disgust with the physical world has only increased. Twelve years ago, he burned the hedonistic Romans with his scorn; now, he literally incinerates Judean farmers with his fiery gaze, a power he has developed, it seems, during his twelve-year vision quest.

As with Rabbi Yohanan and Resh Lakish—in my opinion, the two stories are authored by the same anonymous hand—we can see how destructive the fiery power of Heaven is without a watery earthly filter.

Apparently, the Holy One concurs:

A heavenly voice rang out and said to them, "Did you go out to destroy my world? Return to your cave!"

What else could they do?
They go back, and they sit there an additional twelve months.

A KIND OF EINSTEINIAN relativity enters our story here. Surely this thirteenth year feels longer to them than the previous twelve years combined. Originally, as they fled the Roman death sentence, the cave offered them life. Now, life exerts a counterforce: the desire to leave the cave. Twelve years of heavenly pursuits quickly become four seasons in Hell. Recognizing this second stint in the cave as a divinely ordained punishment, Rabbi Shimon finally cries out, "Even the judgment of the wicked in Gehenna is for only twelve months!"

(According to tradition, the souls of the dead in the purgatorial realms remain there for no more than one year.)

In response, a heavenly voice again resounds, "Come out of your cave!"

THOUGH WORKING, as always, in extreme miniature—tiny scenes, small gestures—the Aggadist has captured something profound here. How truly human Rabbi Shimon appears in this moment. After twelve brutal years of life as a desert saint, he seems to have lost all sense of commonality with what he surely despises as the all-too-human race. Rigorously self-disciplined, a physical renunciate, he's had little trouble living in the splendid isolation of his cave, indulging his ascetic inclinations.

(I'm reminded of a Leonard Cohen lyric: "I needed so much to have nothing to touch. I've always been greedy that way.")

The moment the external compulsion for this solitude is relieved, however, though he may share no other trait with his fellows, the desire to live, to live among others, and to live freely, reasserts itself. Though he may be blind to it, in this way at least, he's no different from the rest of humanity.

FATHER AND SON venture out again, and once again, they see simple people going about their worldly and spiritually unheroic lives. (Not everyone is elevated enough to merit being fed by a miraculous carob tree and stream of water.) Still, the gall rises in their throats. Perhaps involuntarily. Rabbi Shimon's son, Rabbi Elazar—named, here, for the first time in our story—seems not to have gotten the heavenly memo, and his father must ameliorate the harm he causes: "Every place that Rabbi Elazar struck, Rabbi Shimon healed."

Rabbi Shimon has taken the twelve-month reprimand more to heart. "My son," he says, "you and I are enough for the world," meaning: *The presence of two such holy and elevated masters on this frail, pathetic planet, populated by sinners of all stripes, is enough to turn back the wrath of the Holy One, and to keep him from destroying the earth utterly* (a possibility that seems to exist from the time of Noah to at least the end of the Book of Malachi).

Rabbi Shimon seems to have conveniently forgotten, at least from the evidence of our tale, that, when it comes to the destruction of the earth, the Holy One appears more worried about Rabbi Shimon and his son than the other way around.

EVERY PLACE *that Rabbi Elazar struck, Rabbi Shimon healed.*

Destruction and healing: with the unearthly powers he has developed in his seclusion—that terrible gaze—Rabbi Shimon is able to heal as well as destroy. Still, his forbearance towards other people, which may hold fast during the days of the week, is sorely tested as the Holy Sabbath draws near.

Our story continues:

Friday afternoon at the approach of the Sabbath, they saw an old man holding two twigs of myrtle running at twilight.

On any day, twilight is a time of uncertainty and confusion, not still day, not yet night. But on Friday afternoon, the issue is even more vexed. Has the Sabbath, with all its prohibitions, arrived or not? If so, carrying even as light a load as two myrtle twigs is forbidden.

By now, we know our protagonists well enough to anticipate their responses. As I imagine the scene, Rabbi Elazar, catching sight of the old man at the point of desecrating the Holy Sabbath, casts his fiery red gaze upon him, ready to incinerate him, when his father, no less a fanatic, but mindful of Heaven's remonstrations and of the uncertainties of the twilight, places a restraining hand upon his son's chest, heaving in outrage, and suggests to him that they investigate before pronouncing a death sentence.

Appearances can be deceiving, after all. That's part of the difficulty of living in the material world. Though physical surfaces may refer to a deeper reality, they conceal this reality as well, and everything, seen as though through a glass darkly, must be interpreted.

The interrogation begins:

"They asked him, 'Why do you have these?'"—meaning the two myrtle twigs.

"He answered, 'In honor of the Sabbath.'"

A pious gesture! He's bringing the fragrant twigs home, as today one might flowers, to make the Sabbath more beautiful, more pleasing.

But not so fast!

"Wouldn't one have been enough?"

"One," he tells them, "is for *remember*, the other for *keep*."

(There are two versions of the Ten Commandments in the Torah, after all, one in the Book of Exodus, the other in the Book of Deuteronomy. The first exhorts the spiritual aspirant to *remember* the Sabbath, the second to *keep* it. Rashi reconciles the discrepancy by explaining that the Holy One spoke two words with a single breath.)

The irony is thick here. In the twilight, nothing is clear. On the border between two worlds, a thing can easily resemble its opposite. Here, a man rushing home to honor the Sabbath, his head filled with biblical verses, his heart full of love for the Holy One's Creation, might appear, to the ungenerous eye, as a vile Sabbath desecrator.

Allowing the old man to live, presumably detaining him no longer, lest twilight give way to night and he find himself actually carrying on the Sabbath, Rabbi Shimon offers his son a benedictory teaching: "See how the commandments are beloved by Israel!" he says to Rabbi Elazar.

And the story tells us: "And their minds were put at ease."

PINHAS BEN YAIR, Rabbi Shimon's son-in-law, enters the story here, and with his appearance, Rabbi Elazar disappears without a word from the text. This dreamlike substitution is no coincidence. As Rabbi Shimon returns to civilization, to the world of loaves and pitchers, after thirteen years in his cave, his wild son, his natural son, the son with whom he lived in the desert, is replaced by a son-in-law, a son made, not by blood, but by the conventions of human society.

Rabbi Pinhas ben Yair could not be more different from Rabbi Elazar. Humble, pious, conscientious, restrained, he's the author of a well-known Talmudic statement:

> Zeal leads to fastidiousness, fastidiousness to cleanliness, cleanliness to abstinence, abstinence to purity, purity to holiness, holiness to humility, humility to fear of sin, fear of sin to pious conduct, pious conduct to the holy spirit, and the holy spirit to the resurrection of the dead.

This statement is the thesis of *The Path of the Just*, an eighteenth-century how-to manual for sainthood; and the stories we have of Rabbi Pinhas ben Yair, as we will later see, illustrate that he himself mastered these attributes, climbing the ladder of this eleven-step program of self-perfection to its highest rung: the ability to raise the dead.

Unlike Rabbi Elazar's eye, Pinhas ben Yair's gaze is neither fiery nor destructive. People do not perish in his sight. On the contrary, they're restored to life under the tearful benevolence of his gaze.

When Pinhas ben Yair hears that his father-in-law has left his cave, he goes out to greet him. He takes him to the bathhouse in Tiberias. Massaging Rabbi Shimon's flesh, he sees that there are cracks in Rabbi Shimon's skin, a result of having spent years buried in sand. Rabbi Pinhas ben Yair begins to cry, and the tears flowing from his eyes cause Rabbi Shimon to cry out. Rabbi Pinhas says to him, "Woe to me that I have seen you in such a state!"

The scene has a beautiful ambiguity. Pinhas ben Yair is moved to tears by Rabbi Shimon's wretchedness. That much is clear. Imagine a homeless man after thirteen punishing years of living in the Mojave. He takes off the only clothes he has worn all those years, and you see the ruin of his body. What's not clear is whether Rabbi Shimon's cries are an emotional response to Pinhas ben Yair's weeping or if Pinhas ben Yair's salty tears falling on his parched and cracked skin make Rabbi Shimon cry out.

How subtle is his pain?

This scene in the bathhouse resonates against the earlier scene in the cave. Without an outside reference, as mirrored reflections of each other, two sand pillars with human heads looking into each other's faces, Rabbi Shimon and Rabbi Elazar didn't—or perhaps couldn't—register the disastrous changes occurring simultaneously to their bodies. Pinhas ben Yair, on the other hand, a humane man planted firmly within human society, sees the toll thirteen years in the wilderness have had on Rabbi Shimon, and he's distressed by it, to the point of tears. As a mirror, he reflects back to Rabbi Shimon a vastly different image than Rabbi Elazar did. Beneath the moist gaze of Pinhas ben Yair, the image of the wild ascetic, the sandy obelisk with a human head, morphs into that of a near-corpse moldering in a shallow, unmarked grave.

Still, unconcerned with earthly comforts, Rabbi Shimon is reluctant to write the experience off as a total loss. Playfully mocking Rabbi Pinhas's locution,

> Rabbi Shimon answered him, "Fortunate are you to have seen me in such a state. Were it not for this state, you would not have seen me at all!"

A droll bit of comedy; though on a deeper level, a gentle tug-of-war is occurring between the two men over whose interpretation of Rabbi Shimon's wilderness years will prevail. If, as Bishop Berkeley states a millennium and a half after our story takes place, *to be is to be perceived*, how we are seen may in fact determine something essential about ourselves. But Rabbi Shimon will have none of it. In fact, he resists his son-in-law's interpretation so completely, insisting that his ostensible misery is actually his good fortune, that in a literal reading of their lines, the two men appear to be arguing over whether *Pinhas ben Yair and not Rabbi Shimon* is the fortunate or unfortunate one: *Woe is me that I have seen you in such a state. Fortunate are you to have seen me in this state.*

The body, however, cannot be deceived by such heady distinctions.

The Aggadist, in our story, is quite clear-sighted about the importance of the eye, the importance of the act of seeing and of being seen. He knows that a gaze may confer or restore or even deny life. By *seeing* the scholar in Resh Lakish, Rabbi Yohanan made him into one. Blind to the scholar in him, Resh Lakish consigned the water carrier to an eternal life bereft of the one thing he thirsted for: the living waters of Torah.

Here, in the bathhouse, beneath Rabbi Pinhas ben Yair's moist gaze, the tears falling on Rabbi Shimon's skin reawaken his senses. His nonverbal cries are reminiscent of a newborn's. And just as Pinhas ben Yair replaces Rabbi Elazar as the son in the story, the bathhouse—as an image, as a stage setting—replaces the dry grave-like cave, serving as a kind of lush womb, in which Rabbi Shimon is reborn, restored to life.

FOR ALL ITS HARSHNESS, the experience of exile and return has profoundly altered Rabbi Shimon:

> Originally, when Rabbi Shimon would pose a problem, Rabbi Pinhas ben Yair would solve it with twelve solutions. In the end, when Rabbi Pinhas ben Yair would pose a problem, Rabbi Shimon bar Yohai would solve it with twenty-four solutions.

While the years in the cave with his son may have invigorated his intellect, the afternoon with his son-in-law in the bathhouse seems to have opened his heart. Along with marketplaces and bridges, as you'll recall, bathhouses were singled out for Rabbi Shimon's scorn. But now, his body repaired—perhaps even made beautiful—in a bathhouse under the benevolent, restorative care of his son-in-law, Rabbi Shimon conceives a complementary desire: "Since a miracle has occurred," he says, "I will go and repair something."

He is following biblical precedent. In chapter 33 of the Book of Genesis, after many years of exile, having fled his brother Esau's murderous wrath, Jacob is at last reunited with his violent twin.

As I said in chapter 1, in the rabbinic imagination, Esau, often conflated with Rome, is associated with all the physical pleasures of the world—sex, power, money—while Jacob, "a simple man of tents," a scholar, represents the rabbinic alternative: creativity, goodness, charity. Having against all expectations survived the reunion with his dark-hearted twin, Jacob arrives intact at the city of Shechem.

Various voices—Rav's, Samuel's, Rabbi Yohanan's—commenting in the margins of our story, interpret this to mean that Jacob arrives in Shechem with his body, his wealth, and his knowledge intact. In appreciation for his safe arrival, he mints a new coin in honor of the city, and he establishes bathhouses and marketplaces there.

Coins, bathhouses, marketplaces: these are familiar motifs.

"IS THERE SOMETHING that needs repairing?" Rabbi Shimon asks, following the patriarch's precedent, and he's told, "There's a place that has a questionable status in regards to ritual purity, and it's a bother for the priests to detour around it."

The priests, the Kohanim, held to a stricter form of ritual purity, cannot walk through a cemetery or any area that contains a dead body without defiling themselves. Rabbi Shimon, intent upon a remedy, asks: "Is there somebody who can vouch for the presumption of purity here?"

In other words: *If this place were once an established cemetery, then, of course, nothing can be done. The field will always be off-limits to the Kohanim. But if it's merely a question of a corpse having been temporarily placed or forgotten here, the field might be redeemable.*

An old grandfather says to him, "Here, ben Zakkai used to cut lupines, a portion of which were given to the priests."

This is the answer Rabbi Shimon needs. If, as the old grandfather testifies, the priests used to accept lupines from here, it follows that the field was once pure and may be redeemed. Further proof: Rabban Yohanan ben Zakkai was himself a priest. He would never have been picking lupines in a cemetery.

On the word of this old man, Rabbi Shimon sets about the difficult work of ritually purifying the field.

"Wherever it was hard," we're told, "he purified it; wherever it was soft, he marked it" to warn of impurity.

There's a difference of opinion about the methods he uses, whether he marks off the impure areas or raises and removes corpses through mystical means, but in the end, he purifies the land, creating, as it were, a shortcut for the priests.

A shortcut is a kind of bridge. If you're keeping track, then, bathhouses and bridges, two of the three things he originally denigrated, have now been elevated.

The old grandfather, however, is—not unlike Rabbi Shimon—a garrolous man. Like Rabbi Shimon, the old grandfather doesn't know when *not* to speak, and here, he exclaims in sarcastic wonderment, "Bar Yohai has declared a cemetery ritually *pure!*"

PRAISE. SILENCE. CONDEMNATION.

Inhabit the scene for a moment. Imagine how this old grandfather must grate on Rabbi Shimon's nerves! Not only has Rabbi Shimon worked, presumably for a long time under a hot sun, restoring the field to a state of ritual purity, but the work surely has had a symbolic significance for him: a near corpse himself, he too has been brought back to life. His labor in the field has been a kind of homeopathic self-repair, like curing like. And if all that weren't annoying enough, it was upon the word of this very man that Rabbi Shimon undertook the immense labor in the first place!

His remonstrance is as elegant as it is cutting. He tells the old man:

> If you had not been together with us, or even if you had been together with us and were not counted amongst us, you would be correct speaking this way, but now that you were together with us and were counted amongst us, people will say, "Even prostitutes fix each other's hair."

Even a prostitute, competing with other prostitutes for clients, will help beautify her competitors!

Doesn't it stand to reason that scholars would enhance one another?

The change in Rabbi Shimon is remarkable. An additional repair has now been made beyond the original necessary three. Prostitutes, denigrated along with bathhouses, bridges, and marketplaces in his opening speech, are elevated here in the same way Rabbi Judah might have elevated them, seeing something good in an otherwise blighted thing.

This makes the comedy of the next moment even more troublesome.

Here is another old man, like the old man carrying the myrtle twigs, a man whom Rabbi Shimon might have destroyed, but whom he spared. We've learned the story's pattern: wholesale destruction (*Every place they gazed upon was immediately consumed by fire*) to partial destruction (*Every place Rabbi Elazar struck, Rabbi Shimon healed*) to the sparing of an innocent, righteous man (*See how the commandments are beloved by the people of Israel*), to at last the sparing of a not-so-innocent, not-so-righteous fellow.

Our expectation is that, having repaired himself homeopathically through working the field—transformed like the field, he too is no longer an old cemetery filled with corpses—he will look upon this old grandfather with a benevolent, restorative gaze.

Instead: "Rabbi Shimon gazed at the old man and his soul departed."

The fiery gaze returns. Rabbi Shimon has reverted to his old fiery ways.

HAVE YOU COME OUT TO DESTROY MY WORLD?

Perhaps it's merely a moment of backsliding. After all, Rabbi Shimon has repaired and elevated bathhouses, bridges, and prostitutes. Perhaps there's hope yet for a complete restoration. All that is left is the marketplace, and following the story's logic, that's where our next scene occurs. "Rabbi Shimon went out to the marketplace," we're told, and whom should he encounter there, but his old student Judah ben Gerim, whose verbal indiscretions, we recall, led to Rabbi Shimon's thirteen years of exile in the first place?

Fortunate are you to see me in this state.

On the one hand—or better yet: viewed through a begrudging eye—those thirteen years were difficult and punishing, a terrible deprivation. Viewed through a generous eye, however, those long, terrible years were also an unprecedented opportunity for intense and focused study during which Rabbi Shimon not only received the mystical teachings of the *Zohar* but also developed his personal powers.

Face-to-face now with the author of his troubles, how will he react?

"This one is still alive!" Rabbi Shimon exclaims to himself. Confirming that it is indeed Judah ben Gerim, "He gazed upon him and turned him into a stack of bones."

Our story ends here.

ESSE EST PERCIPI: *To be is to be perceived.* A gaze can confer or restore life: beneath Pinhas ben Yair's caring regard, Shimon bar Yohai is gently eased back into wholeness. But looks can also kill. Like the field Rabbi Shimon repairs, this story is littered with corpses: Judah ben Gerim, the old grandfather, the farmers working in their fields on the day Rabbi Shimon and his son set out, like the undead in a horror movie, from their cave. All these people are destroyed by a look, by a blazing eye. (Even Rabbi Shimon's life is threatened when he draws the unwanted attention of the Roman government: Survival means disappearing from sight.)

Again and again, as I've said, the Talmud anticipates the work of Samuel Beckett. In his play *Happy Days*, for instance, Beckett buries his protagonist up to her neck in sand. His fictions and dramas are filled with extreme cases of human wreckage—the blind, the lame, the broken—and certainly no figure in the Talmud is presented with as much Beckettian panache as Nahum ish Gamzu.

Nahum is actually from a town called Gimzu. He is Nahum ish Gimzu, Nahum, the man from Gimzu, but—we seem to be in the world of Irish literary precedents—in a *Finnegans Wake*–like pun, he is called Nahum ish Gamzu, which literally translates into *Nahum the Man of This Too*.

See for yourself if he doesn't belong on Beckett's stage:

> They said of Nahum ish Gamzu that he was blind in both eyes, and missing both arms and legs. His entire body was covered in boils, and he lay in a bed, the legs of which stood in pails of water, so that ants could not crawl on him.

If this weren't bad enough:

> His house was tottering, and when his students suggested removing his bed and all his furniture from the house . . .

One must save a life before saving property.

> . . . he told them, "My children, first take all my furniture and then my bed and me, for you can be assured that as long as I am in the house, it will not collapse."

While an ordinary person may not rely on miracles, an elevated master is above the law of nature, it seems. According to Nahum, the house, which should fall, will not fall as long as he is inside it, the cosmic merit of his goodness somehow holding everything aloft.

His students follow his instructions: "They took out the furniture and then removed his bed"—with Nahum in it, of course—"and the house immediately collapsed."

His students said to him, "Master, since you are a completely righteous person, why did all this happen to you?" He replied, "My children, I brought it all upon myself."

He tells them how:

Once, I was on my way to my father-in-law's. I had three donkeys, one laden with food, one with drink, and a third with assorted delicacies. A poor man came and stood before me on the road, and he cried, "Master, give me food!" I said to him, "Wait until I unload one of the donkeys." But before I could do so, he died. I fell on my face and cried out, "May my eyes, which took no pity on your eyes, become blind. May my hands, which took no pity on your hands, be cut off! May my legs, which took no pity on your legs, be cut off!" And my mind did not cool down until I said, "Let my entire body be covered in boils!"

Nahum ish Gamzu understands that the work of compassion begins with the eyes. He blames his eyes for not seeing clearly, for not seeing compassionately. With his many donkeys groaning with food, he is blind to the fact that the man confronting him is starving. Had his eyes seen clearly, his legs would have run to the man, his hands would have fed him.

His students take this in. "Woe to us," they say, echoing Pinhas ben Yair, "that we have seen you in such a state," and Nahum, echoing Rabbi Shimon, replies, "Woe to me if you didn't."

IN THE RABBINICAL moral calculus, suffering expiates sin, and a traditional reading of this story would have Nahum, a man of perfect righteousness, pleased to have bartered away his body as an act of atonement for his inadvertent error. In this way, he will arrive in the next world free of the blemish of having allowed a man to die.

The internal logic of the story, however, insists upon a different reading. If the house is able to stand miraculously as long as Nahum is in it, the laws of nature abrogated in deference to the holiness of his person—then, really, there's no point in moving him out. His students, however, have seen his condition more accurately than he has—the house is clearly on the point of collapse—and they rescue him from it in the nick of time. *This is the very act he failed to perform on behalf of the starving man.* There, he was blind to the extremity of the starving man's condition, just as, here, he's blind to the nearly fatal extremity of his own.

This shouldn't surprise us. This blindness to the danger and the darkness in the world is the condition that earned Nahum his nickname. Why did they call him Nahum ish Gamzu, literally, Nahum the Man of This Too? Because no matter what happened to him, he always says, "*Gam zu l'tova*—This, too, is for the good."

The story:

> It once happened that the people of Israel wanted to send a gift to the court of Caesar. They discussed the question of who should go, and they decided to send Nahum ish Gamzu because he was used to miracles.

They assumed that in dealing with Rome, they'd be in need of one.

> They sent him with a chest filled with precious stones and pearls. On his way, he lodged at an inn for the night, and thieves stole the contents of his chest and filled it with earth.

This way, the weight of the chest would remain the same, and Nahum wouldn't perceive that anything had been taken from it. When eventually he discovers the dirt, he doesn't panic. "*Gam zu l'tova*," he says to himself. "This, too, is for the good."

Without fear, one presumes, he proceeds on his way.

> And when he arrived and presented the gift, they saw that the chest was filled with dirt, and Caesar wanted to kill all the Judeans, certain they were mocking him.

"This, too, is for the good," Nahum says, still unperturbed.

Our old friend, the prophet Elijah, appears. Disguised as one of the royal counselors, he tells Caesar, "Perhaps this dirt is the same earth that their father Abraham possessed. When he threw it on his foes, it turned into arrows and his enemies' arrows turned into straw."

As a proof, Elijah cites a verse from the Book of Isaiah—*He made his sword like dirt, his bow like wind-blown straw*—and nobody in Caesar's court (another miracle!) wonders why this courtier they've never seen before is able to quote the Hebrew Scriptures so fluently.

As it turns out, there is one city in their vast empire that the Romans haven't been able to conquer. There, they test the dirt as a secret weapon, and the city falls.

Then they brought the earth to the royal treasury, and they filled the chest with precious stones and pearls and sent Nahum off with great honor.

As blind as ever to the dark side of human nature, he stays at the very same inn on his way back home. The thieves are surprised to see him, surprised to see him alive. "What did you bring as a gift that such great honor should be repaid to you?" they ask.

"Whatever I took from here," he says, "I brought to there."

Imagining that the dirt of their town possesses some magical property, they demolish their homes digging it up. They bring it to the royal palace with predictably bad results—the dirt, a mighty weapon in Nahum's hand, turns to straw in his enemies'—and naturally Caesar has them executed.

A CERTAIN ONE-SIDEDNESS —or should I say one-sightedness?—is under critique here. Though *Gam zu l'tova*, finding the best in every situation, might elevate a Rabbi Judah to a position of prestige or allow a Nahum ish Gamzu to skate through a complicated Rube Goldberg–like political trap unharmed, surviving his encounters with both Caesar and the thieves, there's a dark side to this happy innocence and a price to pay for it. One risks becoming too complacent about one's own suffering and the suffering of others. Blind to the extreme suffering of the starving man, Nahum is equally blind to his own self-neglect.

This twin-sidedness of *Gam zu l'tova* is presented in the comedy and the tragedy of the two stories above, and it's interesting to note that, in the story of Rabbi Shimon, there seem to be two of everything as well: two sets of eyes (one fiery, one watery); two words from the Holy One's mouth; two myrtle branches; two old men; two sons; two marketplaces; two bridges; two bathhouses; two men named Judah; two men who speak in the opening scene, two who remain silent; two incarcerations in the cave, two exits from it; two cultures (Roman, rabbinic); two hideouts (the House of Study, the cave); two scorchings in the beginning of the story, two in the end; two periods of twelve (first years, then months).

The appearance of the running man concretizes this theme of doubleness as an explicit element in the narrative, and he appears, interestingly enough, in the exact center of the story, serving as a kind of hinge between its two parts, and of course, he's holding the symbol of this doubleness: the two myrtle branches.

Wouldn't one be enough for you? Rabbi Shimon asks.

The comedy and suspense of this moment are so delicious—having managed to restrain their fiery destructiveness during the workweek, the two hotheaded gunslingers, intent on reforming themselves, are put to a more difficult test as the Sabbath approaches; any moment now, they may incinerate the poor fellow—that our attention is distracted from the fact that in carrying those two myrtle branches, the running man brings onstage an explicit statement of the story's themes.

Wouldn't one be enough for you? Rabbi Shimon asks. One: one culture, one modality of being, either rabbinic or Roman, sacred or earthly, societal or wild, physical or spiritual, male or female.

But no, the running man says, two are necessary. Just as the Holy One spoke one word that was heard as two different utterances—*remember* and *keep*, the first a positive commandment, the second a negative commandment; the first urging action, the second restraint; the first from the sphere of open flowing love

(called *Hesed* in the Kabbalah), the second from the sphere of re-
stricted, bounded love (*Gevurah*) — the Torah itself opens with an
image of oneness birthing two: *In the beginning, the Holy One created Heaven and earth.*

This sense of twoness is alien to Rabbi Shimon, however. He
has no need for Heaven *and* earth. His Torah — the esoteric Torah
of the *Zohar* — is received, via the mortifications of the cave, outside the world of human society and as near to the other world
as one can get while remaining yet alive. He and his son are no
longer fit for earthly life. Upon their first entrance into the world
from the cave, they're more like fiery cherubim than men. Only
upon their second entrance is Rabbi Shimon able to restrain himself. Rabbi Elazar, however, is not, and the older man must undo
the damage his impetuous son creates: *Every place Rabbi Elazar
struck, Rabbi Shimon healed.*

We two are enough, Rabbi Shimon tells his son. Our twoness —
striking and healing — is sufficient for the world, but this is a one-
sided sense of twoness, and the Aggadist sketches out the issue in
a more complete way: there is a soul and there is a body, he seems
to say, and *the two* must serve the divine in holiness, the two must
serve the Holy One. The soul, a sojourner in these earthly spheres,
an exile from the supernal realms, must *remember* the Sabbath;
while the body, born, as the Mishnah states, from a putrid drop
and destined for a place of dust, maggots, and worms, must *keep*
the Sabbath. Rabbis Shimon and Elazar, concerned with the needs
of the soul alone and too focused on Heaven, perceive the normal
workaday world as degraded and fallen. Why deal with earthly
things at all? Rabbi Shimon asks. Isn't one — oneness, the holy
one — enough for you?

The fiery eye of the dry cave, the watery eye of the bathhouse: the
running man already knows what Rabbi Shimon must learn. It's
a simple matter of optics: depth comes from a binocular perspective. Human beings live in twoness, and there is an upside to
Roman civilization (*They've established markets, they've established
bridges, they've established bathhouses*) and a downside to a monas-
tic life lived only for the sake of Heaven (*Have you come out to destroy my world?*).

HUMAN BEINGS LIVE IN TWONESS: These existential polarities extend to the three dimensions of space (up/down, east/west, north/south), the one dimension of time (past/future), and the fifth dimension of morality (good/evil). And the tension between these primary oppositions—between the demands of Heaven and the desires of earth—runs like a braided red thread through the fabric of the Torah's sacred law as well.

For two years, two ancient wisdom schools, the School of Hillel and the School of Shammai, debated each other over a crucial question: *Is it better to have been born or not?* The question is originally posed, according to tradition, by King Solomon in the Book of Ecclesiastes: "I counted the dead who have died more fortunate than the living who are yet alive, and happier than each are they who have never been born."

I imagine the debate as a kind of philosophical Manhattan Project, the best and the brightest minds living together in seclusion, though perhaps in two camps, working to reach a consensus on what, after all, is not a small issue.

This is not the first time the two schools have debated. The Schools of Hillel and Shammai debated each other for three years over the question of which school could claim supremacy for its views. At the end of three long years, a voice from Heaven declares, "These and these are both the words of the living God."

(We cannot escape Rabbi Shimon's question. It haunts this debate as well: *Isn't one enough for you?* Must there really be two *authentic* versions of the living word of God?)

Still, a society needs a practical bottom line. Though the words of a living God might be hard to pin down, when it comes to law, even sacred law, human beings can follow only one opinion, and so it was decided that, in practice, the law will follow the views of the School of Hillel.

Why?

Because the Hillelists "were easygoing and forbearing, and they would study their own opinions as well as the opinions of the School of Shammai, and they would even mention the teachings of the School of Shammai before their own."

This dichotomy of styles seems to derive from the general

natures of the founders of the two schools. Everyone knows the story of the would-be convert who asks each man to teach him the entirety of the sacred law while he stands on one leg. Shammai picks up a stick—he was a builder, his defenders claim, and the stick merely a yardstick he wished to use as a visual aid in discussing correct proportions as a path to righteousness—but the heathen, feeling threatened, runs out. Hillel, on the other hand, tells the man, "What is hateful unto you, do not do to your fellow. That is the whole of the Torah. The rest is commentary. Now, go and learn."

TO HAVE BEEN BORN or not to have been born? That is the question.

According to Ecclesiastes, not to have been born is the preferable alternative.

Like physicists looking into new and strange quanta, the Schools of Hillel and Shammai explore this issue for two years. They're not discussing—as we would be discussing—whether life is enjoyable or not. Theirs is a universe that, at its core, is moral, and so in more precise terms, the issue for them is: in a world full of temptation and error, a world that is a famine for the soul but a feast for the senses, where dense materiality can so easily extinguish the bright and vulnerable flame of the sacred, is it worthwhile for the soul to risk the journey through this dark vale, risking its own endarkenment, in exchange for the opportunity to elevate and illuminate the physical world through the acts of goodness, kindness, and mercy one might (or might not) perform as a temporary resident here?

Let's face it: even were the stakes not so high, life is at best a battering and a bruising affair. The soul can so easily lose its way, becoming lost in hatred, jealousy, fear, depression, addiction. Certainly, from a theocentric point of view, the risks far outweigh the benefits.

TWO YEARS IN, the two schools are still at loggerheads. Unable to reach a consensus, they put it to a vote: *Is it better or not to have been born?* Shammai's stricter view prevails. "They conclude: it's better for a person not to have been created than to have been created."

A lot of good this does us all, each of us already having been created, and we can sense the hand of the Hillelists in the practicality of the concluding proviso: "But now that he has been created, let him *search* his deeds."

Meaning, some suggest, a person's *past* deeds. Let him reflect upon his past sins, so that he may repent. "Although others have it: Now that he has been created, let him *examine* his deeds." Meaning his future deeds. Let him carefully consider the goodness of his *future* deeds.

Search and *examine* in Hebrew are nearly identical words— יפשפש and ימשמש—and the two interpretations seem to be the result of a typographical ambiguity. Are those *pehs* (פ) or *mems* (מ)? This slight variation creates a world of difference, and it seems clear which version belongs to the School of Shammai and which to the School of Hillel, the one pessimistic, dwelling on an unchangeable past, the other optimistic, hopeful for an as-yet-unlived future.

In our story of Rabbi Shimon and the cave, eyes search and eyes examine. The searching eye searches for sin, for failings, for shortcomings—this is the fiery eye that burns and destroys—while the examining eye, like a doctor's eye, a critical diagnostician's eye—like Pinhas ben Yair's eye in the bathhouse—looks for what needs repairing, whether it's Rabbi Shimon's cracked skin or a field filled with corpses. (Think how carefully Rabbi Shimon must have *examined* that field: *Wherever it was hard, he purified it; wherever it was soft, he marked it to warn of impurity.*)

The searching eye, finding fault, responds with fire and destruction (whether it's Noah's world or Lot's Sodom), while the examining eye, finding faults, responds with tears and reparation (*The Holy One heals the brokenhearted and binds up their wounds*). The searching eye belongs to the School of Shammai, the examining eye to the School of Hillel; and though both heed the words of the living God, the School of Hillel is superior, we're told, because it integrates its opposite. It understands that a two-point perspective creates depth. Close one eye, rely on one eye alone, and you lose your bearings.

Humility, gentleness, forbearance, characteristics of Hillel, are the key. That, in terms of practical law, the School of Hillel's viewpoint prevails over the School of Shammai's, we're told, "teaches you that whoever humbles himself, the Holy One raises up. Whoever raises himself up, the Holy One lowers. Whoever searches for prominence, prominence flees from him. But whoever flees from prominence, prominence searches for him. And whoever forces time, time forces him, but whoever yields to time, time yields to him."

NOW, WE MIGHT ASSUME that Rabbi Shimon is a disciple of the School of Shammai, but this is not the case. His teacher is Rabbi Akiva, whose teachers, Rabbis Joshua ben Hananiah and Eliezer ben Hyrcanus, were students of Rabban Yohanan ben Zakkai, whose teacher was Hillel. Though Rabbi Shimon is firmly planted in the traditions of Hillel, he seems not to have fully integrated them into his way of life.

At the beginning of our story, contemplating the glories of Roman civilization, he's full of fiery condemnation. His twelve years in the cave only exacerbate his sense of impatience with the world. Worse: the unworldly powers he attains through these twelve punishing years of self-mortification and study confer upon him the ability to demolish anything he disdains.

What happened to the easygoing, forbearing Hillelist? you might wonder.

This disruption in the chain of continuity occurs at the very moment Rabbi Shimon receives his rabbinic ordination:

Rabbi Abba said: "Formerly, each master used to ordain his own pupils: thus, Rabban Yohanan ben Zakkai ordained Rabbi Eliezer and Rabbi Joshua; Rabbi Joshua ordained Rabbi Akiva; Rabbi Akiva ordained Rabbi Meir and Rabbi Shimon. But when Rabbi Akiva added, 'Let Rabbi Meir sit in the first place,' Rabbi Shimon's face turned pale. At this, Rabbi Akiva said to Rabbi Shimon, 'Isn't it enough for you that I and your Creator recognize your strength?'"

This being passed over, a great wounding to his *amour propre,* seems to create a bitterness in Rabbi Shimon—"Learn my rules," he later tells his students, "for my rules surpass the very best of Rabbi Akiva's rules"—and this bitterness extends also towards the Romans, towards his wife, towards the plowers and the sowers, towards the running man, towards the old grandfather, towards Judah ben Gerim, towards anyone, in fact, who stands in opposition to his will.

Our Aggadist could not be clearer about condemning this unharnessed fury: according to our story, the Holy One himself rebukes Rabbi Shimon, sending him back to his cave for a thirteenth purgatorial year. This countereducation continues with his encounters with the running man and Pinhas ben Yair, and also with his clearing the field of corpses. Imagistically, he is clearing the corpses out of his own personal history, a symbolic atonement for the murder of the plowers and the sowers. In emulation of them, he must work the field, bringing life from it, breathing life into it, atoning for their deaths and sanctifying their work.

The question with which this great act of atonement begins— *Is the field a cemetery or merely a place where a dead body or two have been left?*—resounds in a personal way for Rabbi Shimon. At this point in the story, he must surely be asking the same question about himself: Is *he* a cemetery, intentionally full of the dead, or have a corpse or two just happened to have been mislaid here?

Can he, like the field, be redeemed and made pure?

Through the events of the story, he lives out a complete cycle of the soul's transmigration: sentenced to death, judged by the heavenly court, purified in the purgatorial fires of Gehenna, he is, at last, born anew. But has he changed? Has he, at last, doused his Shammaitic fire and embraced the gentleness and forbearance of the Hillelist teachings?

Bar Yohai has declared a cemetery ritually pure! the old grandfather exclaims, and we can hear this exclamation in two ways, either as a cry of wonder in celebration of Rabbi Shimon's remarkable resurrection of the field and of himself, or as a mocking statement of sarcastic derision. That he addresses Rabbi Shimon in the third person implies the presence of an audience. (This moment, of course, is paired with Elijah's gentle use of the same locution.) But is the old grandfather publicly humiliating Rabbi Shimon or elevating him in public?

This same ambiguity muddies the story Rabbi Shimon's student Judah ben Gerim tells, the story that sets our story in motion. Was Judah ben Gerim informing on Rabbi Shimon, denouncing him to the authorities, or was he, in fact, bragging about his beloved teacher's fearlessness in the face of Roman oppression, elevating him in the circle of their friends?

We don't know. The story doesn't tell us. All we know is how Rabbi Shimon reacts to both the old grandfather and Judah ben Gerim. Seeing with a critical eye and hearing with a critical ear, Rabbi Shimon hears only criticism and betrayal. Both the old grandfather and Judah ben Gerim are, like Rabbi Shimon, intemperate in speech, and perhaps this cuts too close to the bone for him. Hard upon his clearing of the field, both are immediately consigned to his private cemetery—the old grandfather perishes, Judah ben Gerim is turned into a stack of bones—and Rabbi Shimon is back exactly where he began, his rebirth betrayed.

SOPHOCLES'S PLAY, *Oedipus Rex*, begins with an image of a sick city. Thebes is sick because it is harboring a murderer, a man guilty, as well, of incest. Through his searching and his examination, Oedipus, the king of the city-state, discovers to his dismay that he himself is the guilty party. He blinds and exiles himself, and the tragedy ends on a dark note, Sophocles unable apparently to end on the happy note that the play itself forecasts: the restoration of health to the city.

This is, of course, the correct aesthetic choice. It's hard to imagine a happy ending—a sigh of relief on the part of the Thebans, leaves returning to the trees, wheat sprouting in the fields, birds chirping—while Oedipus, blind and broken, is led into exile off-stage by his sister-daughters.

Rabbi Shimon's story, too, opens with an ailing city, a Jerusalem oppressed by an occupying force. In an odd symmetry with *Oedipus Rex*, the issue of the city drops out of our story as well, though, here, it's not so much a failure on the part of the story-teller as on the part of the protagonist.

Our story reads as a typical hero tale: a character, separated from his society, performs amazing deeds in the wilderness and returns with a boon to share with the entire community. Sensitive to the failings of human nature, however, the Aggadist invests our "hero" with all sorts of all-too-human traits. Yes, Rabbi Shimon must leave his home and his family; yes, he faces a great trial; yes, he returns home from this quest with an extraordinary power, the ability to incinerate his enemies. But instead of using this hard-won ability for the good of the community—that is to say, against the Roman occupiers—he uses it to settle personal grudges against his fellow countrymen.

Oedipus ends, broken by tragedy but also exalted by it and utterly transformed. Rabbi Shimon attempts a self-transformation, but he ends up more or less restored to his old self, transformed neither by his hero's quest nor by the boons with which he returns from it.

Even worse: His failure to integrate his experience plays out in the lives of his sons.

Rabbi Elazar ben Rabbi Shimon (flourished c. 3910/end of second century CE)

RABBI ELAZAR, THE SON OF RABBI SHIMON, ONCE met a detective who was assigned to catch thieves. Rabbi Elazar asked: "How can you recognize them? Are they not like wild beasts that prowl at night and hide during the day? Perhaps you sometimes arrest the innocent and leave the guilty free?"

The detective answered: "What can I do? It's the king's command." Rabbi Elazar: "Come, I will teach you what to do. At nine o'clock in the morning, go into a tavern. Should you see a man dozing with a cup of wine in his hand, inquire about him. If he is a disciple of the wise, you may assume that he has risen very early in the morning to pursue his studies; if he is a day laborer, that he is up early to do his work. Or perhaps he works at night, hammering metal. But if he's none of these, he's a thief and you should arrest him."

The report of this conversation was brought to the king's attention, and the decision was (as the proverb puts it) "Let the reader of the message become the messenger."

Rabbi Elazar, the son of Rabbi Shimon, was accordingly sent for and was appointed to arrest thieves. Rabbi Joshua ben Korhah sent word to him, "O Vinegar, son of Wine! How long will you deliver up the people of our God for slaughter!" Rabbi Elazar sent back: "I weed out thorns from the vineyard." Rabbi Joshua replied, "Let the Owner of the Vineyard come and himself weed out its thorns."

One day a mere fuller met him and called him "Vinegar, son of

Wine!" Rabbi Elazar said to himself: "Since he is so insolent, he must surely be a felon." So he gave the order to his attendants: "Arrest him!" and they arrested him. When Rabbi Elazar's anger cooled, he went back in order to secure the fuller's release, but could not do so. Then he applied to himself the verse "He who guards his mouth and his tongue, keeps his soul from troubles." When they subsequently hanged the fuller, Rabbi Elazar stood under the gallows and wept. His disciples said to him, "Master, do not grieve, for this fuller and his son together raped a betrothed maiden on the Day of Atonement."

At this, Rabbi Elazar laid his hand on his belly and exclaimed, "Rejoice, my innards, rejoice! If matters you were in doubt about fall out this way, how much more so matters about which you are certain! I am well assured that neither worms nor decay will have power over you!"

Nevertheless, his conscience had no rest. So he was given a sleeping draught and taken into a marble chamber, where his abdomen was opened. Out of it baskets and baskets of fat were removed and placed in the sun during Tammuz and Av, yet the fat did not putrefy. Consequently, he applied to himself the verse "Even my flesh rests secure."

Yet even so, Rabbi Elazar ben Rabbi Shimon's conscience continued to trouble him. He therefore invoked painful afflictions upon himself, so that although sixty sheets were spread under him in the evening, sixty basins of blood and pus were removed from under him in the morning. Every morning his wife prepared a mixture of sixty kinds of fig pap for him, and when he ate it, he recovered.

But his wife did not permit him to go to the House of Study, so that the sages would not press him. In the evening, Rabbi Elazar would invite his afflictions back, saying, "Come back, my brethren and friends!" And in the morning, he would say to them, "Depart lest you disturb my studies!"

One day his wife, overhearing him, cried out: "So it is of your own volition that you bring these afflictions upon yourself and to pay for their treatment, you squander the money of my father's house." With that taunt, she went off to her father's house, in defiance of her husband. Just then, sixty mariners were sailing on the sea. When a huge wave crested over them and was about to sink their vessel, they rose up in prayer, saying, "O God of Elazar, answer us!" and the sea's wrath abated. When the mariners reached dry land, they brought Rabbi Elazar a gift of sixty slaves bearing sixty purses. The slaves prepared a mixture of sixty kinds of fig pap for him, and he ate it, applying to himself the verse "Torah is like the merchant ships, fetching food stuffs from afar."

One day, Rabbi Elazar's wife said to her daughter, "Go and find out how your father is faring, how he is now." She went to him and on her arrival her father said to her, "Go tell your mother that our wealth is still greater than that of her father's house."

He ate, drank, and recovered, then went to the House of Study. Sixty specimens of blood were brought before him, and he declared all the specimens pure. But the sages criticized him, saying, "Is it possible that there was not even one specimen about which there might have been some doubt?" He responded, "If it is as I have said, let all the future children borne by these women be males; if not, let there be one female among them." All the children were males and were named Elazar after him.

In his last illness, Rabbi Elazar's arm once happened to be exposed and his wife both laughed and wept. She laughed because she said to herself: How happy I am—how happy my lot that I have been able to cleave to the body of so righteous a man! She wept because she said: Alas the body of so righteous a man is destined for the dust.

As he was dying, he said to his wife, "I know that the sages are angry with me and will not properly attend to my burial. Let my body repose in the attic, and do not be afraid of my presence there."

Rabbi Samuel bar Nahmani said: "Rabbi Jonathan's mother told me that the wife of Rabbi Elazar ben Rabbi Shimon had told her, 'He lay in his attic not less than eighteen nor more than twenty-two years. Whenever I ascended there, I would examine his hair, and if even a single hair happened to fall out, blood would spurt forth. One day, when I saw a worm issue from his ear, I was much grieved. But then he appeared to me in a dream and told me to think nothing of it. "This has happened," he said, "because I once heard a disciple of the wise being belittled and did not protest as I should have done.""'"

Whenever two people in a lawsuit came before him, they stood at the door, and each stated his case. Then a voice would issue from the attic, saying, "So-and-so, you are liable; so-and-so, you are in the clear."

One day, Rabbi Elazar's wife was quarreling with a neighbor woman who cursed her, "May you be like you husband, who had no proper burial!" Consequently, the sages said, "Now that Rabbi Elazar's being unburied has come to be known, it is not right to have it continue thus."

Others say: "Rabbi Shimon bar Yohai appeared to the sages in a dream and said to them, 'I have a dear child among you, whom you refuse to bring to me.' Then the sages decided to attend to his burial. But the townspeople of Akhbera would not let them, because during all the years that Rabbi Elazar ben Rabbi Shimon lay asleep in his attic, no wild beast had come to their town. However, one day—it was the eve of the Day of Atonement—while the people of Akhbera were preoccupied, the sages sent word to the townspeople of Biri, and they took his bier down and carried it to the cave where his father was buried. When they found a snake coiled at its entrance, they said to it, 'Snake, O snake, open your mouth and let go of your tail, so that a son may join his father.' At that, the snake opened its mouth and they were able to enter."

BABYLONIAN TALMUD,
TRACTATE *BAVA METZIA* 83B–84A

Memo Three B

Rabbi Pinhas ben Yair
(first third of the third century CE)

WHILE RABBI PINHAS BEN YAIR WAS ON HIS WAY TO ransom captives, he came to the River Ginnai. "O Ginnai," said he, "split your waters for me, that I may pass through you." The river: "You are traveling to do the will of your Maker; I, too, am flowing to do the will of my Maker. You may or may not accomplish your task. I am certain to accomplish mine."

Rabbi Pinhas: "If you will not split, I shall decree against you that no water ever pass through you again." The river split. A certain man who was carrying wheat for Passover happened to be there. So Rabbi Pinhas told the river, "Split for this man also, since he is occupied with performing a sacred commandment." The river split again. Now, an Arab who had joined them earlier during the journey was there too, and Rabbi Pinhas once again told the river, "Split for this one as well, so that he should not say, 'Is this how a fellow traveler is treated?'" The river split a third time.

His disciples asked, "Can we cross it too?" Rabbi Pinhas replied, "He who feels certain that never in his life has he put his fellow to shame can cross and suffer no harm." Rav Joseph explained: "How great is this man, greater than Moses and the six hundred thousand Hebrews for whom the Red Sea split! For there, it split only once, but here it split thrice!"

Continuing on his journey, Rabbi Pinhas came to a certain inn, where some barley was placed before his donkey, but she would not eat. The barley was sifted, but the donkey would not eat. It was carefully picked, still the donkey would not eat. "Perhaps," suggested Rabbi Pinhas, "the barley has not been tithed?" The barley was tithed, and then the donkey ate it. Rabbi Pinhas said, "This poor creature is on a journey to do the will of her Creator, and you try to feed her untithed grain!"

His disciples asked him, "Our master, did you not teach us that he who purchases grain from an unlearned person for an animal is exempt from the obligation about grain that may not have been tithed?" Rabbi Pinhas replied, "But what can I do with this poor creature if she chooses to be strict with herself?"

When Rebbi heard of the arrival of Rabbi Pinhas, he went out to meet him and asked him, "Will you please dine with me?" "Certainly," Rabbi Pinhas answered. Rebbi's face at once brightened with joy. So Rabbi Pinhas said, "Did you suppose that I had vowed not to derive benefit from a son of Israel? Oh, no. The people of Israel are holy! But there are some who desire to benefit others and have not the means; while others have the means, but not the desire, and it is written, 'never dine with a niggardly man, never fancy his dainties,' etc. But you have the desire and also the means. However, right now I am in a hurry, for I am engaged in fulfilling a commandment. But on my return, I will come and visit you."

When Rabbi Pinhas returned, he happened to enter Rebbi's courtyard by a gate near which some white mules were standing. He exclaimed, "The Angel of Death is in this house, and I'm to dine here!" As soon as Rebbi heard what Rabbi Pinhas had said, he went out to him and announced, "I shall sell the mules." Rabbi Pinhas replied, "'You shall not put a stumbling block before the blind.'" "I shall abandon them." "You would be causing damage as they run wild." "I shall hamstring them." "There is a prohibition against inflicting pain on living creatures." "I shall kill them." "That would be counter to the ruling prohibiting wanton waste."

As Rebbi kept pressing Rabbi Pinhas, a mountain rose up between them. Then Rebbi burst into tears and said, "If in their lives, how much more so after their deaths!"

BABYLONIAN TALMUD, TRACTATE *HULLIN* 71A–B;
JERUSALEM TALMUD, TRACTATE *DEMAI* 1:3, 22A.

Rabbi Judah ben Gerim
(c. 3910/end of second century CE)

RABBI JONATHAN BEN ASMAI AND RABBI JUDAH BEN Gerim took leave of Rabbi Shimon bar Yohai in the evening. In the morning, they returned and took leave of him again. He said to them, "Did you not already take leave of me last night?" They said to him, "You have taught us, our master, that a student who takes leave of his teacher and who remains staying overnight in the city must take leave of him a second time."

BABYLONIAN TALMUD, TRACTATE *MOED KATAN* 9A.

Chapter 3

Towards the Hearts of Sons

AN EXPERIMENT WAS PERFORMED BY SOCIAL SCIEN-
tists at Harvard: people the world over were given envelopes containing various sums of money. Sometimes large, sometimes
small. The envelopes also contained instructions. Some of the
people were instructed to spend the money on themselves. The
others were instructed to spend the money on other people. At
the end of the day, no matter what the sum, the people who spent
the money on other people reported being happier than the people
who spent the money on themselves.

With a very few exceptions, this was true worldwide, and it
makes sense, I suppose. We are born wanting—wanting food,
wanting shelter, wanting love. We arrive on this planet with nothing and very little ability to get anything. At least not on our own.
If, as infants, we were kept alive by powerful-seeming people who
gave us food and shelter and love, it follows that, by providing love
and food and shelter for others later in our lives, we ourselves feel
strong, powerful, independent, *life-giving*. In other words: happy.

THE TALMUDIC VIEW OF LIFE, it seems to me, can be boiled
down to six areas of concern. It's as though the writers of the *Aggadah* had sent us six memos—six memos from the last millennium—reminding us of these six concerns. A perfect action, a
holy action, a *righteous* action, successfully addresses all six.

The first memo reminds us to take care of HEAVEN. You can imagine a little yellow Post-It stuck to your refrigerator door: REMEMBER: TAKE CARE OF HEAVEN! The Talmudic worldview is theocentric, after all, and it's our responsibility to water HEAVEN daily, as though it were a garden, with our prayers and blessings and acts of goodness, kindness, and mercy. The second memo reminds us to take care of EARTH, to be good stewards of the biosphere. Preferable though it may be to have never been born, now that we're born, we need a place to live. The better we care for the EARTH, if only in terms of agriculture, the better the EARTH cares for us. The third memo reminds us to take care of the ANCESTORS, the people who preceded us in time, who in the great copulatory chain of being are the infinitely regressing causes of which we are the most recent or one of the most recent effects. Our ANCESTORS live through us now, and we mustn't do anything to retroactively shame or humiliate or dishonor them. The same is true for our DESCENDANTS, the subject of the fourth memo. We must make certain our actions are beneficial for our DESCENDANTS, most of whom have yet to appear (or who may never appear but who are present, nevertheless, *in potentia*). No one, for instance, enjoys having a mass murderer for a grandfather. The fifth memo reminds us to take care of our SELF, and the sixth to take care of OTHERS.

A graphic model of this picture might resemble a Calder mobile hanging in dynamic tension, with HEAVEN above us, the EARTH below us, the ANCESTORS behind us, the DESCENDANTS before us, the SELF at the center, and OTHERS all across the lateral circumference.

Like a mobile, this six-point system is dynamic. An imbalance in one area disturbs the entire field.

As human beings, no matter how grounded in a tradition, we live with a finite sense of consciousness in temporary and ever-shifting circumstances, and as a consequence, we tend to improvise, to bootstrap our lives. It's all on-the-job training, and because of our limited knowledge, we often prefer one memo over the others.

We all know people who even deny the existence of such concerns. The proud atheist denies the obligation to HEAVEN, the greedy developer his obligation to the EARTH. The religious zealot will destroy the EARTH and the fullness thereof (including you and your neighbors) to perform the will of HEAVEN. In my experience, most people's default modes are set to SELF with little interest in OTHERS. And yet, as we all know, the person who privileges OTHERS at the complete expense of SELF is courting disaster.

As we see from the stories in this book, when any of these six reference points is out of balance, *all* six are. Take Rabbi Yohanan as an example. Privileging HEAVEN above EARTH by placing the state of Resh Lakish's soul above his physical existence, Rabbi Yohanan allows his concern for OTHERS—for Resh Lakish, in this case—to overwhelm his concern for SELF. As a result, both men are destroyed. Rabbi Yohanan additionally loses his connection with his DESCENDANTS—Resh Lakish's son, his nephew, is the only male child of the family—and his obligation to his ANCESTORS, to the people who came before him, is disturbed: he is no longer alive in the world to create goodness and mercy, as a consequence of his ANCESTORS' lives.

Rabbi Yohanan's wiser and more beautiful sister, on the other hand, though she appears in the pages of the Talmud for no more than three or four lines, balances all six concerns with grace and beauty. (For this reason, she is, for me, a hidden heroine of the Talmudic enterprise.) Her actions demonstrate a balanced regard for her SELF as well as for the OTHERS in her life. She loves both her husband *and* her brother: her own sense of well-being depends upon their well-being, and in advocating for forgiveness, she is giving to all three of them. She acts as well for the benefit of the family line, giving to both her ANCESTORS and her DESCENDANTS. Resh Lakish's son needs a father. He could use a loving, mentoring uncle. We've seen how his own orphanhood numbed Rabbi Yohanan's emotional life. The last thing his sister wants is for this psychic wound to keep reverberating through the generations of their family. We can only imagine that the souls of her parents would be pleased if their two orphaned children had at last found a stable home, free of the disruptions and disconti-nuities their own deaths caused in their children's lives.

HEAVEN is also better served by the continuation of the holy companionship of Rabbi Yohanan and Resh Lakish: together, the two served the Holy One through study and the performance of good deeds in a way that neither of them could do alone, their holy work bringing goodness and mercy to the EARTH.

WITH RABBI SHIMON BAR YOHAI, we see how the fire of HEAVEN, blazing through his burning gaze, scorches everything he comes into contact with. Privileging HEAVEN above all else, his default mode set closer to SELF than to OTHERS, he moves through life with a scorched-earth policy, burning up, sometimes literally, sometimes verbally, anyone who stands in opposition to him: the Romans, the farmers, the old grandfather, his chatty student. He has shrugged off his obligation to the EARTH (the farmers), to OTHERS (the Romans, his wife), to his ANCESTORS (the old grandfather, as well as the line of his teachers, all the way back to Hillel). HEAVEN and SELF—a poisonous cocktail—are the only obligations Rabbi Shimon appears to acknowledge, and, as we'll see, his one-sided, one-sighted, unrepentant stance has grave implications for his DESCENDANTS, the sons who come after him.

THIS SPLIT IN Rabbi Shimon's character, his failure to integrate a Hillel-like compassion with a Shammai-like sense of proportion, is lived out in the next generation by his sons, Rabbi Elazar, his wilderness son, the son he possesses by blood, and Rabbi Pinhas ben Yair, his civilized son-in-law, the son he possesses through social convention.

Both sons suffer equally through a one-sidedness of their own, Rabbi Elazar carrying on his father's fiery path through the world, and Rabbi Pinhas ben Yair, despite his goodness and his kindness, causing suffering for those he cares about as well.

LET'S TAKE A LOOK AT Rabbi Elazar first.

A boy of enormous appetites even in his youth, he enters the Talmudic stream of stories as a bit of a bruiser:

> Some donkey drivers, wishing to buy grain, came to his father's house, where they saw Rabbi Elazar seated near the oven from which his mother kept taking out loaves of freshly baked bread. As she took them out, he kept eating them, until he had consumed all the troughs of bread. "What a shame!" the donkey drivers said. "A pernicious snake must be lodged in this young man's belly."

They are donkey drivers, of course, and not dietitians, but to their untrained eye, the malady appears potentially catastrophic: "He may well bring famine on the world!" they say.

Young Elazar overhears them. As sensitive to slights as his father, he's quick to act upon his resentment:

> When they went out to fetch their load, he took hold of their donkeys and hoisted them onto the roof. When they returned, they looked for their donkeys but could not find them until they raised their eyes and saw them on the roof.

"Perhaps you said something to offend him?" Rabbi Shimon asks when the drivers complain to him. For his part, he's understandably annoyed, and he rebukes them:

> "Why did you say something that might make him the victim of the evil eye? Was it *your* food he ate? Do *you* have to pay for his food? Did not the Holy One who created him also create food for him? Nevertheless, go and tell him in my name to fetch the donkeys down, and he will do so."
>
> The second feat was even more striking than the first. In taking up the donkeys, Elazar had hoisted them up one by one; in bringing them down, he carried them down two by two.

Though relishing Elazar's Esau-like strength, the Aggadist is equally eager to assure us this strength does not persist into his later life as a scholar: "Once he began to study Torah, however, he could not carry even his own cloak."

Still, though he may have lost his brawn, a bit of his brutishness remains.

IT SHOULDN'T SURPRISE US. Rabbi Shimon seems not to have concerned himself with Elazar's education. The boy grows up untutored and wild. Rabbi Yossi—yes, this is the same Rabbi Yossi who responded to Rabbi Judah's praise of Roman culture with silence—chooses not to remain silent here. Taking Elazar aside, Rabbi Yossi tells him, "You come from the stock of righteous men, and yet you are not a student of Torah."

He begins "teaching him one chapter of Scripture, then a second and then a third." When at last he brings the boy to school, Elazar's rough appearance inspires loathing, even in the teachers: "When Rebbi saw him, he asked Rabbi Yossi, 'Did you have to bring such a one as this with you?' Rabbi Yossi said, 'He comes from the stock of Rabbi Shimon bar Yohai.'"

According to another tradition, it's not Rabbi Yossi, but the prophet Elijah, who convinces Elazar to dedicate his life to the holy Torah. Elazar is working as a porter at the time, and, here, we see clearly that the child is father of the man:

"One time, Elijah the prophet came to him, disguised as an old man, and he said to him, 'Get a beast of burden ready for me.'"

The consummate professional, Elazar asks the old man, "And what do you have to load on the animal?"

"This baggage, my cloak, and myself as a rider," Elijah replies.

More interested in profits than in prophets, Elazar reasons to himself: "Look at this old man—I could load him onto my back and carry him to the end of the world, yet he says to me, 'Get a beast of burden for me!'"

Because Elijah insists upon riding, Elazar puts the old man and his baggage on his own back and takes him "up mountainsides, down into valleys, and across fields of thorns."

The animal side of Elazar's nature is in the ascendant here, and when the prophet, playing his usual mind-altering tricks, bears down with all his weight upon him, Elazar brays like a donkey: "Old man, old man, ride more lightly. If not, I shall throw you off!"

The angels of his better nature arrive, and Elazar offers Elijah a chance to rest. "He took him to a field, set him down under a tree, and gave him something to eat and drink."

After he eats, Elijah asks him where all this heavy labor is getting him, wondering if it wouldn't be better for him to take up the vocation of his forebears—i.e., the Torah—to study its sacred laws and to follow its holy paths. Elazar asks Elijah if he will teach him, and "according to some, Elijah taught Elazar Torah for thirteen years."

This version of the story reaches the same conclusion as the first: so much of Elazar's animal strength is spent in his studies that, afterwards, "he could not even carry his own cloak."

THOUGH, I'M AFRAID, this transformation from donkey to rider doesn't proceed without a hitch.

Despite years of immersion in his holy studies—I'm counting thirteen years with Elijah and thirteen with his father in the cave, although from a mythic point of view, those may have been the same thirteen years—the coarser attributes of Elazar's mulish character stubbornly resist refinement, and the next time we see him, though he's riding firmly atop his own animal—having mastered his baser instincts, he's graduated imagistically from beast of burden to man—the mulish side of his character remains:

> It happened that Rabbi Elazar, the son of Rabbi Shimon, was coming home from his teacher's house in a town called Migdal Gedor. He was riding on a donkey and traveling along a riverbank. He rejoiced greatly and was feeling very proud of himself, for he had learned much Torah. There chanced upon his way an exceedingly ugly man. He said to him, "Peace be upon you, my teacher," but he did not return the greeting.

Thanks to the fog of ambiguous pronouns—*he said to him*—we do not really know at this point who is speaking to whom. This ambiguity is pregnant with possible meanings. Though the ugly man seems merely to be greeting Rabbi Elazar with the respect due a scholar—*Peace be upon you, my teacher*—by story's end, he will turn out to be the teacher, having taught Rabbi Elazar a lesson. In fact, according to Rashi, the ugly man is none other than the prophet Elijah, Rabbi Elazar's old teacher, returned, again in disguise, to continue what seems to be his never-ending tutorial with his mulish charge.

Rabbi Elazar, unlike Nahum ish Gamzu upon spotting the starving man, does not bound off his donkey. Neither does he look with rapid or too-tardy compassion upon this other who has crossed his path. On the contrary, he replies, "Empty One! How ugly is that man! Are all the people of your city as ugly as you?"

Ambiguities abound. Once again, it's not clear who is being addressed as "Empty One!" Is Rabbi Elazar speaking to himself? At this point, he doesn't appear to be speaking directly to the ugly man. Is Rabbi Elazar perhaps addressing the Holy One in this way? It's unlikely and yet, the Holy One seems to have entered the equation, since the ugly man replies, "I don't know. But go and tell the Potter who made me, 'How ugly is this vessel you have made.'"

One way or the other, the Holy One has been insulted—an ugly thing to do—and the story at last clears up the ambiguity concerning its speakers: "When he realized he had sinned, he got down from the donkey, prostrated himself before him, and said, 'I have spoken to you out of turn. Forgive me!'"

But the ugly man is not so easily appeased.

"He answered him, 'I will not forgive you until you go to the Potter who made me and tell him, "How ugly is this vessel you have made."'"

Rabbi Elazar is in something of a jam. Having elevated himself above the ugly man—not only is he sitting astride his ass, he has come from Migdal Gedor, which translates literally as *an enclosed tower*: there is no town by this name—he has grown haughty and sinned. Realizing this and regretting it, he lowers himself to the ground. The imagery is complex: by lowering himself, he is actually raised. (We remember the words of the School of Hillel: *Whoever humbles himself, the Holy One raises up.*) But the ugly man will have none of it. The slight is not towards him, he is rigorous in maintaining, but towards the Holy One, the divine Potter whose omnipotence and omniscience Rabbi Elazar, stuffed to the point of self-congratulation with Torah, has insulted.

The comedy is rich. A prisoner of his own repentance, hoisted by the petard of his own arrogance, in dire need of forgiveness, Rabbi Elazar follows the ugly man all the way to the ugly man's city, where the very people he has maligned—*Are they all as ugly as you?*—come out to greet him, saying, "Peace be upon you, Teacher, Teacher, Master, Master!"

The ambiguity thickens. Not only is it unclear which of the two men the crowd is addressing—perhaps the double vocative indicates that both are being addressed; or perhaps it's how the Aggadist writes dialogue for a crowd—but since the phrase is a variation on the words that started this whole fracas, it's possible that the crowd is taunting Rabbi Elazar. Or maybe they're not, but thanks to his guilty conscience, perhaps Rabbi Elazar hears it that way.

Finally, the ugly man asks, "Who are you calling 'Teacher, Teacher'?"

(I presume he knows who is the Master, Master of this situation.)

The people say to him, "This man who's traveling behind you."

"If this is a teacher," the ugly man says, "may there not be many like him among the people of Israel!"

"Why so?"

"He did such and such to me."

Imagine Rabbi Elazar's sorrow and regret as his own ugliness is exposed and expounded upon in so public a way. The people, listening to the ugly man's story, however, counsel mercy. "Forgive him nevertheless," they say, "because he is a man of great Torah."

"For your sakes, I will forgive him," the ugly man says, "provided he reforms himself and refrains from this ugly habit."

Chastened, Rabbi Elazar immediately enters a House of Study, and there, he expounds, "A person should always be soft, like a reed, and not hard like a cedar. And this is why the reed deserves to have pens drawn from it, pens which scribes use to write Torah scrolls, phylacteries, and mezuzahs," the holiest of sacred objects.

Soft/hard, reed-like/cedar-like, flexible/inflexible: we've arrived once again at the difference between the Schools of Hillel and Shammai.

A MYTH, THEY SAY, is an event that never happened, but which is always happening. Still, the chronology of these stories is a bit washy, and it's unclear exactly *when* Rabbi Elazar turns from the path of arrogance and hostility to embrace the gentler Way of the Reed. The confusion is part of his character, I think. My suspicion is that, despite his good intentions, the "easygoing forbearance" counseled by the School of Hillel eludes Rabbi Elazar throughout his life and even beyond the moment of his death.

THE AGGADISTS CONTRIBUTE all sorts of stories to the Talmud's full-to-bursting compendium of tales, including—as we will see here—a *noir*, the sort of dark detective story Albert Camus admired Dashiell Hammett for writing. And as we'll see, Rabbi Elazar's internal drama, this wrestling in his soul between his own fiery nature and the Way of the Reed, plays out against a background of double-dealing and intrigue.

In his later life or in his midlife perhaps—all we know is that his father is no longer alive—Rabbi Elazar meets a detective whose job is to catch thieves for the Roman government.

"How can you recognize them?" Rabbi Elazar asks this fellow. "Are they not like wild beasts that prowl at night and hide during the day?" Also, he worries: "Perhaps you sometimes arrest the innocent and leave the guilty free?"

"What can I do?" the detective says. "It's the king's command."

We can almost hear a shrug of helplessness underscoring this line of dialogue.

"Come," Rabbi Elazar says, responding to the poor man's plight, "I will teach you what to do. At nine o'clock in the morning, go into a tavern. Should you see a man dozing with a cup of wine in his hand, inquire about him. If he is a disciple of the wise, you may assume that he has risen very early in the morning to pursue his studies; if he is a day laborer, that he is up early to do his work. Or perhaps he works at night, hammering metal. But if he's none of these, he's a thief and you should arrest him."

The tale turns in on itself. Like a mirror facing another mirror, the scene reflects the very themes it discusses: things are not always what they seem. In broad daylight, the innocent may appear guilty, the guilty innocent, the righteous wicked, and the wicked righteous. The wicked and the righteous so resemble each other in the broad light of day, in fact, that you may be speaking to a wicked person without realizing it.

This detective, for example.

Rabbi Elazar imagines that the man is moral, that compelled against his will to do the king's bidding, he is chafing under this coercion, worrying as Rabbi Elazar does that, in the process, the innocent may find themselves swept up in an indiscriminate dragnet. Imagining that the man is suffering, Rabbi Elazar responds by creating a plan that might relieve his suffering and salve his conscience.

In truth, though, this detective hardly seems righteous. *What can I do? It's the king's command* is perhaps less a cry of helplessness and more a statement of moral indifference. He has shrugged off Rabbi Elazar's concerns. He does his job, though it's an immoral job. Less a detective, he's more an informer, really, turning his own people in to the occupying powers, and yet, feeling victimized himself, he refuses to see himself as culpable in any way.

Rabbi Elazar does not share this moral blindness. His sense of morality is crystal clear: though thievery is immoral, the government is illegitimate and oppressive; working for the occupiers is a morally dubious activity; compelled to do so, one must make absolutely certain that only the guilty are apprehended. If his scheme for apprehending thieves appears ludicrous—is there nowhere else a thief might be at nine a.m. but in a tavern?—that's because its principal aim is not to aid the detective in capturing thieves but to deceive him—gently, gently—into sparing innocent scholars and simple laborers.

Has Rabbi Elazar learned nothing in all these long years of occupation? Just as his father's incautious words were carried back to the occupying government, so now are Rabbi Elazar's. Word reaches him from the government: "Let the reader of the message become the messenger." In other words: *You claim to know so much about catching thieves, let's see* you *be the detective!*

Rabbi Elazar is immediately sent for and appointed to arrest thieves.

WELL, IT CERTAINLY *is* hard to tell the wicked from the righteous, with the wicked hiding themselves in the broad light of day! The conversation with the detective no longer seems quite so innocent. Was it, in fact, a conversation or an interrogation? For who else but the detective would have reported Rabbi Elazar's words to the king?

The two men, it turns out, were gulling each other. Attempting to con the detective, Rabbi Elazar never noticed that he was being conned.

How could he be so blind? A deeply buried psychological issue is at play here: though the detective openly advertises himself as both immoral and uncaring, for some reason Rabbi Elazar doesn't take him at his word. Taking his own uprightness for granted, Rabbi Elazar takes the detective's presumed uprightness for granted as well. Attempting to gull the detective, Rabbi Elazar is blind to the detective's snare; worrying on behalf of the detective that innocent people might fall into his trap, Rabbi Elazar falls into the trap as well.

This is a detective story, after all, and the clues are laid out in front of Rabbi Elazar, although he doesn't seem to see them: in addition to its being possibly both a statement of helplessness and a statement of indifference, *What can I do? It's the king's command!*

may also be a proclamation of loyalty, a publicly proclaimed loyalty oath to the king, which Rabbi Elazar chooses for some reason not to hear.

AS A RESULT of his naïveté, Rabbi Elazar finds himself working as an informant for the same occupying power that sentenced his father to death. But it's even worse than that: except in cases of extreme lawlessness, the Torah forbids the turning of one's fellow in to a foreign government, *especially* in capital cases.

No wonder Rabbi Joshua ben Korhah sends a strongly worded message to Rabbi Elazar. "Vinegar, son of Wine!" it reads. "How long will you deliver up the people of our God for slaughter!"

Unlike the detective, Rabbi Elazar doesn't blame the king for compelling him to do this questionable work.

"I weed out thorns from the vineyard," he writes back, pruning the people of Israel of its evildoers.

Rabbi Joshua ben Korhah fires back: "Let the Owner of the Vineyard come and himself weed out its thorns!"

OURS IS A STORY OF SONS.

According to some—though not to all—Rabbi Joshua ben Korhah is the son of Rabbi Akiva. (*Korhah* means *bald*; and Rabbi Akiva was famously bald.) If that is the case, the subtext of this scene is deeply resonant. Here, we have the son of a man executed by the Romans admonishing a man whose father was sentenced to death by the Romans for working as an informer for that same occupying government.

In any case, with this epithet— *Vinegar, son of Wine!*—the ghost of Rabbi Shimon walks onstage. Like the ghost of Hamlet's father, he haunts this drama in ways both subtle and plain.

OUR STORY CONTINUES:

"One day a mere fuller met [Rabbi Elazar] and called him 'Vinegar, son of Wine!'"

In the ancient world, a fuller scoured cloth with his feet, ankle deep in tubs of human urine, whitening the cloth and cleansing it of impurities. (A source of ammonium salts, urine was a taxable commodity throughout the Roman Empire.) The fabric was then stretched on large frames called tenters and fastened to the frame by tenterhooks—this is where the phrase *on tenterhooks* comes from—before being thickened through a matting process, and finally rinsed with fresh water of its foul-smelling urine.

The appearance of the fuller in our story sounds an ominous note. Or it should for Rabbi Elazar. The fuller has arrived to put the moral squeeze on him. It's time for Rabbi Elazar to come clean, and the process won't be an easy one. No, I'm afraid there's going to be a lot of scouring, squeezing, stretching, and human waste.

Elsewhere in the Talmud—a happy coincidence for us!—Rabbi Joshua ben Korhah is quoted as saying, "The messenger of a person is like the person himself." Meaning: a messenger has the legal status of the person who sends him. By repeating his message, the lowly fuller essentially stands in for Rabbi Joshua ben Korhah. But Rabbi Elazar, in addition to being willfully blind—he couldn't see the detective for who he was: a dangerous man on the prowl—is also willfully deaf: unable to hear the echo of Rabbi Joshua ben Korhah's admonition in the fuller's taunt, he's deaf to the fuller's true self:

Rabbi Elazar said to himself, "Since he is so insolent, he must surely be a felon!"

So he gave the order to his attendants: "Arrest him!" and they arrested him.

LIKE HIS FATHER BEFORE HIM, Rabbi Elazar finds it hard to tweeze his personal grudges out from the skein of earthly and divine justice. Like his father as well, he navigates an unruly path between striking and healing. When his anger cools, though, Rabbi Elazar is filled with remorse. How could he not be? He's committed a terrible sin, the sin he tried to keep the detective from committing: he's turned a fellow in to a foreign government, a man innocent of all crimes but the insolence of having insulted him.

A repentant and remorseful Rabbi Elazar attempts to secure the fuller's release, but he's unable to do so. A petty subaltern, he forgot for a moment that the authority the government has given him over his fellow countrymen gives him no authority *within* the government.

At last, the treachery of the detective is fully revealed. Rabbi Elazar has been tricked into causing a murder. He's been warned by two witnesses, Rabbi Joshua ben Korhah and the fuller, but he has insolently pursued the course of his own destruction. *Since he is so insolent, he must be a felon.* His questions to the detective ring out now in tones of heavy irony: *How do you recognize the wicked? How do you make certain the innocent are not unfairly punished?*

In remorse, he applies to himself the verse "He who guards his mouth and his tongue keeps his soul from troubles."

"When they subsequently hanged the fuller," we're told, "Rabbi Elazar stood under the gallows and wept."

His conscience aching, he weeps beneath the gallows, concerned for the fuller certainly, but concerned as well, if not more so, with the black stain of this arrogant sin upon his own soul: twice warned away from his quisling activities, he ignored all entreaties, and now an innocent man has paid with his life for Elazar's sinful arrogance!

Rabbi Elazar's students attempt to comfort him: "Master, do not grieve, for this fuller and his son together raped a betrothed maiden on the Day of Atonement."

This is a trifecta of sin. Or even a pluperfecta, if such a thing exists. Let us take this in for a moment: sacred law prohibits a father and son from having sex with the same woman; sex with a woman betrothed to another man is considered adultery; one must refrain from sexual relations on the Day of Atonement; and the girl in question, according to some commentators, was a minor, no older than twelve and a half.

This late-breaking news ushers in a terrible comic reversal. Perhaps Rabbi Elazar's agony of conscience is a bit premature. We can imagine his internal dialogue. Sex with a betrothed minor is a capital offense! Granted, the biblical punishment for that crime is stoning. But since all persons executed by the Sanhedrin, the ancient Supreme Court of Israel, were hanged afterwards, perhaps a Roman hanging isn't entirely inappropriate. Perhaps the Owner of the Vineyard *has* merely been using him as a pruning hook to weed the thorns from his vineyard, after all:

> At this, Rabbi Elazar laid his hand on his belly and exclaimed, "Rejoice, my innards, rejoice! If matters you were in doubt about fall out this way, how much more so matters about which you are certain! I am well assured that neither worms nor decay will have power over you!"

Despite the simplicity of his aesthetic palette, the Aggadist here seems to understand human nature deeply. The story has come to a complex pass with a beautifully sketched picture of moral relativity. Having rejected Rabbi Joshua ben Korhah's admonition to let the Holy One prune his own vineyard, Rabbi Elazar now hides behind this very notion as his defense: acting upon instinct, he has been used as a tool by the Vintner himself to prune away an evil thorn.

Rabbi Elazar's conscience, however, will not let him rest. If nothing else, he's versed sufficiently in the sacred law to know, his great intuitive innards aside, that justifying his actions against the fuller is a stretch, and that the magnitude of the fuller's sins cannot ameliorate his own.

The crux of his quandary goes even deeper. Identified in this story emphatically as a son, Rabbi Elazar is the soured, vinegary descendant of an exquisite wine. (Or so Rabbi Shimon is remembered.) The fuller has a son as well, but where we might expect to find him—wailing beneath his father's hanged body—we find Rabbi Elazar instead: an image of paternal abandonment.

Abandoned by his father—abandoned, as an adult, by him in death; left by him, as a child, untutored and wild—Rabbi Elazar has been left as well to finish the psychological integration that Rabbi Shimon failed to achieve on his own between lightness and darkness, between repairing and striking.

RABBI ELAZAR IS ENORMOUSLY OBESE. For all of his gastronomic reassurances, his mind is still not at ease. Since he's a detective, he decides, like a character in a postmodern film *noir*, to investigate himself:

> So he was given a sleeping draught and taken into a marble chamber, where his abdomen was opened. Out of it baskets and baskets of fat were removed and placed in the sun during Tammuz and Av, yet the fat did not putrefy.

Tammuz and Av are the hot summer months of the year. That his fat does not putrefy, Rabbi Elazar takes as a sign—or I suppose, given the era, as scientific and medical proof—of his righteousness, and he applies to himself a verse from the Psalms, "Even my flesh rests secure."

In context the verse is even more emphatic:

> I bless the Lord who has guided me; my conscience admonishes me at night. . . . I shall never be shaken. My heart rejoices, my whole being exults, and even my flesh rests secure.

(A small note: The months of the Hebrew calendar, oddly enough for a culture that claims to eschew syncretism, have Babylonian names. Tammuz means *deity* and Av means *father*. Metaphorically, then, Rabbi Elazar conducts the search of his conscience under the searing light of his own godlike father.)

Rabbi Ishmael is a great friend of Rabbi Elazar's. Like Rabbi Elazar, he, too, is enormously obese. In fact, when they hug each other in greeting, their bellies are so large, we're told, that a cow could pass between them. Not only are they twins in their great love for each other, but this presentation of them is apt in other ways: each is the son of an illustrious father—Rabbi Ishmael is the son of the silent Rabbi Yossi—and both find themselves working as detectives for the Roman government, informing on their countrymen.

In Rabbi Ishmael's case, no less a luminary than the prophet Elijah appears in order to rebuke him. "How long will you hand over the people of Israel to their slaughter?" Elijah says, repeating the words of Rabbi Joshua ben Korhah; and Rabbi Ishmael tells him exactly what the detective tells Rabbi Elazar: "What can I do? It's the king's command!"

The prophet has a better, more straightforward answer for Rabbi Ishmael than Rabbi Elazar had for the detective. "Your father fled to Asya," he tells him. "You should flee to Laodicea."

THERE'S A LINE from a song by Jackson Browne that goes: *Down on a half-darkened street, Father's and son's lives repeat.*

Presented as a kind of intermission between the two acts of Rabbi Elazar's passion, this moment involving Rabbi Ishmael and the prophet Elijah recapitulates some of our story's themes—a son's helpless reenactment of his father's life; the uneasy, imperfect solutions to life under occupation—while raising a new question as well: if the prophet Elijah appears occasionally *without* disguise to offer help and guidance, why does he *always* appear to Rabbi Elazar *in disguise*?

In other words: why must Rabbi Elazar always be *tricked* into spiritual growth and heightened clarity—tricked by the old traveler, tricked by the ugly man, gently deceived by the whisperer at the entrance of his father's cave, tricked by the detective and even by the fuller, who, although the story doesn't explicitly reveal this, are certainly manifestations of the prophet in disguise?

Just as Rabbi Shimon differed from Rabbi Yossi in his inability to hold back his scorching denunciations, Rabbi Elazar differs from Rabbi Ishmael in his inability to do anything but move forward into a fight. Like his father, Rabbi Elazar is quick on the emotional draw. Heated, passionate, impulsive, he relies (quite literally) on his gut. This behavior almost necessarily creates for him the kind of trouble that requires reflection and regret. This is not true with the cooler heads and calmer hearts of Rabbi Yossi & Son. They hold themselves back, preferring silence, exile, and cunning to personal and political tumult. It's a different temperament that refrains from action, a different kind of life with smaller mistakes and gentler revisions.

In meeting Elijah, one always learns the truth. His appearance cleanses the doors of perception. With this in mind, I think we can say: it's not that Elijah appears undisguised to Rabbi Ishmael and in disguise to Rabbi Elazar. Rabbi Ishmael simply recognizes the prophet for who he is when he appears. Rabbi Elazar, on the other hand, is the sort of person who learns through making poor choices, through making mistakes, through charging into action, through speaking too hastily, too bluntly, too loudly, and too often. A life lived as impetuously as his—and as his father's—is a life requiring reflection and regret. Only in retrospect does Rabbi Elazar realize that he has encountered the prophet, only upon reflection does he see the hand of the Holy One in his troubles and his woes.

DESPITE THE GREAT SUCCESS of his operation—the fat of his innards did not putrefy under the hot summer sun—still Rabbi Elazar's conscience continues to nag at him. (We can imagine the phrase *Vinegar, son of Wine!* ringing like a refrain in his ears.) He's guilty, and he knows he's guilty. *He* is a thorn in the vineyard of the Holy One: *he* has stolen a man's life, but no Roman court will try him, no rabbinical court convict him, no executioner carry out his death sentence:

> He therefore invoked painful afflictions upon himself, so that although sixty sheets were spread under him in the evening, sixty basins of blood and pus were removed from under him in the morning. Every morning his wife prepared a mixture of sixty kinds of fig pap for him, and when he ate it, he recovered.

Every night, in a ritual of self-denigration, attempting to cleanse his soul, Rabbi Elazar takes on the role of the fuller, plumping up sixty sheets of felt with his own bodily fluid. Though the Aggadist is not explicit about this, we can imagine that, previously corpulent and self-satisfied, Rabbi Elazar is slowly turning into an emaciated renunciate, a guilt-ridden hermit, in fact.

"His wife would not permit him to go to the House of Study, so that the sages would not press him." (*Press*, a verb not unrelated to both legal interrogation and laundry work.)

Like his father before him, Rabbi Elazar has fled the House of Study for a cave-like hideout, only this time, it's his fellow rabbis who threaten him over his association with his old enemy, the Romans, and not vice versa. Though a woman and not a carob tree shelters and feeds him now, his life resembles the life he shared with his father in the cave: a life of prayer and study alternating with long moments of self-mortification:

> In the evening, Rabbi Elazar would invite his afflictions back, saying, "Come back, my brethren and friends!" And in the morning, he would say to them, "Depart lest you disturb my studies!"

Alone as he may feel, he is not entirely alone: he has his afflictions. *Come back, my brethren and friends!* he calls to them. (A beautiful turn: his afflictions, these new brothers and friends, have replaced the brothers and friends who have been afflicting him with a guilty conscience.) One day, however, his wife hears his crying out. She knows that others are oppressing her husband, but that her husband is oppressing himself is news to her.

"So it is of your own volition that you bring these afflictions upon yourself!" she says. "And you squander the money of my father's house." She means: to pay for his treatments, the extra meals, all the ruined clothes and bedding.

Furious, she leaves him and returns to her father's house.

AS SHE WALKS out the door, Heaven itself offers a dramatic demonstration of support for Rabbi Elazar:

> Just then, sixty mariners were sailing on the sea. When a huge wave crested over them and was about to sink their vessel, they rose up in prayer, saying, "O God of Elazar, answer us!" and the sea's wrath abated. When the mariners reached dry land, they brought Rabbi Elazar a gift of sixty slaves bearing sixty purses.

The slaves prepared a mixture of sixty kinds of fig pap for him, and he ate it, applying to himself the verse "Torah is like the merchant ships, fetching food stuffs from afar."

His atonement appears to be working. Or at least it's not unreasonable for him to think so. And if his wife imagines that, for the sake of her fig pap fund, he might call her back, she's sadly mistaken. When she asks their daughter to look in on him, Rabbi Elazar says, "Go tell your mother that our wealth is still greater than that of her father's house." And so he has no need of her.

Assuming that Heaven has forgiven him and that his atonement is complete, he eats, drinks, and recovers. He returns to the House of Study. He's back in business now, working as a different kind of detective: "Sixty specimens of blood were brought before him, and he declared all the specimens pure."

Sixty specimens of blood?

An explanation is required: according to the sacred law, a woman cannot sleep with her husband while she's menstruating. Five hues of blood are deemed impure; all others are pure; and it takes an expert like Rabbi Elazar to make that determination.

Sixty women, sixty specimens of blood, sixty "pure" verdicts: it seems statistically excessive, and his rabbinical colleagues question him about it: "Is it possible that there was not even one specimen about which there might have been some doubt?"

(Doubt, our old theme, reappears: *How can you recognize them? Isn't it possible that you might sometimes apprehend the innocent and let the guilty go free?*)

"If it is as I have said," Rabbi Elazar declares, "let all the future children borne by these women be males; if not, let there be one female among them."

We're told: "All the children were males and were named Elazar after him."

Another miracle vouching for Rabbi Elazar's perfect integrity! However, as we will come to learn in chapter 4, the law is not in Heaven anymore. Heaven may have a vote, but not a veto, and miracles do not exonerate a man before the cold, hard facts of the law. Speaking on behalf of the sages, their leader Rebbi says, "How much procreation was eliminated by this evil"—by Rabbi Elazar's tenure as an informer—"from the midst of Israel!"

In other words: sixty rights do not undo untold wrongs. Sixty new sons named Elazar do not exonerate an informer.

The sages do not, will not, forgive him.

THIS MORAL STANDOFF persists until beyond the end of Rabbi Elazar's life. As he lies dying, he says to his wife, "I know that the sages are angry with me and will not properly attend to my burial." He wants to be buried with his father, but his colleagues do not consider him worthy of the honor. And so he tells his wife, "Let my body repose in the attic, and do not be afraid of my presence there."

Time passes. The sages begin to forget about him. Or so it seems. The narrative gets hazy; the rest of the story comes to us through a chain of rumors:

> Rabbi Samuel bar Nahmani said: "Rabbi Jonathan's mother told me that the wife of Rabbi Elazar ben Rabbi Shimon had told her, 'He lay in the attic not less than eighteen nor more than twenty-two years. Whenever I ascended there, I would examine his hair, and if even a single hair happened to fall out, blood would spurt forth.'"

Though dead, Rabbi Elazar doesn't seem to be decomposing. In fact, he still adjudicates cases:

> Whenever two people in a lawsuit came before him, they stood at the door, and each stated his case. Then a voice would issue from the attic, saying, "So-and-so, you are liable; so-and-so, you are in the clear."

Finally:

> "One day," his wife is said to have said, "when I saw a worm issue from his ear, I was much grieved. But then he appeared to me in

a dream and told me to think nothing of it. 'This has happened,' he said, 'because I once heard a disciple of the wise being belittled and I did not protest as I should have done.'"

A confession. At last. At the end of this long detective story, the guilty party is at last found. After twenty-odd years on the case, Rabbi Elazar finally discovers his own crime: *This has happened because I once heard a disciple of the wise being belittled and did not protest as I should have done.*

He's like a character out of Kafka. Unaware that he's under suspicion, he stages his own trial, playing all the parts: detective, criminal, accuser, prosecutor, witness, defender, and judge. The worm, the malady he looked for in his innards, was hiding in his brain. No wonder the fuller's belittling of him—*Vinegar, son of Wine!*—rankled. Though held to a higher standard of decorum, he was guilty of the same crime: belittling a Torah scholar. (*If he is so insolent, he is surely a felon!*) The fuller had a secret sin, and Rabbi Elazar had a secret sin, secret even to himself. (*How can you recognize them? Do they not hide during the day? Mightn't you sometimes apprehend the innocent and let the guilty go free?*)

NOTHING LASTS FOREVER, and the sages finally permit Rabbi Elazar to be buried. Some say it came about because, one day, Rabbi Elazar's wife was quarreling with a neighbor who cursed her: "May you be like your husband, who had no proper burial!" When the sages heard this, they said, "Now that Rabbi Elazar's being unburied has come to be known, it is not right to have it continue thus." Others say that Rabbi Shimon himself appeared to the sages in a dream. "I have a dear child among you, whom you refuse to bring to me," he told them.

Still, it wasn't easy. The townspeople of Akhbera, north of Tiberias, protested. While Rabbi Elazar "lay asleep in his attic," no wild animals had attacked their town—*Are they not like wild beasts that prowl at night?*—and the Akhberians were hoping to keep things exactly as they were.

Stealth and deception—our old themes—are required. Waiting

until the eve of the Day of Atonement when the Akhberians are otherwise engaged, the sages send word to the people of Biri, a town farther north, to remove Rabbi Elazar's bier from the attic and to carry it to the cave where his father is buried.

There, as a kind of cordon sanitaire, they find a snake encircling the cave, its tail in its mouth. "They said to it, 'Snake, O snake, open your mouth and let go of your tail, so that a son may join his father.' At that, the snake opened its mouth and they were able to enter."

Teacher, teacher; master, master; snake, snake: curious doublings. Putting aside the Edenic resonances of the image of the snake, as well as Jung's notions of the Ouroboros, the serpent that swallows its own tail, a symbol, some say, of self-reflectivity, and others, of the cyclic nature of things, both appropriate here, the image speaks to me of a dangerous self-poisoning. Rabbi Shimon and Rabbi Elazar are joined once again in their cave, too fiery, too biting, too destructive for earthly life.

THIS IS HOW Rabbi Elazar ends his life.

If he carries the darker hues of Rabbi Shimon's unintegrated character, what happens to the son-in-law, who embodies his lighter attributes of patience, healing, and caring?

How does Pinhas ben Yair fare, wandering in the plains of Israel and Judea?

UNLIKE RABBI ELAZAR, Rabbi Pinhas ben Yair is an attractive figure, well thought of by his contemporaries and also by those who come after him:

> Rabbi Zeira said in the name of Rava bar Zemina, "If the former generations were like the sons of angels, we are like the sons of men; and if the latter generations were like the sons of men, we are like asses—and not even the asses of Rabbi Hanina ben Dosa and Rabbi Pinhas ben Yair, but just ordinary asses!"

We've seen how the iconography of the donkey plays out in the life of Rabbi Elazar, embodying his baser, more elemental nature. With Pinhas ben Yair, it's exactly the opposite:

> While Rabbi Pinhas ben Yair was on his way to ransom captives, he came to the River Ginnai. "O Ginnai," said he, "split your waters for me, that I may pass through you."

The river is disinclined to grant this request. A pious and theology-minded river, the Ginnai tells Rabbi Pinhas ben Yair, "You are traveling to do the will of your Maker; I, too, am flowing to do the will of my Maker. You may or may not accomplish your task. I am certain to accomplish mine."

"If you will not split," Rabbi Pinhas tells the Ginnai, "I shall decree against you that no water ever pass through you again!"

A credible threat, it seems. In any case, the river obeys. And just as we're beginning to think of Moses splitting the Red Sea, the Aggadist underscores the point by sending onstage from the wings "a certain man who was carrying wheat for Passover," the holiday commemorating the Hebrews' Exodus, under Moses's leadership, from Egypt.

"Split for this man also," Rabbi Pinhas tells the Ginnai, "since he is occupied with performing a sacred commandment," bringing wheat to be milled into flour for *matzah*.

The Ginnai splits again.

> Now, an Arab who had joined them earlier during the journey was there too, and Rabbi Pinhas once again told the river, "Split for this one as well, so that he should not say, 'Is this how a fellow traveler is treated?'"

The river splits a third time.

Rabbi Pinhas's students are traveling with him, and they ask, "Can we cross it too?"

Rabbi Pinhas tells them, "He who feels certain that never in his life has he put his fellow to shame can cross and suffer no harm."

Since the story remains silent on whether the river splits and the students cross, we can assume that they don't. Who would risk the danger? Shaming your fellow is too easy a crime to commit.

A Rav Joseph, commenting on the story from the sidelines, like a voice in a Greek chorus, remarks at this point, "How great is this man, greater than Moses and the six hundred thousand Hebrews for whom the Red Sea split! For there, it split only once, but here it split thrice!"

(*Thrice*: another indication, perhaps definitive, that Rabbi Pinhas's disciples do not feel up to crossing the Ginnai, a querulous river that probably is already feeling fairly cross.)

The comparison with Moses is not incidental, especially when we recall that, despite his greatness or perhaps because of it, Moses is left standing on a mountaintop, staring longingly into a land he cannot enter.

But more on this later.

RABBI PINHAS'S heralded donkey finally enters the picture:

> Continuing on his journey, Rabbi Pinhas ben Yair came to a certain inn, where some barley was placed before his donkey, but she would not eat. The barley was sifted, but the donkey would not eat. It was carefully picked, still the donkey would not eat. "Perhaps," suggested Rabbi Pinhas, "the barley has not been tithed?"

> Meaning: Perhaps the portion belonging to the priests has not been separated out from it.

> The barley was tithed, and then the donkey ate it. Rabbi Pinhas said, "This poor creature is on a journey to do the will of her Creator, and you try to feed her untithed grain!"

> His students, who have caught up with him after somehow fording the river, ask, "Our master, did you not teach us that he who purchases grain from an unlearned person for an animal is

exempt from the obligation about grain that may not have been tithed?" Rabbi Pinhas replied, "But what can I do with this poor creature if she chooses to be strict with herself?"

A fascinating reversal: while his brother-in-law Rabbi Elazar is depicted as resembling a donkey, toting the prophet Elijah uphill and downhill on his back, Pinhas ben Yair's donkey resembles her enlightened master, elevating herself through asceticism. Rabbi Pinhas himself has taken on certain spiritual restrictions: "It is said of Pinhas ben Yair that never in his life did he say grace over a piece of bread that was not his own"—he accepts no invitations, relying only on the generosity of the Holy One—"and that from the day he reached maturity, he did not avail himself even of his own father's table."

In other words, he has elevated his animal nature through a life lived impeccably. We remember that he is not only the author of the eleven-step program of self-perfection that leads the spiritual aspirant from zeal to the resurrection of the dead—*Zeal leads to fastidiousness which leads to cleanliness which leads to . . .*—but as we see from the following two stories, he has completed all the steps.

First zeal and fastidiousness:

When Rabbi Pinhas ben Yair was living in a city in the south, two poor men came there seeking a livelihood. They had with them two large bags of barley, which they deposited with Rabbi Pinhas, but they forgot about them and went away. Year after year, Rabbi Pinhas ben Yair sowed the barley, reaped it, gathered it, and stored it in a granary. After a lapse of seven years, the two men returned and asked for their barley. Rabbi Pinhas ben Yair recognized them and said, "Fetch camels and asses, and come take your stores."

Then resurrection of the dead:

A story is told of a pious man who used to dig cisterns, pits, and holes to contain water so that those who come and go may drink. His daughter was on her way to her wedding, when she crossed a river and was swept away. All the people came to the pious man seeking to comfort him, but he refused to be comforted. Even when Rabbi Pinhas ben Yair came to comfort him, he refused.

Rabbi Pinhas asked, "Is this the man you regard as pious?" And the people replied, "Our master, the man has been doing such good deeds, and yet such a thing befell him!" Rabbi Pinhas: "Is it possible that the Holy One would chastise with water a man who honored his Creator with water?" Just then a rumor reverberated in the city: *the Daughter of So-and-So is back*! Some say that, as she fell into the water, she was held up by a branch of a thorny tree. Others say that an angel in the likeness of Rabbi Pinhas ben Yair came down and saved her.

NO SOONER HAS his stellar asceticism been alluded to in our story than it is sorely tested. When Judah the Patriarch, the Nasi, the leader of the generation—known simply as Rebbi (Teacher)—hears that Rabbi Pinhas ben Yair is passing through town, he goes out to greet the illustrious traveler.

"Will you please dine with me?" Rebbi says.

Based on all we know about him—he hasn't dined even at his father's table since he was thirteen—we may imagine he will not accept the invitation, but Rabbi Pinhas answers, "Certainly."

Rebbi's face brightens with joy.

Seeing his expression, Rabbi Pinhas says, "Did you suppose that I had vowed not to derive benefit from a son of Israel? Oh, no! The people of Israel are holy." But he explains, "There are some who desire to benefit others and have not the means; while others have the means, but not the desire. . . . But you have the desire and also the means. However, right now I am in a hurry, for I am engaged in fulfilling a commandment"—the ransoming of captives is a divinely ordained commandment—"but on my return," Pinhas assures Rebbi, "I will come and visit you."

Rabbi Pinhas's reputation seems to precede him. It's clear from the subtext of their conversation that Rebbi has heard of his vow "not to derive benefit from a son of Israel." The joy in Rebbi's face—how beautifully human—speaks to his delight at having an exception made in his case. And why shouldn't one be? Rebbi is the patriarch, the Nasi, the leader of the generation, the redactor of the Mishnah. He's the son and student of Israel's most illustrious men, and he regularly dines with the Roman emperor Antoninus.

Certainly, Rabbi Pinhas is right to be careful in eating from the table of an unlearned person or, as he says, a poor person who might wish to honor a saint, but who hasn't the means to do so. But Rebbi, as Pinhas himself points out, has both the desire and the means—he's in fact quite wealthy—and certainly the two are equals in terms of piety.

Still, a vow is a vow, and a close reading of Rabbi Pinhas's monologue will reveal that, after asking a question (*Did you suppose that I had vowed not to derive benefit from a son of Israel?*) and making a series of statements (*The people of Israel are holy. . . . Some desire to benefit others and have not the means, others have the means, but not the desire, but you have the desire and the means*), he has promised only to visit Rebbi and not to dine with him (*But on my return, I will come and visit you*).

It's a strange moment. Why wouldn't Pinhas ben Yair simply tell Rebbi the truth? Perhaps he's concerned about shaming or embarrassing him. That the river obeys Rabbi Pinhas's command, we remember, is proof that he has never shamed another person. Or perhaps at that moment his own desire, the desire to dine with Rebbi, outweighs his means, his ability, thanks to his vow, to do so.

In any case, when he returns, he's as good as his word. He comes to Rebbi for a visit. However, upon entering Rebbi's courtyard, he sees two white mules standing inside it.

"The Angel of Death is in this house," he exclaims, "and I'm to dine here!"

In a note that resonates beyond the simple meaning of the text, Rashi explains that Rabbi Pinhas has referred to the two mules as the Angel of Death because white mules are known to kick and inflict wounds that never heal.

Gracious as ever, Rebbi offers to sell the offending animals, but

Rabbi Pinhas demurs. "'You shall not put a stumbling block before the blind,'" he says, quoting Scripture, meaning that one cannot sell dangerous animals to an unsuspecting person.

"I shall abandon them," Rebbi says.

"You would be causing damage as they run wild," and this is another prohibition.

"I shall hamstring them."

"There is a prohibition against inflicting pain on living creatures."

"I shall kill them."

(We can perhaps hear Rebbi's temper flaring in this line, for surely if hamstringing the mules is painful, how much more so cutting their throats?)

Rabbi Pinhas: "That would be counter to the ruling prohibiting wanton waste."

The two men, so much alike, devolve into the white mules they're arguing over: stubborn, dangerous, full of kicks and bites, they've completely hamstrung each other. They can't run wild, kick over the traces of the reins of holiness they've placed upon themselves. Neither can they abandon each other nor can they help from causing each other pain, from wasting the opportunity to dine together, the opportunity to receive an honored guest, the opportunity to be honored, the opportunity to delight in each other's company.

"As Rebbi kept pressing Rabbi Pinhas, a mountain rose up between them," we're told, although whether this is a literal mountain or a figurative mountain is impossible to say. Though the mountain may seem a figure of speech, we must remember that this is a story whose opening scene features a talking river. Perhaps at the story's end a literal mountain comes to Rabbi Pinhas's aid. (Perfect bookends: the river ceases to be a barrier, while the mountain, appearing out of nowhere, becomes one.)

WHAT AM I TO DO *with the poor creature if she chooses to be strict with herself?*

Rabbi Pinhas asks this about his donkey, but he may as well ask the same question about himself. The same high level of piety that allows him to cut across natural barriers miraculously places a natural barrier between him and his fellow. Though Pinhas ben Yair is on a mission to redeem captives, there is no redemption for these two mulish men. Rabbi Pinhas cannot free them from the vow that holds them both captive.

The polar opposite of Rabbi Elazar in terms of spiritual refinement, Rabbi Pinhas is equally one-sided, it appears. He is a prisoner of his own goodness, and despite that goodness—and I suggest this gently, not wishing to complain about goodness, a rarity in this world—or perhaps like Moses, *thanks* to his goodness, he winds up on a mountaintop, far from the people of Israel.

As the mountain divides them, Rebbi bursts into tears. "If in their lives," he cries, "how much more so after their deaths!"

A cryptic, idiomatic statement, open to interpretation, and generally interpreted to mean, *If, in their earthly lives, these elevated masters can achieve so much holiness, imagine the good works they'll perform when the physical world no longer constrains them.*

A pietistic reading, to be sure, and a nonsensical one. In the Talmudic worldview, the dead do not perform good works. Though Rebbi may be weeping in heartfelt admiration over Pinhas ben Yair's holiness, he may also be trembling at the terrible inhuman cost such human greatness requires.

"If, in their lives, the saints forgo simple earthly pleasures," we could read the line, "how much more so after their deaths will they feel bereft?"

This reading makes a kind of sense, since, according to a statement in the Jerusalem Talmud, "In the World to Come, a person will be called to account for any good thing his eyes saw, but of which he did not eat."

Greatness is always one-sided, and great holiness, the Aggadist seems to be telling us, comes at a great cost. A mountain separates these two men: Rebbi beholds Rabbi Pinhas ben Yair from an impassable distance. True, Rabbi Pinhas is doing extraordinary good in the world. His spiritual athleticism is cultivating an abundant harvest. He's ransoming captives from the Roman government and reviving the dead, whether it's his father-in-law in the bath or the cisternman's daughter in the river. Still, I can't help feeling compassion for the small boy who, in the name of piety, renounces his place at his father's table; or for the grown man spending years conscientiously harvesting barley that its owners haven't given a second thought to; or for the wandering saint incapable of allowing himself to be feted by the Nasi.

I empathize with Rebbi's desire to feed such a person, to take care of him, to offer him the gift of food and drink and a companionable evening of talk. But as Rebbi recognizes in his weeping, like Rabbi Shimon in his cave, Rabbi Pinhas ben Yair is far out there, away at a high altitude in a wilderness of his own creation, unreachable beyond uncrossable mountain passes.

———

"HAD I STOOD AT MOUNT SINAI at the time when the Torah was given to Israel," Rabbi Shimon proclaims, "I would have asked the Holy One to create two mouths in a person, one to be occupied with Torah, and the other to serve all his other needs."

Thinking better of it, he retracts his statement: "If, when a person has only one mouth, the world can barely endure all the informing it does, how much less if he had two!"

Of all the many types of people Rabbi Shimon despises— plowers, sowers, Romans, garrulous men—he despises none more than those who collaborate with the Roman government— tax collectors, quislings, and especially informers.

As I've said, it's a matter of speculation whether, in the wake of Rabbi Shimon's impassioned denunciation of the Roman occupiers, Judah ben Gerim went directly to the authorities to inform on his teacher or whether, without malicious intent, he mentioned the conversation, perhaps even in tones of glowing approval, to his peers or perhaps to his parents, and that this is how word got out.

Perhaps Judah ben Gerim's parents said something to the authorities. This is what I suspect. Converts to monotheism—that is the meaning of the word *Gerim*; *Judah ben Gerim* is Judah son of converts—perhaps they found their allegiance to their new tribe a little shaky in a time of danger. Perhaps, as Rabbi Shimon worries about his wife, they were tortured into confirming the story.

Though some commentators call Judah ben Gerim a malicious ignoramus, this characterization seems unjustified to me, and it certainly ignores his history with Rabbi Shimon. Elsewhere in the Talmud, Judah is depicted as an accomplished scholar, well beloved by his teacher Rabbi Shimon.

Before things go south between them, the two, in fact, have a highly cordial relationship:

Rabbi Jonathan ben Asmai and Rabbi Judah ben Gerim took leave of Rabbi Shimon bar Yohai in the evening. In the morning, they returned and took leave of him again. He said to them, "Did you not already take leave of me last night?" They said to him, "You have taught us, our master, that a student who takes leave of his teacher and who remains staying overnight in the city must take leave of him a second time."

The gesture so impresses Rabbi Shimon, he not only calls Judah ben Gerim and his companion "men of stature," but he advises his son, Rabbi Elazar, to go to them to receive a blessing:

They said to him, "What are you doing here?" He said to them, "My father said to me, 'Go to them so that they might bless you.'" They said to him, "May it be the Holy One's will that you sow and not reap, that you take in and not bring out, bring out and not take in. May your house be destroyed and your inn inhabited, may your table be disturbed, and may you not see a new year."

Completely confounded, Elazar returns to his father. "It wasn't enough that they didn't bless me," he complains, "but they caused me pain!"

"What did they say to you?" Rabbi Shimon wonders.

"This and this they said to me."

Rabbi Shimon explains:

These are all blessings. *That you sow and not reap* means you will beget children and they shall not die. *That you take in and not bring out* means that you will take in daughters-in-law and your sons shall not die so that the daughters-in-law will not go away. *Bring out and not take in* means that you will beget daughters and their husbands will not die and cause them to return to you. *May your house be destroyed and your inn inhabited*: this world is compared to an inn, the next world to a house. May your grave, your house in this world, go long unused, while your inn, your home in the next world, be long inhabited. *Let your table be disturbed* means by the activity of many children. And *may you not see a new year* means may your wife not die and you have to marry another.

A student is an intellectual son, and Rabbi Shimon and Judah ben Gerim are clearly close. Mutually respectful, the two speak the same language. They understand each other's riddles. It's hard to imagine that Judah ben Gerim would intentionally inform upon his revered master—though, certainly, such things happen and have happened—and it's equally hard to imagine that his hatred of informers explains or justifies the murderous vitriol Rabbi Shimon feels towards Judah ben Gerim when, spying him in the marketplace, he turns him into a stack of bones.

Certainly Rabbi Shimon is riled up by his own weakness for intemperate speech, a weakness he sees in the younger man whose bragging about his teacher's verbal vehemence sent him on the run, but it goes deeper than that, I think. Everything is revealed by his name. Judah ben Gerim—a native of Judea (*Judah*) born of strangers (*Gerim*)—he is a man who lives in two cultures simultaneously. He is, in a sense, a bridge, a bridge between the two cultures our story concerns itself with: Romans and Judeans; or—more elementally—them and us.

This is a bridge too far for Rabbi Shimon. Asked by the events of the story to cross it, he refuses. Instead, he burns the bridge up. Having turned a cemetery into a bridge for the priests to walk through, he reverts to his old self and turns Judah ben Gerim, a bridge between two cultures, into a cemetery, a collection of bones.

And of course, in doing so, Rabbi Shimon becomes exactly like the Roman government he despises: oppressing the scholars, issuing death sentences, all in service to himself.

It's a grand defeat. Unable to repair this split within himself, he leaves the work of healing to his sons in the next generation, and we see where this leaves them. Pinhas ben Yair winds up alone on a distant mountaintop, Rabbi Elazar lies frozen between life and death in a draughty attic, and Judah ben Gerim sinks to the earth as a clatter of bones.

Rabban Gamliel II of Yavneh (flourished 3850–3875/90–115 CE), Rabbi Joshua ben Hananiah (flourished 3850–3890/90–130 CE), and Rabbi Eliezer ben Hyrcanus (flourished c. 3830–3945/70–185 CE)

DURING A DISCUSSION IN THE ACADEMY ON THE ritual purity of the oven of Akhnai, Rabbi Eliezer ruled the oven ritually clean, while the majority of the sages ruled it ritually unclean. Rabbi Eliezer brought a number of proofs to support his view, but they were all rejected by his colleagues. He finally said, "If the Law is as I say, let this carob tree prove it," whereupon the carob tree uprooted itself and moved one hundred cubits out of its place.

They said to him, "A proof may not be brought from a carob tree."

He said, "If the Law is as I say, let the waters prove it," where-upon a stream reversed its flow. The sages said, "A proof may not be brought from the water."

He said, "If the Law is as I say, let the walls of the House of Study prove it," whereupon the walls began caving in. Rabbi Joshua then reprimanded the walls: "If Torah scholars are having a legal argument with each other, who are you to interfere?"

The walls did not collapse completely, in honor of Rabbi Joshua, but they did not straighten, because of the honor of Rabbi Eliezer, and they remain leaning to this day.

Rabbi Eliezer then said to them, "If the Law is as I say, let it be proved from Heaven," whereupon a heavenly voice came out and announced, "Why do you dispute with Rabbi Eliezer? The Law is as he states in every instance." Rabbi Joshua arose and said, "The Law is not in Heaven!"

Rabbi Jeremiah explained that the Torah has already been given to us at Sinai, so we pay no attention to heavenly voices since it has already been written, "One must follow the majority."

Rabbi Nathan met Elijah the prophet and asked him, "What did the Holy One, blessed be he, do at that hour?" Elijah replied, "He laughed and said, 'My children have overruled me, my children have overruled me!'"

On that day, all the objects that Rabbi Eliezer had previously declared ritually clean were burnt in fire. A vote was taken and Rabbi Eliezer was excommunicated; and then they said, "Who will go and inform him?"

"I will go," Rabbi Akiva said. "Perhaps an unfit person will go and inform him and bring about the destruction of the entire world."

Rabbi Akiva clad himself in black garments, wrapped himself in black, and sat before him at a distance of four cubits.

Rabbi Eliezer asked him, "Akiva, why is today different from all other days?" Rabbi Akiva answered, "Master, it appears to me that your friends are separating from you," whereupon Rabbi Eliezer tore his garments, removed his shoes, sat upon the ground, and cried. At that time, a third of the olive crop, a third of the wheat crop, and a third of the barley crop of the world were smitten. And some say even dough already in a woman's hands became spoiled!

A great blow occurred that day. For every place on which Rabbi Eliezer set his eyes went up in flames, and it even happened that Rabban Gamliel was traveling aboard a ship when a huge wave rose up, threatening to capsize the boat and drown him. He said, "It appears to me that this is on account of Rabbi Eliezer ben Hyrcanus." Then he stood on his feet and he called out and he said, "Master of the Universe, it is known and revealed to you that I have not acted for my own honor or for the honor of my father's house, but for your honor, that disputes not proliferate in the House of Israel." At this, the sea calmed down.

Ima Shalom, the wife of Rabbi Eliezer, was the sister of Rabban Gamliel. From that time on, she did not let Rabbi Eliezer fall on his face. One day, she thought that it was the new month, when *Tahanun* isn't recited, but she had confused a full month with a deficient one. There are those who say that a poor person came and stood at the door, and she took bread out to him. Either way, she afterwards found Rabbi Eliezer falling on his face in the prayer.

She said to him, "Arise, you have killed my brother!" In the meantime, it was proclaimed that Rabban Gamliel had indeed died. When Rabbi Eliezer asked her how she had known that this would happen, she responded, "I have a tradition from my father's house that 'When all the gates of Heaven are locked, the gate of a broken heart remains open.'"

BABYLONIAN TALMUD, TRACTATE *BAVA METZIA* 59B.

IT HAPPENED THAT A CERTAIN STUDENT CAME BE-fore Rabbi Joshua, and he asked him, "The evening prayer—is it elective or obligatory?" He answered him, "Elective." Then he came before Rabban Gamliel and asked him, "The evening prayer—is it elective or obligatory?" He replied, "Obligatory." He said to him, "But Rabbi Joshua told me it's elective." Rabban Gamliel said to him, "Wait until the shield-bearers enter the House of Study."

When the shield-bearers entered the House of Study, the question was asked, "The evening prayer—is it elective or obligatory?" Rabban Gamliel replied, "Obligatory." He then said to the sages, "Is there among us a man who disputes this ruling?" Rabbi Joshua said to him, "No." Rabban Gamliel said to Rabbi Joshua, "But in your name it was said to me that you declared the evening prayer elective! Joshua, stand on your feet and let them testify against you!"

Rabbi Joshua stood on his feet and said, "Were I alive and he dead, the living might contradict the dead, but since he is living and I am living, how can the living contradict the living?"

Rabban Gamliel continued sitting and lecturing, and Rabbi Joshua remained standing on his feet, until all the people murmured and said to Huzpit the Interpreter "Stop!" and he stopped. They said, "How long will Rabban Gamliel go on humiliating Rabbi Joshua! On New Year's Day last year, he insulted him! In the matter of the firstborn in the incident with Rabbi Zadok, he insulted him! And now, he insults him as well! Come! Let us depose him! Whom shall we appoint? Shall we appoint Rabbi Joshua? He is involved in the matter. Shall we appoint Rabbi Akiva? Perhaps Rabban Gamliel will cause punishment to befall him because he does not have the merit of righteous ancestors. Rather, let us appoint Rabbi Elazar ben Azaryah, for he is wise, and he is wealthy, and he is ten generations from Ezra the Scribe. He is wise, so that if he is asked something, he will be able to answer. He is wealthy, so that if one is needed to deal with the House of Caesar, he too will be able to go and deal with them. And he is ten generations from Ezra the Scribe, so that he possesses the merit of righteous ancestors."

So they came and said to Rabbi Elazar ben Azaryah, "Is it pleasing to the master to become the head of the academy?" He said to them, "I will go and consult with the members of my household." He went and consulted with his wife. She said to him, "Perhaps they will remove you from the post as well." He said to her, "Let a person use a precious glass cup one day, and the next day, let it break." She said to him, "But you have no white hairs in your beard."

That day, Rabbi Elazar ben Azaryah was eighteen years old. A miracle occurred for him and eighteen streaks of white appeared in his beard. It was in reference to this that Rabbi Elazar ben Azaryah said, "I am like a seventy-year-old man," not "I am a seventy-year-old man."

That day, they removed the doorkeeper and permission was granted to all students to enter, for before that, Rabban Gamliel had a rule: "Any student whose inside is not like his outside may not enter the study hall!" That day, many benches were added. Rabbi Yohanan said, "Abba Joseph ben Dostai and the rabbis disagree about the matter. One says four hundred benches were added, and one says seven hundred benches."

Rabban Gamliel was dispirited. He said, "Perhaps, God forbid, I have withheld Torah from the people of Israel!"

They showed him a dream of white pitchers filled with ash. But that was not the case. It was only to put his mind at ease that the dream showed him this.

There was not a single law that had thus far been left unresolved in the study hall which they did not resolve the day Rabbi Elazar ben Azaryah was installed as Nasi. Even Rabban Gamliel did not withhold himself from the House of Study even for a moment. As we learned: that day, Judah, a would-be Ammonite convert, came before them in the study hall. He said to them, "What is the law? May I enter the congregation by marrying a daughter of Israel?" Rabban Gamliel said to him, "You are forbidden to enter the congregation." Rabbi Joshua said to him, "You are permitted to enter the congregation."

Rabban Gamliel said to him, "But is it not already stated 'An Ammonite and a Moabite shall not enter the congregation of the

Lord'?" Rabbi Joshua said, "But do Ammon and Moab reside in their places? Sancheiriv, King of Assur, long ago came up and confused all the nations." . . . Immediately they permitted Judah to enter the congregation.

Rabban Gamliel said, "Since this seems to be the case, I shall go and appease Rabbi Joshua."

When he reached Rabbi Joshua's house, he saw that the interior walls of the house were black. He said to Rabbi Joshua, "From the walls of your house, it appears that you are a smith or perhaps a coal maker."

Rabbi Joshua said to him, "Alas for the generation whose leader you are! For you know nothing of the suffering of Torah scholars or how they support themselves and how they are nourished!"

Rabban Gamliel said to him, "I have spoken excessively against you. Forgive me!"

Rabbi Joshua paid him no heed.

Rabban Gamliel said, "Do it for the sake of the honor of my father!"

Rabbi Joshua was appeased.

They said, "Who shall go and inform the sages?" A certain fuller said to them, "I will go." Rabbi Joshua sent him with this message to the House of Study: "Let him who is accustomed to wear the robe wear the robe. Shall he who is not accustomed to wear the robe say to him who is accustomed to wear the robe: remove the robe and I shall don it?"

Rabbi Akiva said to the sages, "Lock the doors so that the servants of Rabban Gamliel do not come and harass the rabbis!"

Rabbi Joshua said, "Better I should go to them myself."

He came and knocked on the door. He said to them, "Let the sprinkler son of a sprinkler sprinkle. Shall he who is neither a sprinkler nor the son of a sprinkler say to the sprinkler son of a sprinkler: your water is cave water and your ashes cinders?"

Rabbi Akiva said to him, "Rabbi Joshua, are you appeased? Did we do this for any reason other than your honor? Tomorrow you and I will arise and go to Rabban Gamliel's door."

They said, "How shall we do this? Shall we remove Rabbi Elazar ben Azaryah? We have a tradition that in matters of sanctity we elevate but do not lower. Let one master lecture one week and the other one week. This will lead to jealousy. Rather, let Rabban Gamliel lecture three weeks and Rabbi Elazar ben Azaryah one week."

And that student was Rabbi Shimon bar Yohai.

BABYLONIAN TALMUD, TRACTATE *BERAKHOT* 28A.

Chapter 4

The Gate of a Broken Heart

THESE THINGS ARE DIFFICULT TO MEASURE, BUT I imagine I've spoken enough about rock 'n' roll in a book about the tales in the Talmud. Still, if you'll indulge me, I'd like to draw your attention to George Harrison's *All Things Must Pass*. The album, Harrison's epic three-record solo debut following the breakup of the Beatles, includes two versions of the song "Isn't It a Pity."

In those days—this was 1970, ancient history now, I know— vinyl LPs, or *records*, as we called them, unlike CDs, contained data on both sides, and—as quaint as it may now seem—the physical act of listening to a record actually contributed to the music's dramatic structure. The end of the last song on Side One, for instance, created a kind of entr'acte while the listener flipped the record over, and the second-to-last track on Side Two (or Side Four in Harrison's case), before the denouement of the final song, served usually as the record's climax.

Prime real estate in terms of song placement in the days before shuffle mode, these are where Harrison places his two versions of the song. "Isn't It a Pity (Version One)" provides a stirring conclusion to the album's first side, and "Isn't It a Pity (Version Two)" is its penultimate track (excluding the instrumental jams comprising the third record).

The two versions of the song differ in a number of ways. Version Two is leaner, simpler, shorter, while Version One clocks in at over seven minutes and ends with a long, swelling coda of singers reminiscent of the coda that concludes the Beatles' "Hey Jude." In fact, a minute twenty or so from the song's end, about halfway into the coda, the chorus of singers slyly introduces the *nah nah nah-nah-nah* motif from "Hey Jude" as a countermelody.

This is a musician's artful intertextuality. As any Beatlemaniac knows, according to the received lore, Harrison had wanted to score each of the singer's lines in "Hey Jude" with an answering line from his guitar, but Paul McCartney, the song's composer and its singer, shot down the idea.

McCartney annoys Harrison by reminding him of the issue in a subsequent disagreement the two men have—this one filmed and included in the movie *Let It Be*—in which McCartney once again attempts to micromanage Harrison's playing, driving Harrison temporarily out of the group.

The two versions of "Isn't It a Pity" are Harrison's answer to McCartney. The sampling from "Hey Jude" in the coda of "Isn't It a Pity (Version One)"—a song that decries *how we take each other's love and cause each other pain*—makes clear exactly who the singer has in mind; while, in Version Two, the tasteful and restrained way the guitar comments upon each of the singer's phrases surpasses in subtlety and beauty McCartney's stripped-down arrangement of "Hey Jude."

In the gentlest of ways, with these two versions of his song, Harrison addresses McCartney and demonstrates to him—and to us—how shortsighted and wrong his musical choices have been.

IN *TAHANUN*, the twice-daily prayer of supplication, the suppliant asks, if he must fall, to fall into the hands of the Holy One, where mercy is abundant, and not into human hands, where, by inference, it is not. As we all know, human beings too often make a hell for one another out of the life we share on earth, and as Harrison seems to have known, our closest comrades are sometimes the worst offenders.

Similar motifs constellate around a trio of men linked in a creative dynamic in the Talmud: Rabban Gamliel II, Rabbi Joshua ben Hananiah, and Rabbi Eliezer ben Hyrcanus. They appear in two stories concerning trouble in the House of Study. One story is a comedy, the other a tragedy.

Now, according to Orson Welles, the difference between comedy and tragedy is where you end your story. Though worlds may be torn apart, fortunes dashed or raised, hopes realized or lost, in comedy, order is restored in the end and things return more or less to how they were, while in tragedy, everything remains broken and in a state of entropy.

As far as Welles is concerned, it doesn't seem to matter where you *begin* a story, and the reason for this is simple: all stories begin with a loss of innocence, a disruption of the status quo, a shaking of a character's foundation, and the only essential narrative question, really, is: Will innocence be regained?

By *innocence*, I don't mean a renewed sense of naïveté. Rather, I'm talking about a *knowing* innocence, a *clever* innocence, an innocence born — paradoxically — out of experience. In tragedy, knowledge is gained; in comedy, wisdom. In tragedy, the heart breaks; while in comedy, the heart, through the experience of breaking, learns to love more fully and more wisely.

(I'm speaking of comedy here, and not satire. In satire, no matter how much the characters learn, the audience remains smarter.)

It's unclear which of our stories in the House of Study — the comedy or the tragedy — comes first. This is part of the Aggadist's blurry sense of chronology. In terms of their emotional tones, the comedy feels earlier to me than the tragedy. Still, the excommunication of Rabbi Eliezer in the tragedy and his absence in the comedy suggest the opposite tack.

We've arrived at a sort of Georg Büchner/*Woyzeck* moment. When Büchner, a German novelist and playwright, died in 1837, not only was his most famous play, *Woyzeck*, unfinished, he'd left the scenes on his desk in no particular order. Editors and directors since have attempted to piece the work together, not in its definitive form — it's a puzzle lacking a single solution — but in ways that make sense dramatically, each version a different play with slightly different emphases. The same is true here: the scenes lie before you on your desk, and you're free to order them in either way. Either way, you can defend your choice. So which scene comes first? Both stories begin with a loss of innocence, but which loss is primary and which is secondary?

I'll split the difference. I'll begin with the opening scenes of the tragedy, break off in the middle, segue into the comedy, and return to the tragedy for its final scenes.

THE OVEN OF COILED SERPENTS.

From the earliest mists of history, at least for biblical man—from the Seventh Day of Creation, in fact—a coiled snake has been the harbinger of a loss of innocence and the painful gaining of knowledge, if not wisdom. So let us start with a coiled snake.

According to tradition, Akhnai's oven—the Oven of Coiled Serpents—was so called not because it belonged to a person named Akhnai, but because, when it was brought into the House of Study, the sages surrounded it like a coiled snake. The question ostensibly before them: *Can this oven be made ritually pure?*

As with the Justices of the US Supreme Court, every case adjudicated by the sages determines theo-legal precedent. Here, we can presume that either something happened to this oven that made it ritually impure or that the question of whether such an oven could be made ritually pure proved so difficult that the case is kicked up the rabbinic chain to its highest level.

Opinions in the House of Study are, as always, divided.

Because the oven is made out of separate clay coils, one placed on top of the other, with sand in between the coils, Rabbi Eliezer holds that the oven is not a single utensil and is therefore not susceptible to ritual impurity. The rest of the sages disagree: the oven's external coating of mortar and cement makes the coils a single utensil, one therefore susceptible to impurity.

(On a deeper level, we understand that the sages are discussing something more essential to the moment in which they find themselves: the relationship of the individual to his society. To reformulate the question: Can a single part be impure without threatening the purity of the whole?)

Imagine Rabbi Eliezer's frustration.

According to his teacher, Rabban Yohanan ben Zakkai, "If all the sages of Israel were placed on one pan of a scale, and Rabbi Eliezer ben Hyrcanus were placed on the other pan, he would outweigh them all in wisdom."

(Even Moses, on one of his not infrequent trips to Heaven, having overheard the Holy One reciting a law in Rabbi Eliezer's name, is so impressed by the not-yet-born scholar that he requests of the Holy One that Rabbi Eliezer issue from his family line.)

Still, though Rabbi Eliezer advances all the arguments in the world—these are the words of the story—he's unable to convince his colleagues of his view. At last, in frustration, he cries out, "If the Law is as I say, let this carob tree prove it!"

And the carob tree outside the House of Study uproots itself and immediately moves one hundred cubits—some say even four hundred cubits—from its customary place.

The sages are not impressed.

"A proof may not be brought from a carob tree," they tell him.

Rabbi Eliezer redoubles his efforts:

He said, "If the Law is as I say, let the waters prove it," whereupon a stream reversed its flow. The sages said, "A proof may not be brought from the water."

Rabbi Eliezer's temper seems to be rising:

He said, "If the Law is as I say, let the walls of the House of Study prove it," whereupon the walls began caving in.

It's a Samson-among-the-Philistines moment, and you will perhaps remember that these three elements—a carob tree, water, and shelter—sustained Rabbi Shimon bar Yohai and his son in their cave. The very fundamentals of life appear to be at stake, and the House of Study, the house that shelters them all, is threatening to collapse.

Rabbi Joshua steps forward to rebuke the walls. "If Torah scholars are having a legal argument with each other, who are you to interfere?" he tells the walls.

A stalemate is reached: Out of deference to Rabbi Joshua, the walls do not collapse, but in deference to Rabbi Eliezer, neither do they straighten up again completely. Indeed, we're told, they're still out of whack to this very day!

(If I may interrupt the flow of the story once more: the House of Study, with its eternally-on-the-point-of-falling-but-not-quite-falling walls, captures, as an image, not only the state of the sages' house, but the state of the Holy One's house as well, the Temple. Our story takes place in the wake of the Roman siege of Jerusalem, when the sages, fearing the fall of the Temple, flee to the port city of Yavneh, and the image of the Holy Temple, eternally rebuilding, eternally falling, remains central to rabbinic concerns to this very day.)

Back to our story: Rabbi Eliezer, it seems, has one more card up his sleeve. "If the Law is as I say," he says, "let it be proved from Heaven!"

And immediately, a heavenly voice rings out, "Why do you dispute with Rabbi Eliezer? The Law is as he states in every instance."

This is impressive. Dramatic. Authoritative. Definitive. Or so one might presume.

The sages, after all, are discussing the terrestrial application of a Heaven-sent legal system, given by the Holy One to humanity through Moses at the summit of Mount Sinai in the midst of thunder and lightning, to the blast of ram's horns.

But no.

Rabbi Joshua once again arises—he stands on his feet, in the vernacular phrase—and declares, "The Law is not in Heaven!"

This is a quotation from Scripture, Deuteronomy 30:12–14, to be exact, in which the prophet Moses exhorts the children of Israel:

Surely this teaching I enjoin upon you this day is not too baffling for you nor beyond your reach. It is not in the Heavens that you should say, "Who among us can go up to the Heavens and get it for us so we can hear it and keep it?" It is not across the sea so that you should say, "Who will cross the sea and get it for us, so that we will be able hear it and keep it?" It is something very close to you. It is in your mouth and in your heart.

Rabbi Jeremiah—a voice from a chorus of later, though still quite ancient, rabbis—breaks into our story at this point to explain that the Law, given into the hands of human beings at Mount Sinai, is no longer the possession of Heaven. The sages must interpret and apply it.

This is all well and good, although Rabbi Jeremiah seems to be speaking less to the reader of the Talmud and more to the Holy One, who in his omniscience, one might imagine, needs no such reminder.

We pay no attention to a heavenly voice, as Rabbi Jeremiah explains, because the Holy One already wrote in the sacred law given at Sinai that *One must follow the majority.*

Here, Rabbi Jeremiah is quoting Scripture as well. Diligent students, we turn to chapter 23, verse 3 of the Book of Exodus, where we discover that the verse he's citing means exactly the opposite. The verse literally reads: "You shall *not* follow after the majority to do evil." And the verb—the second person singular, obscured, of course, in the English translation—addresses the individual, not the collective, exhorting him to stand firm against a wrong-turning majority.

Exactly the circumstances, one imagines, that Rabbi Eliezer feels he is facing.

(The passage Rabbi Joshua references from Deuteronomy, likewise written in the second person singular, is addressed to the individual. Together, these two passages might suggest: *Don't give in to the mob. Listen to your own heart. It's not that complicated.*)

In any case, let's look at the facts. In refutation of *all* the arguments in the *world*, plus four magical proofs, what does Rabbi Joshua have? One freely interpreted verse (*The Law is not in Heaven!*), a single magical proof (the walls of the House of Study obey his word as deferentially as they do Rabbi Eliezer's), the muscle of the crowd, and one extratextual note of support offered seven generations later by Rabbi Jeremiah, who, it seems, feels he can, like Rabbi Joshua, interpret Scripture with a free hand, standing it on its head.

(After all, does it *really* follow logically that, since one is forbidden to follow the majority into evil, one *must* follow the majority into good, and what if that "good," according to all the arguments of the world, appears to the lone man as evil?)

I must say, the sages seem unsure of themselves. A certain doubtfulness haunts the margins of the tale. In fact, the next thing we're told is this: "Rabbi Nathan met Elijah the prophet and asked him, 'What did the Holy One . . . do at that hour?'" meaning in the moment Rabbi Joshua and Rabbi Eliezer had their magical throwdown.

According to Elijah, "[The Holy One] laughed and said, 'My children have overruled me, my children have overruled me!'"

Decisive, it seems. Authoritative. Persuasive. But on closer examination, a terrible irony is at play here: his arguments and his magic having failed, Rabbi Eliezer, in frustration, calls upon Heaven, and Heaven answers him with a voice announcing for all to hear that Rabbi Eliezer's position is, *as always*, the correct one; and though Rabbi Joshua has declared heavenly voices legally null and void, the story itself, filled with doubt concerning the sages' actions against him, pulls the Holy One onstage from the wings, as it were, and allows him to give exactly the same sort of testimony on Rabbi Joshua's behalf that Rabbi Joshua has declared inadmissible on behalf of Rabbi Eliezer.

Even worse: the voice from Heaven is heard by all, while the report of the Holy One's laughing acquiescence is reported third-hand: *according to our anonymous narrator, Rabbi Nathan heard it from the prophet Elijah that the Holy One . . .*

Now, as grateful as I am for the image of a laughing deity allowing his errant children their head—so much for the so-called *vengeful* Old Testament God of the Jews—still, you have to wonder: what is going on here? Magic is used to repudiate magic; heavenly voices, deemed inadmissible, are admitted, after the fact, as evidence; Scripture, quoted as authoritative, is made to mean the opposite of what it says.

How certain are the sages that their opinion is correct? Is there no room for believing that they may in fact *be* wrong and that, since the sacred law governs morality, in *being* wrong, they are *doing* wrong, following the majority into evil?

IT'S NOT CLEAR exactly what happens next. Or it's not clear exactly why. Scholars in both the academic and rabbinic worlds have speculated on the presumptive crimes of Rabbi Eliezer, arguing that he is guilty of everything from following the rulings of the School of Shammai to becoming heretically involved with the new Christian cult, dabbling in its secret orgiastic rites.

Whatever the reason they've turned against him, the sages, as people do when in pursuit of a dubious course, kick their efforts up a notch, and they decide to place Rabbi Eliezer under a rabbinic ban—a single impure coil, in their view, after all, can contaminate an entire oven—and they do so with a burning vehemence:

> On that day, all the objects that Rabbi Eliezer had previously declared ritually clean were burnt in fire. A vote was taken and Rabbi Eliezer was excommunicated; and then they said, "Who will go and inform him?"

"I will go," Rabbi Akiva says.

Rabbi Akiva is the student of Rabbi Eliezer *and* Rabbi Joshua. He is their most beloved pupil, in fact, and he's clearly worried over the reverberating consequences of this rash move.

"Perhaps," he says, "an unfit person will go and inform him and bring about the destruction of the entire world."

We have to understand this clearly: These are powerful men, towering intellectuals. They have a long history together, and they're involved in a conflict, the underlying and—except for Rabbi Akiva—*unacknowledged* emotional currents of which have turned dark and threaten to turn darker still, pulling them into a vortex of passion and unreason. After all, like Samson pushing over the pillars, Rabbi Eliezer was willing to bring down the walls of the House of Study, destroying himself along with everyone present. (*Philistines!* we can imagine him thinking.)

Rabbi Akiva alone seems aware of the danger: the entire world—or certainly *his* entire world—is imperiled.

PERHAPS IT'S NOT CLEAR from our story so far that Rabbi Joshua and Rabbi Eliezer are and have been for many years the most devoted of friends. Students of Rabban Yohanan ben Zakkai, they share a palpable love for each other, referring to each other alternatively as "my master" or "my son," depending on who is asking a question of whom. Unusually harmonious and close, they're a sort of salt-and-pepper team, another iteration of the complementary pairs we keep seeing in these tales. Though they're partners, learning and teaching together, in their personal histories, in their approach to sacred scholarship, like salt and pepper, they couldn't be more black and white.

Rabbi Joshua, for example, believes that wisdom derives from the head—the center of wit, imagination, ratiocination—while Rabbi Eliezer maintains that it comes from the heart, the seat of memory. For all of his advanced thinking, Rabbi Joshua is something of a misogynist; Rabbi Eliezer, on the other hand, lives surrounded by strong women. While Rabbi Joshua is quite poor, Rabbi Eliezer not only comes from a wealthy family, he also, though temporarily disowned by his father, becomes wealthy as an adult. He is extraordinarily handsome. When he teaches, we're told, his face shines with the brilliance of the sun, and beams of light emanate from his head as they did from the head of his ancestor Moses. Rabbi Joshua, on the other hand, is so ugly that when he meets the daughter of Caesar, she cannot hold her tongue:

"What a pity!" she says. "Such glorious wisdom in so ugly a vessel!"

He takes his revenge.

"My child," Rabbi Joshua says to her, "in what kind of vessel does your father keep his wine?"

"In earthenware vessels."

"Ordinary people keep their wine in earthenware vessels," he tells her. "Important persons, like yourselves, should keep their wine in vessels of silver or even of gold."

The daughter runs to tell this to her father, and he immediately transfers his wine into silver and golden vessels, thereby souring it.

Caesar sends for Rabbi Joshua immediately. "Why did you give my daughter such advice?"

"I merely asked her the same question she asked me."

"But are there not learned people who are handsome?"

"There are," Rabbi Joshua tells him. "But if these handsome people were ugly, they'd be even more learned."

Rabbi Joshua grew up steeped in Torah. An older sage even recalls that his mother used to bring his cradle into the House of Study so that, as an infant, his ears would become attuned to the holy words spoken there. Rabbi Eliezer had no parent devoted to sacred things, and no easy path to the rabbinate. Quite the opposite: his father actually forbade him from becoming a scholar of the Torah.

It's a bit of a Cinderella story:

Rabbi Eliezer was twenty-eight years old and had not yet studied. It happened that once his brothers were plowing arable land belonging to their father, while he was given stony land to plow. He sat down and wept. His father asked him, "Why are you crying? Are you unhappy because you have been given stony soil to plow? Until now, you have been plowing a stony plot, but now you will have arable land to plow!"

But when Eliezer started to work the fertile ground, again he sat down to cry. His father asked him, "Why are you weeping? Is it because you do not like working on the stony plot?" Eliezer: "No, that is not the reason." His father: "But then why are you crying?" Eliezer: "I weep only because I desire to learn Torah." Hyrcanus: "Look, you are twenty-eight years old, and you want to study Torah? Get married, have children, and take *them* to school!"

A short while later, Eliezer told his father, "I shall go to Jerusalem to study Torah with Rabban Yohanan ben Zakkai." His father:

"You will not get a taste of food until you have plowed a full furrow." The next morning, Eliezer woke up early and plowed the furrow, but as he finished, his cow fell and was maimed. He thought: "It is fortunate for me that this accident occurred, for now I shall flee to Rabban Yohanan ben Zakkai in Jerusalem."

Because he lacked food, on the way he ate clods of earth. When he reached the academy of Rabban Yohanan, he sat down before him and wept. When Rabban Yohanan asked him why he was weeping, Eliezer told him, "It is my desire to study Torah." The rabbi questioned him. "Have you never studied at all?" The answer was no. Rabban Yohanan began by teaching him the most elemental things, the *Sh'ma*, the Prayer, the Grace after Meals, and two laws each day.

Now poverty, not wealth, defines Eliezer's life:

On the Sabbath, Eliezer would review what he had learned and absorb it. Because of his poverty, he went eight days without eating and emitted a foul odor from his mouth. Rabban Yohanan noticed this and asked him, "Eliezer, my son, have you eaten anything today?" Eliezer remained silent. Again the question was put to him and again he did not reply. Rabban Yohanan declared, "By our life! Today you will eat with me." Eliezer spoke up, "I have already eaten at my lodgings." Rabban Yohanan ordered his students, "By your lives, investigate the matter!"

They went through all the streets of Jerusalem, asking the innkeepers, "Do you have a student in your rooms?" The answer was always in the negative until they came to a certain woman and, to their question, she replied, "Yes." They inquired, "Does he have anything here?" She told them, "He has a single sack into which he places his head and sucks as on a wine sack." They asked her to show it to them, which she did at once. They looked into it and saw only some earth. They asked her, "Has Eliezer not eaten with you at all today?" She answered, "I thought he was eating with his teacher."

They went and told this to Rabban Yohanan, who cried out, "Woe to you, Eliezer, that your lot was neglected among us, but I tell you now that as a foul odor came from your mouth, so in the future will the fragrance of Torah issue from your mouth to the ends of the earth." Rabban Yohanan provided him with food on a regular basis, and soon he was completely healed.

Rabbi Eliezer studies with Rabban Yohanan for three years. Meanwhile at home, his brothers, like wicked stepsisters, are hatching his disinheritance:

They told their father Hyrcanus, "See what your son Eliezer has done to you! He left you in your old age and went off to Jerusalem. Go up there and pronounce a vow that he will never inherit any of your property." Hyrcanus listened to them and went.

Not a ball, as in the story of Cinderella, but a celebration nonetheless:

It happened that the day Hyrcanus arrived was a day of celebration for Rabban Yohanan ben Zakkai. All the greatest men of the land were his guests, among them Ben Zizit Ha-Kaset, Nakdimon ben Guryon, and Ben Kalba Savua. When Rabban Yohanan heard that Hyrcanus had come, he had him seated among these important people. Hyrcanus felt uneasy.

(Perhaps he's worried that, seated among the grandees, he'll be hit up for a donation.)

Rabban Yohanan fixed his eyes upon Eliezer and said to him, "Begin and expound." Eliezer begged off. "I cannot; I am like a cistern that cannot give off more water than has been poured into it. So too I am unable to speak words of Torah other than what you have taught me." Rabban Yohanan spoke up, "No, my son, you are more like an ever-flowing fountain that brings forth its own waters."

He urged him to begin, and his fellow students also pressed him. Whereupon, he stood up and began. He expounded upon subjects of learning that had never been heard before! His face shone as with the brilliance of the sun, and beams of light emanated from his head as they had from the head of Moses. So absorbed were they all that no one noticed if it was day or night.

Then Rabban Yohanan stood up, kissed Eliezer on his head, and said, "Blessed are you, Abraham, Isaac, and Jacob, that such a descendant has come from your loins!"

Hyrcanus inquired, "Of whom is he speaking this way?" They told him, "Of Eliezer, your son." He declared, "Then he should not have spoken so. Instead he should have said, Blessed am *I* that such a person came from *my* loins!"

Hyrcanus stood up on a bench and called out to the people of Jerusalem who were there, "My masters, I had come here to disinherit my son Eliezer by an oath. But now all my possessions will go to him and his brothers will inherit nothing!"

Had Jakob and Wilhelm Grimm edited the text, the feet of these wicked brothers might next have been amputated, but forgiveness and forbearance are ancient rabbinic virtues:

Rabbi Eliezer said to him, "Had I sought landed property from the Holy One, blessed be he, he would have granted it to me, as it is said, 'The earth is the Lord's and the fullness thereof.' Had I asked the Holy One for silver and gold, he would have given it to me, as it is said, 'Silver is mine and gold is mine—says the Lord of Hosts.' But all that I seek from the Holy One is to study his Torah."

Rabbi Eliezer and Rabbi Joshua's different backgrounds perhaps explain their different approaches as scholars. Left as an infant in the House of Study as though it were a day-care center, Rabbi Joshua feels free to innovate when it comes to sacred law: Informed by Rabbi Eliezer that the fast declared by the people of Lod on the holiday of Hanukah is a violation of rabbinic law, Rabbi Joshua rises from the fast, washes—forbidden on a fast day—and tells the people, "Now go and observe a fast as a penalty for having fasted on Hanukah!"

Rabbi Eliezer, on the other hand, nearly thirty when he learns the basics, is so conservative he claims—despite the evidence from our story—to have never taught a word that he hasn't heard first from his teacher:

They said to Rabbi Eliezer, "Are all your words only what you have heard from your teacher?" He replied, "You are forcing me to say something that I have not received from my teachers. In all my days, no man has preceded me to the House of Study; I have never slept in the House of Study, neither a fixed sleep nor a nap; and I was always the last to leave. I've never engaged in frivolous talk, nor have I ever said a thing which I have not heard from my teacher."

Marvelously, it turns out that even *this* claim is modeled upon the life of his teacher Rabban Yohanan ben Zakkai, about whom it is said:

All his days, he never engaged in frivolous talk; he never walked four cubits without studying Torah and wearing phylacteries. He never meditated in unclean alleyways. No man ever preceded him into the House of Study; he never slept in the House of Study, neither a fixed sleep nor a nap; . . . he was always the last to leave the House of Study . . . and he never said something which he had not heard from his teacher.

Certainly, the innovator in Rabbi Joshua needs the conservationist in Rabbi Eliezer. As every musician knows, without a strong theme, no variation is possible. Rabbi Joshua seems aware of this, too.

Once, for example, "Rabbi Joshua came into the House of Study and began kissing the stone on which Rabbi Eliezer sat. 'This stone is like Mount Sinai,' he said, 'and he who sits on it is like the Ark of the Covenant.'"

Rabbi Eliezer's chair is unmovable, inflexible, obdurate as stone. It *is* stone. In Rabbi Joshua's view, the place from which Rabbi

Eliezer teaches is as fundamental to the faith as Mount Sinai. "You are more valuable to Israel than the orb of the sun," Rabbi Joshua will tell an ailing Rabbi Eliezer on his deathbed. "The orb of the sun is only for this world, while you, my master, are for this world and the World to Come."

Their similarities and their differences are subtly illustrated by their nearly twin credos:

Rabbi Eliezer said: "If all the seas were ink, and all reeds pens, and Heaven and earth scrolls, and all mankind scribes, they would not suffice to write the Torah that I have learned, even though I abstracted from it no more than a man would take by dipping the tip of his painting stick into the sea."

Rabbi Joshua: "If all the seas were ink, and all reeds pens, Heaven and earth scrolls, and all mankind scribes, they would not suffice to write down the Torah I learned, even though I abstracted from my masters' teaching no more than a man would take when dipping the point of a pen into the ink tube."

Rabbi Eliezer's image is of a man cleaning his pen; Rabbi Joshua's of a man preparing to write. The traditionalist enters the picture at the end of the work, the innovator at its beginning. Tradition and innovation share a long and rocky marriage in rabbinic culture, and in the story of Akhnai's oven, we are witnessing their divorce. Though the two friends have spent many years teaching together in mutual love and admiration, the innovator has now kicked the traditionalist out of the house, and the delicate balance of their mutually beneficial relationship is thrown out of whack.

EACH TIME, WHEN, for good or ill, the structure of their society is threatened, Rabbi Akiva's is a calming voice. His metamorphosis from violent rustic to wise-hearted sage—which I'll elaborate more fully in chapter 5—has been slow and hard won. He embodies that paradoxical archetype of the big-muscled fellow who could kill you but who would rather not.

Exquisitely aware of the dangers in informing Rabbi Eliezer of the ban, Rabbi Akiva, as though he were defusing a bomb, takes every precaution, proceeding as tactfully as the prophet Elijah did in calling the news of his amnesty into Rabbi Shimon's cave.

What did Rabbi Akiva do? the Aggadist asks. "Akiva clad himself in black garments, wrapped himself in black"—he puts on the mantle of mourning, as a person under a rabbinic ban must do— "and sat before [Rabbi Eliezer] at a distance of four cubits," another requirement of a ban.

The somber clothing, the sitting upon the ground, the distance: gently, Rabbi Akiva raises the issue of excommunication visually before having to explain to Rabbi Eliezer the cold, hard facts.

Perhaps Akiva is in mourning, we can imagine Rabbi Eliezer thinking. *Is it possible* Akiva *has been placed under a ban?* The sympathy and concern these thoughts stir up in Rabbi Eliezer are emotions from the cooler side of the heart's spectrum, and they do much to quench the outrage and the woundedness he might otherwise—and properly—feel.

"Akiva, why is today different from all other days?" he asks.

The question—the opening question from the Passover Seder— is freighted with allusive meaning. Is Rabbi Eliezer hoping for freedom from bondage? Does he fear forty years of wandering in the desert of exile?

"Master," Rabbi Akiva explains, "it appears to me that your friends are separating from you."

Note the gentleness and the slow approach to the heart of this bitter matter. He addresses Rabbi Eliezer respectfully as his teacher, answering him with a hazy sense of passive subjectivity: though Rabbi Eliezer has been violently pushed out of their circle, for Rabbi Akiva, it seems as though the sages have separated themselves from him as its center.

Having been prepared by Rabbi Akiva, Rabbi Eliezer receives this terrible news without resistance. He accepts the ban, as prescribed, with signs of mourning: "Rabbi Eliezer tore his garments, removed his shoes, sat upon the ground, and cried."

Though not entirely destroyed, the world is still smitten:

At that time, a third of the olive crop, a third of the wheat crop, and a third of the barley crop of the world were smitten. And some say even dough already in a woman's hands became spoiled! A great blow occurred that day. For every place on which Rabbi Eliezer set his eyes went up in flames.

Thanks to the imperfect chronology of our two stories, at this point we must leave off from the tragedy—we will return to its continuation later—and pick up the comedy. In the comedy, as I've pointed out, Rabbi Eliezer has disappeared from the House of Study, so it makes sense that the story follows his excommunication. Perhaps his presence served as a buffer between Rabbi Joshua and Rabban Gamliel, because with Rabbi Eliezer absent, tensions between these two men come to a head:

It happened that a certain student came before Rabbi Joshua, and he asked him, "The evening prayer—is it elective or obligatory?" He answered him, "Elective."

This, as I understand it, is the correct answer. Sacred law obligates a man to pray the morning and afternoon prayers with a cohort of no fewer than nine of his fellows. For many reasons, not excluding the dangers of the night—darker in the ancient world than in our own—the evening prayer falls outside this obligation. Still, in a beautiful example of rabbinic hyperthink, by performing it regularly, a person may *elect* to make the evening prayer *obligatory* upon himself.

You'd think the matter settled, but as it turns out, this same fellow "came before Rabban Gamliel and asked him, 'The evening prayer—is it elective or obligatory?'" To which Rabban Gamliel replies, "Obligatory."

"But Rabbi Joshua told me it's elective," the student says.

Rabban Gamliel must feel threatened. He reaches immediately for a military metaphor. Meaning the sages, he tells the student, "Wait until the shield-bearers enter the House of Study."

A LITTLE BACKSTORY here might be helpful.

We have to ask the question: If a third of the world belongs to Rabbi Eliezer, sustained by his will and his place in the circuit of holiness, to whom do the other two-thirds belong, the two-thirds Rabbi Akiva attempted through his gentleness to protect?

Surely to Rabbi Joshua and to Rabban Gamliel.

These three together, with their long history and their triangular association, are the necessary pillars of the world they share. Formed before the fall of the Temple, this deltoid relationship is cemented during the chaos and confusion of that time. (As I have said, the falling in of the walls of the House of Study is a visual echo of the Temple's collapse.) All three of these men are caught up in that moment of chaos and collapse, and their lives depend on one another's.

In 3828 (or 68 CE), Jerusalem has been under siege for three and a half years, surrounded by the forces of Vespasian, a general in the Roman army. Rabban Yohanan ben Zakkai is the last surviving disciple of Hillel. His nephew ben Batiah has thrown in his lot with the Zealots, resistance fighters who believe that, with the help of the Holy One, they can triumph over Rome's superior military force.

Three rich men, the same three who attend Rabbi Eliezer's Cinderella ball, Nakdimon ben Guryon, Ben Kalba Savua, and Ben Zizit Ha-Kaset, have stocked the city's storehouses with a twenty-two-year supply of staples. Unfortunately, they've put ben Batiah in charge of these storehouses, and he burns them to the ground, hoping, in this way, to compel the people into rising up and fighting against the Romans for food.

When his uncle, Rabban Yohanan ben Zakkai, hears of this, he cries out, "Woe!"

Word reaches ben Batiah. "Your uncle cried out, 'Woe!'" he's told.

Ben Batiah has his uncle brought before him. "Why did you cry out, 'Woe'?" he says.

It's an interrogation. Rabban Yohanan ben Zakkai is aware of this. If his nephew burnt the storehouses to the ground, he's capable of doing anything. Happily, Rabban Yohanan thinks on his feet. "I didn't cry out, 'Woe,'" he says, "but rather 'Whoa!' as an expression of approval."

"And why did you cry out, 'Whoa'?" ben Batiah wants to know.

"Because as long as the storehouses were intact," Rabban Yohanan tells him, "the people would not expose themselves to the dangers of battle."

(A marvelous lesson here: Where better to conceal the truth but inside itself!)

As the Aggadist tells us: "Through the difference between *Woe!* and *Whoa!*, Rabban Yohanan ben Zakkai escaped death."

THE PEOPLE DON'T RISE UP, of course. They don't have the strength. They're starving. Eventually, even ben Batiah, perhaps starving as well, loses his zealotry. His uncle asks him, "How long will you carry on this way, starving the city's people?"

Ben Batiah, a prisoner of his own ideology, asks pitifully, "What can I do? If I say anything, the others will kill me."

Thinking less of his own survival and more of the survival of the Torah, Rabban Yohanan ben Zakkai asks his nephew for help in slipping past the other Zealots who guard the gates of the besieged city.

"Perhaps there's a chance of rescuing something," he says.

The nephew seems to share some of his uncle's wiliness. He tells him, "We've an arrangement among ourselves that none shall leave the city, but the dead. Pretend to be ill, let people come to visit you. Get something with a bad odor, and let the smell become overpowering. Then people will say you have died. Let no one but your students carry you out, so that the guard will not sense that you are light in weight"—the dead are heavy—"and realize that you're alive."

Rabban Yohanan ben Zakkai carries out his nephew's plan to the smallest detail. This time ben Batiah's scheme works. Rabbi Eliezer carries the head of Rabbi Yohanan ben Zakkai's coffin, Rabbi Joshua the feet, and ben Batiah, under the *nom de résistance* Abba Sikra, walks in front.

When they reach the gates of the city, the Zealot guard asks them, "What is this?"

"A dead man," they tell him. "Don't you know that it's forbidden for a corpse to remain in Jerusalem overnight?"

The guard, zealous in his zealotry, suggests piercing the bier with a lance to make certain it contains a corpse. Abba Sikra puts him off: "Then the Romans will say, 'They killed their own teacher by piercing him.'" The guard suggests throwing the body on the ground, but Abba Sikra objects. "Then the Romans will say, 'They killed their teacher by throwing his body down.'"

Untrained, obviously, in the hairsplitting disputation of Talmudic scholars, the guard is stymied, and he lets the cortege pass.

Many difficulties follow, but eventually Rabban Yohanan ben Zakkai stands before Vespasian, having won his patronage by correctly prophesying his elevation in rank to emperor.

Now in charge of the Roman Empire, a grateful Vespasian, preparing to depart Jerusalem, says to Rabban Yohanan, "I'm about to leave this area, and another will be sent in my place. Ask of me something, and I shall grant it."

Rabban Yohanan ben Zakkai asks that Jerusalem be spared. "Ask me for something else," Vespasian says.

After securing that the eastern gate of the city, the gate through which the Messiah is expected, is left intact, and that the citizens be allowed to depart, unmolested, up to the fourth hour, Rabban Yohanan ben Zakkai says (famously), "Give me Yavneh and its sages and the descendants of Rabban Gamliel."

Rabbi Eliezer and Rabbi Joshua have carried Rabban Yohanan ben Zakkai to safety; now Rabban Yohanan secures Rabban Gamliel's life. As the city collapses behind them, their world—the world of the sages—has been ransomed. That ransomed world will come to rest on the pillars of Rabbi Eliezer, Rabbi Joshua, and Rabban Gamliel's shoulders; together, the three possess the qualities that we will soon learn are necessary in leadership—wealth, wisdom, and a noble lineage, qualities none of them alone possesses.

AT THE BEGINNING of this new world, the three of them are in perfect synchrony and balance, everyone working towards the same high purpose, each man assuming identical risks in a high-stakes life-or-death escapade, and each man cognizant of the reminders of all six of our memos: each man's action serves in a perfectly balanced way the needs of HEAVEN, EARTH, SELF, OTHERS, ANCESTORS, and DESCENDANTS.

Not to equate the sacred with the secular, but in Beatle lore, this is the moment when Paul McCartney introduces his young friend George Harrison to his songwriting partner John Lennon on the upper deck of a double-decker bus in Liverpool.

"Go on, go on," McCartney urges Harrison. "Get your guitar out." Complying, Harrison opens his case and auditions, playing a perfect rendition of a popular rocker called "Raunchy."

"He's in the band!" McCartney says, recalling the moment.

The year is 1958, a mere thirteen years after the end of World War II, when much of England still lay in ruins.

UNDER RABBAN YOHANAN ben Zakkai's leadership, the sages repair to the port of Yavneh, a battered and war-tossed remnant. Yavneh is filled with refugees and, for a decade and a half, the sages are mainly concerned with the impossible task of putting back together a society sundered by war and devastated by the catastrophic loss of the Holy Temple.

Though, from all appearances, Rabbi Joshua possesses the superior mind, thanks to his illustrious lineage—he is a descendant of Hillel—Rabban Gamliel is appointed Nasi, the head of the academy, following Rabban Yohanan ben Zakkai's death in 3834 (74 CE), with Rabbi Joshua serving under him as Av Bet Din, his second-in-command.

Now, at the beginning of our story, after nearly a decade and a half in Yavneh, Rabban Gamliel is committed to returning their society to its principal work—its sacred studies, its daily devotions—and under these conditions, it seems, the evening prayer is damn well compulsory!

> When the shield-bearers entered the House of Study, the question was asked, "The evening prayer—is it elective or obligatory?" Rabban Gamliel replied, "Obligatory." He then said to the sages, "Is there among us a man who disputes this ruling?" Rabbi Joshua said to him, "No."

So far, so good. Everyone and everything are in agreement.

But Rabban Gamliel pushes the battle a bridge farther.

"But in your name it was said to me that you declared the evening prayer elective! Joshua," he tells him, not insignificantly stripping him of his title, "stand on your feet and let them testify against you!"

Rabbi Joshua stands, and he says a curious thing: "Were I alive and he dead, the living might contradict the dead, but since he is living and I am living, how can the living contradict the living?"

I presume he's speaking to himself—there is no reaction to his words in the room—though it's not clear to whom he is referring. Perhaps he means the as-yet-unidentified student, suggesting that, if he could lie his way out of this embarrassing situation, he would. More likely Rabban Gamliel is the person he seems to be wishing dead at the moment. I suggest we're privy not to a petulant public rant, but to the private mental formulation of Rabbi Joshua's long-term goals: outlive Rabban Gamliel and overturn his rulings.

IN THE HOUSE OF STUDY, having stood, a member needs the Nasi's permission to sit. In a strategic miscalculation, Rabban Gamliel further humiliates Rabbi Joshua by forcing him to remain standing:

> Rabban Gamliel continued sitting and lecturing, and Rabbi Joshua remained standing on his feet, until all the people murmured and said to Huzpit the Interpreter, "Stop!" and he stopped.

A word of explanation here: as a sort of PA system in the ancient world, a teacher had an interpreter, an aide who, in a stentorian voice, repeated every word he spoke, so that he might be heard by everyone in a large assembly. Rabban Gamliel's interpreter is called Huzpit—we'll meet him again, in greatly reduced circumstances, in chapter 5—and when the shield-bearers, defecting from Rabban Gamliel's defense, defend the poor humiliant Joshua instead, crying out *Stop!*, Huzpit, joining their ranks, stops.

It's a dramatic moment. Rabban Gamliel has, in effect, lost his voice.

"How long will Rabban Gamliel go on humiliating Rabbi Joshua!" the shield-bearers want to know. "On New Year's Day last year, he insulted him! In the matter of the firstborn in the incident with Rabbi Zadok, he insulted him! And now, he insults him as well!"

AGAIN, A FEW backwards-moving words of explanation.

Let's look first at the incident on Rosh Hashanah, the New Year: As part of his responsibilities as head of the High Court, the Nasi establishes the calendar for each year, basing his calculations upon the astronomical testimony of two reliable witnesses. Because Rabban Gamliel has a tradition, handed down to him from the house of his father and even from the house of his father's father, that, between its disappearance and its reappearance, the moon sometimes travels a short route and sometimes a longer one, he accepted, for the year in question, the illogical and unscientific testimony of witnesses who claim to have seen the waning moon in the morning sky and the waxing moon on the evening of the same day.

Other sages—in the commentaries on the margins of the text and in the room itself—decry this decision as absurd. A contemporary of Rabban Gamliel, Rabbi Dosa ben Harkynos, asks, "How can they testify that a woman gave birth when the very next day her belly is still swollen?" Rabbi Joshua agrees, maintaining that, at the very minimum, twenty-four hours must fall between the waning and the waxing moon.

The disparity of opinions is no small matter. According to Rabbi Joshua's view, the holidays of the first month—these include the New Year and the Day of Atonement, the holiest day of the year—occur a day later than they do according to Rabban Gamliel's nonsensical calculations.

Following the Nasi's ruling means, at the very least, undergoing the obligatory Day of Atonement fast on the wrong day.

Which, of course, is nothing compared to *not* fasting on the correct day.

When word reaches Rabban Gamliel that Rabbi Joshua has agreed with Rabbi Dosa ben Harkynos's dissenting opinion, he sends him the following message: "Rabbi Joshua, I issue a decree upon you to come to me with your staff and your money on the day that according to your calculations should be the Day of Atonement."

We can imagine Rabban Gamliel's rationale: Even were the nation not reeling from the loss of the Temple, still, they cannot have two calendars. The people cannot feel free to fast on a Day of Atonement of their own choosing! A Nasi and his Av Bet Din cannot be at cross-purposes, and though the ultimate authority might be wrong, still, for the sake of political coherence, one must adhere to that authority.

Rabbi Joshua is in torment over this fatal turn of events. The moon may be inconstant, but that's only in comparison with the sun. It doesn't travel at varying rates, no matter how illustrious the religious authorities are who hold that it does. Worse, one is forbidden to handle money, to carry, and to travel on the Day of Atonement. How can Rabbi Joshua desecrate this most holy of days?

Rabbi Akiva, his most beloved student, comes to his aid:

He asked, "Master, why are you so distraught?" Rabbi Joshua replied, "Akiva, that man deserves to be laid up in a sickbed for twelve months without the opportunity to issue such an order!"

Rabbi Akiva told him, "I can bring proof that whatever Rabban Gamliel has done is valid, for it is stated, *These are the festivals of the Holy One, holy convocations, that you shall declare them.*"

That you shall declare them: In parsing this verse from the Torah, Rabbi Akiva puts the emphasis on the act of declaration, as though the Holy One has said: "At their proper time or not at their proper time, I have no festivals but these."

Hearing this, Rabbi Joshua took up his staff and his money, and went to Yavneh to Rabban Gamliel on the day on which, according to his own calculations, the Day of Atonement fell. As soon as Rabban Gamliel saw him, he rose from his chair, kissed Rabbi Joshua on his head, and said to him, "Come in peace, my master and my student—my master in wisdom and my student because you accepted my decision. Blessed is the generation in which men of great distinction obey those of little distinction."

All's well that ends well, I suppose, until the incident with Rabbi Zadok, which proves to be another humiliation for poor Rabbi Joshua.

Rabbi Zadok owned a firstborn male calf. Such an animal, if unblemished by any disfiguring mark, possesses a sacrificial sanctity and must be given to a priest who offers it as a sacrifice on the Temple altar. If, after it is surrendered to the priest, the animal is disfigured in any way, the priest may eat it himself.

Rabbi Zadok's calf splits its lip eating barley from a basket woven from peeled willow bark—peeled willow bark is nearly as soft as cloth—rendering it unfit for sacrifice. A suspicion obtains that, in such cases, the owner of the animal might have inflicted the blemish himself, and an investigation is made. Rabbi Zadok is a member of the priestly caste as well as a scholar, and he asks Rabbi Joshua if, because he is learned and therefore trusted to report honestly on the calf's disfigurement, he can, on his own authority, slaughter the animal and, as a priest, eat its meat.

Rabbi Joshua tells him to proceed. As a scholar, he's trusted;

as a priest, he's entitled. But for some reason, not unlike the student who begins our story, Rabbi Zadok asks the same question of Rabban Gamliel.

Once again, Rabban Gamliel takes the opposite tack. Informed by Rabbi Zadok that Rabbi Joshua has permitted him to eat the calf, Rabban Gamliel says, "Wait until the shield-bearers enter the House of Study."

And the whole rigmarole begins, with Rabbi Joshua, forced to stand, wondering how the living might contradict the living, and Rabban Gamliel blithely sitting and teaching until all the scholars in the House of Study can take no more of it and yell to Huzpit the Interpreter to stop, and Huzpit the Interpreter stops.

The only difference is that the second time this happens, following the question about elective or obligatory prayer, the indignation of the scholars in the House of Study is so great that they decide to depose Rabban Gamliel.

THE QUESTION, of course, is whom shall they install as Nasi in his place?

Not Rabbi Joshua: he's personally involved in the matter. Not Rabbi Akiva: without the merit of righteous ancestors to protect him, he'd be mortally susceptible to any punishment Rabban Gamliel might, out of pique, cause to befall him.

What about Rabbi Elazar ben Azaryah?

Rabbi Elazar ben Azaryah is a good candidate. He's wise, he's wealthy, and he's a descendant, ten generations removed, from Ezra the Scribe. (Wisdom, wealth, good lineage: these are the sources of personal power in the ancient rabbinic world.) With his wisdom, Rabbi Elazar ben Azaryah will be able to answer legal questions. With his wealth, like Rabban Gamliel, he'll be able to negotiate with Caesar and Rome. With his illustrious family tree, he'll be guarded from any revenge Rabban Gamliel might cook up.

(This last precaution turns out to be unnecessary. The sages are projecting their own—or perhaps Rabbi Joshua's—malice onto Rabban Gamliel, who, it's clear, hasn't a vengeful bone in his body.)

They put the question to Rabbi Elazar ben Azaryah. "Is it pleasing to the master to become the head of the academy?"

He tells them, "I will go and consult with the members of my household," although he merely asks his wife.

She tells him, "Perhaps they will remove *you* from the post as well."

"Let a person use a precious glass cup one day," he says, "and the next day, let it break."

His wife seems less than enthusiastic and more cautious than he. "But you have no white hairs in your beard," she tells him.

He's only eighteen, but a miracle occurs and eighteen streaks of white appear in his beard. (Which is why, by the way, when he makes an appearance every year in the Passover Hagaddah, he is quoted as saying not "I am a seventy-year-old man" but "I am *like* a seventy-year-old man.")

PREVIOUSLY RABBAN GAMLIEL had a rule: "Any student whose inside is not like his outside may not enter the study hall!" But with a new Nasi in place, the sages set about democratizing the House of Study: "That day, they removed the doorkeeper and permission was granted to all students to enter."

The effect is dramatic: To accommodate the crush of new students, new benches must be added. Some say four hundred new benches were added, while others say as many as seven hundred were needed.

And Rabban Gamliel? Where do we imagine he is on this day? Off sulking somewhere or plotting his revenge? On the contrary, he's in the House of Study, watching as his colleagues carry in four hundred or even seven hundred new benches. The new energy seems to excite him, and he suffers a moment of dispirited self-scrutiny. "Perhaps, God forbid, I have withheld Torah from the people of Israel!" he says to himself.

To quell these fears, alabaster pitchers filled with sooty ash are shown to him in a dream. He interprets his dream to mean: *Though these students might look white on the outside—don't you believe it!—on the inside, they're as black as ash.*

Usually quite invisible as a narrator, the Aggadist intrudes upon the story, making a rare appearance here. "But that was not the case," he informs us. "It was only to put his mind at ease that the dream showed him this."

Nevertheless, the House of Study is buzzing with activity. "There was not a single law that had thus far been left unresolved in the study hall which they did not resolve the day Rabbi Elazar ben Azaryah was installed as Nasi." Even Rabban Gamliel throws himself into the mix—"Rabban Gamliel did not withhold himself from the House of Study even for a moment"—debating Rabbi Joshua and ultimately losing to his nemesis:

> That day, Judah, a would-be Ammonite convert, came before them in the study hall. He said to them: "What is the law? May I enter the congregation by marrying a daughter of Israel?" Rabban Gamliel: "You are forbidden to enter the congregation." Rabbi Joshua: "You are permitted to enter the congregation." . . . Immediately they permitted Judah to enter the congregation.

Resigned to this new world order—perhaps even happy to no longer shoulder the burdens of his former office—Rabban Gamliel makes a momentous decision. "Since this seems to be the case," he says to himself, "I shall go and appease Rabbi Joshua."

ALABASTER PITCHERS FILLED WITH SOOTY ASH.

Though our story does not underscore the detail—the Aggadist, having put in his two *zuzim*'s worth of dream analysis, disappears again into the margins of the page—in arriving at Rabbi Joshua's house, Rabban Gamliel encounters, in waking life, the image from his dream: "When he reached Rabbi Joshua's house, he saw that the interior walls of the house were black."

Rabban Gamliel makes an assumption: "He said to Rabbi Joshua, 'From the walls of your house, it appears that you are a smith or perhaps a coal maker.'"

The black walls are emblematic, not of Rabbi Joshua's trade, but of his poverty; and they function in the story as a Rorschach inkblot that, like the image from his dream, Rabban Gamliel is unprepared to interpret accurately. There, the dream is misinterpreted because Heaven wished to put Rabban Gamliel's mind at ease; here, he misreads the walls out of a sense of upper-class complacency.

Things have changed, however. At this moment, our two antagonists stand on as equal a footing as they ever have. I suppose, as Av Bet Din, Rabbi Joshua even outranks Rabban Gamliel now. In any case, Rabbi Joshua no longer needs to hide his ashy feelings beneath an alabaster façade of politesse. Gamliel, the pampered idiot who decreed the Day of Atonement on the wrong day and who, insecure about his own authority, forced him to desecrate that holiest of days, who has never paid sufficient attention to the moon to observe that its motion does not vary, but who believes, based on nothing more than the opinion of his illustrious forebears, that it speeds up and slows down, taking alternate routes, is standing before him, making the same dunderpated observations as always and, as always, arriving at the same dunderpated conclusions. Rabbi Joshua can bear it no more. Speaking from the heart, he answers Rabban Gamliel in his bitterness.

"Alas for the generation whose leader you are! For you know nothing of the suffering of Torah scholars or how they support themselves and how they are nourished!"

As happens so often in these stories, each of a pair of dark and light twins confronts himself in the mirror of his other. Rabban Gamliel, too, is not what he appears to be. He too is an alabaster pitcher filled with sooty ash. Though he possesses the outward manifestations of leadership—wealth, a good lineage—he lacks the interior quality of wisdom.

In fact, we're told:

This was Rabban Gamliel's conduct: When he walked into the House of Study and said, "Ask," it had been made known to him in advance that there would be no intellectual challenge. But when he entered and did not say, "Ask," it had been made known to him that an intellectual challenge was to be expected.

No wonder he overcompensates, especially in regard to Rabbi Joshua, who, as his exact opposite, is intellectually but not economically or genealogically fit to be Nasi.

Still, as different as they are, they've wound up, in this moment at least, in the same place. Rabban Gamliel may be too pampered, too incurious, and too obtuse, to see deeply enough into Rabbi Joshua's life to feel compassion for him, while Rabbi Joshua sees through Rabban Gamliel completely. However, this seeing-through forfeits for him any compassion he might feel for the suffering of his tormentor.

They're at emotional loggerheads, and Rabban Gamliel does something that, as far as I can tell, is as rare in the Talmudic tales as it is in actual life: he apologizes.

"I have spoken excessively against you," he says to Rabbi Joshua. "Forgive me!"

Rabbi Joshua pays him no heed.

Rabban Gamliel persists. "Do it," he pleads, "for the sake of the honor of my father!"

He means either Hillel, his great-great-grandfather, or Rabban Shimon ben Gamliel, his father, the former Nasi, and one of the ten martyrs of Jerusalem. His illustrious lineage is—and has always been—his trump card. In this moment, we're allowed to witness the effects of this rabbinic power source: Rabbi Joshua is, at last, appeased.

Reconciled, they ask: "Who shall go and inform the sages?"

Our old friend, the fuller, appears, conveniently enough. Volunteering to act as their messenger, the fuller comes to the House of Study, bearing a strange message for the sages there:

> "Let him who is accustomed to wear the robe wear the robe. Shall he who is not accustomed to wear the robe say to him who is accustomed to wear the robe: remove the robe and I shall don it?"

Perhaps because this odd message about robes comes from the mouth of a laundryman—(*Is anybody expecting a delivery?* I imagine the sages asking each other)—no one quite knows what to make of it. The world is topsy-turvy. The revolutionaries become reactionaries. Though upon democratizing the House of Study, they've removed the doorkeeper, now:

> Rabbi Akiva said, "Lock the doors so that the servants of Rabban Gamliel do not come and harass the rabbis!" Rabbi Joshua said, "Better I should go to them myself." He came and knocked on the door.

His message is equally odd, perhaps as a way of convincing them that the first message did indeed come from him:

> He said to them: "Let the sprinkler son of a sprinkler sprinkle. Shall he who is neither a sprinkler nor the son of a sprinkler say to the sprinkler son of a sprinkler: your water is cave water and your ashes cinders?"

This gnomic message is intended, it seems, for Rabbi Elazar ben Azaryah, a *kohen*, a priest. Rabbi Joshua seems to mean: as the office of the priest, who sprinkles the blood of the sacrifices on the Temple walls, is hereditary, so too should be the office of Nasi. Despite his deficiencies, Rabban Gamliel is descended from a long line of Nasi'im, and shouldn't our little world of the study hall, the nucleus inside the greater atom of the cosmos, be restored to its long-standing order?

Rabbi Akiva is once again standing near the door. In his youth, he was something of a bruiser, and it makes sense that he is acting now as a bouncer.

"Rabbi Joshua," he says, "are you appeased? Did we do this for any reason other than your honor? Tomorrow you and I will arise and go to Rabban Gamliel's door."

IT'S NO ACCIDENT that the fuller arrives at this decisive moment. The world of the sages, like a garment, had grown dull and lusterless through long wear and tear. It needs to be scoured and squeezed, violently kicked and shaken out, stretched and thickened. Just as human urine was used in the process of fulling, one might even say that the sages needed to piss on their little community as part of the process of returning it to its former luster.

The story is a comedy: the world, momentarily torn asunder, is restored, with a few improvements, more or less to its original shape. The House of Study has been democratized and enlarged, filled with a buzzing new vitality (personified by Judah the Ammonite convert). Rabban Gamliel and Rabbi Joshua are once again in their former places, their hearts, from all appearances, reconciled. There's only one problem now: how can they remove Rabbi Elazar ben Azaryah?

"We have a tradition that in matters of sanctity we elevate but do not lower."

Having elevated Rabbi Elazar ben Azaryah to the position of Nasi, it's impossible now, despite his wife's concerns that such a thing might occur, to demote him. Worse: if Rabban Gamliel and Rabbi Elazar ben Azaryah take turns, one lecturing one week, the other the next, won't it lead to jealousy?

(Having momentarily woken up in rebellion, the House of Study now lazily returns to sleep, the sages in their happiness forgetting that no sacred rule prevented them from deposing Rabban Gamliel and that jealousy resulting not from shared rule but from Rabban Gamliel's autocracy was the spark that lit their revolutionary conflagration.)

Still, a compromise is reached: Rabbi Elazar will lecture one week out of four, and Rabban Gamliel the remaining three.

ODDLY, THE AGGADIST waits until all the trouble is over and the world of the House of Study is restored to order before asking the long-unasked question: "And the student who sparked the entire incident," the fellow who inquired if the evening prayer was elective or obligatory, "who was he?" The answer: a young Shimon bar Yohai, that once and future conflagrationist, who, you'll recall, will one day in his own future blanch when he is passed over for a superior post by a colleague he considers his inferior, and who, having attained a super power, will use it to settle personal grudges against members of his own tribe rather than directing it against the Roman forces occupying their land. The same patterns seem to be in play here.

AS I'VE SAID, our two stories fit imperfectly together, and it's hard to know which comes first, the comic deposing of Rabban Gamliel or the tragic excommunication of Rabbi Eliezer. Certainly, we can imagine that Rabbi Eliezer, as a conservative voice and as Rabbi Joshua's *haver*, his sacred companion, served as an ameliorating presence between Rabbi Joshua and Rabban Gamliel, and that in his absence the tension between them is allowed to reach its boiling point. Certainly, Rabbi Eliezer's absence plays a part in the comedy—we can assume he has already been placed under a ban—but at the same time, he feels *too* absent here, too absent from the other characters' memories. His ghost doesn't seem to haunt the stage. No one appears worried, for instance, that, having excommunicated Rabbi Eliezer, they're further destroying the structure of their world by deposing Rabban Gamliel.

The alabaster pitcher of comedy is filled with tragedy's sooty ash, and the external sense of happiness conceals a darkness within. Those who forget the past, as we know, are doomed to repeat it. That the sages have so completely forgotten Rabbi Eliezer during the comic deposing of Rabban Gamliel adds to the tragic aspect of the story: though at the end of the comedy their world appears temporarily restored, they are, in fact, tearing it apart.

As it turns out, despite Rabbi Nathan's account of the prophet Elijah's vision of the laughing deity underthrown by his beloved children, despite all the sages' counterproofs and arguments, a guilty conscience remains and, as we see, on the day the sages excommunicate Rabbi Eliezer, another third of the sages' world nearly goes up in flames. Or down to the bottom of the sea:

Rabban Gamliel was traveling aboard a ship when a huge wave rose up, threatening to capsize the boat and drown him. He said, "It appears to me that this is on account of Rabbi Eliezer ben Hyrcanus." Then he stood on his feet . . .

(There's that image again.)

. . . and he called out and he said . . .

(Addressing the supposedly happy-to-have-been-capsized deity.)

> . . . "Master of the Universe, it is known and revealed to you that
> I have not acted for my own honor or for the honor of my father's
> house, but for your honor, that disputes not proliferate in the
> House of Israel."

The Law may no longer be in Heaven, but it seems to have
friends in high places, coming to the defense of Rabbi Eliezer.
Once again, however, evoking his noble lineage, Rabban Gamliel
is able to soothe an unsoothed heart, and the sea leaves off from
its raging.

As always, as Nasi, he is working for the good of the whole. As
we've learned in the scene in which the sages debate the merits of
his possible successors, the Nasi's is a dangerous job. In addition
to wealth and wisdom, one needs the supernatural protection of
righteous ancestors. The protection of living relatives doesn't hurt
either. Though Rabban Gamliel is able to stop the Hand of Heaven
as it descends upon him in the form of a gigantic tidal wave, in
the end, as we'll see when his sister is unable to protect him, he's
undone by a simple prayer.

LIKE RABBI YOHANAN and Resh Lakish, Rabban Gamliel and
Rabbi Eliezer are brothers-in-law. Rabbi Eliezer is married to
Rabban Gamliel's sister, Ima Shalom. Her name means *Mother
of Peace*, and keeping the peace in her family in the wake of her
brother's excommunication of her husband is, one imagines, not
an easy task. Her loyalties are divided. We can see this clearly:
from the moment her husband is banned, Ima Shalom prevents
him from reciting a prayer called *Tahanun*. As a prayer, *Tahanun*
is a cry of the heart. Recited with the head lowered, as though the
supplicant were in a state of exhaustion, it reads in part: "I am ex-

ceedingly distressed. Let all my foes be shamed and utterly confounded. They will regret what they have done and be instantly shamed!"

Tahanun is recited on most days, but not on every day. There are exceptions. Some believe Ima Shalom got her dates mixed up, while others maintain she was distracted, at the decisive moment, by a beggar knocking on her door. In either case, her guard lowered, she leaves her husband at his prayers, and, unsupervised, he prays *Tahanun* for the first time since his banning.

Ima Shalom returns to find Rabbi Eliezer with his head lowered. She understands everything at once. "Arise," she cries, "you have killed my brother!"

No sooner has she said this than a proclamation goes forth from Rabban Gamliel's house: "*The Nasi is dead!*"

"How did you know this would happen?" Rabbi Eliezer asks his wife in amazement.

"I have a tradition from my father's house," she tells him. Which, of course, is Rabban Gamliel's father's house, the same illustrious house that held the nonsensical tradition about the travels of the moon, as well as the house on behalf of which Rabbi Joshua forgives Rabban Gamliel, and on behalf of which the capsizing wave relents.

"When all the gates of Heaven are locked," Ima Shalom explains to her husband, "the gate of a broken heart remains open."

THE GATE OF A BROKEN HEART REMAINS OPEN.

Despite the fact that their argument led to his banishment, Rabbi Joshua and Rabbi Eliezer's love for each other appears undiminished until the end:

When Rabbi Eliezer fell sick, Rabbi Akiva and his companions came to visit him. He was seated in a canopied four-poster bed, and they sat down at a distance of four cubits from him.

In deference to the rabbinic ban.

Their presence here is not a harbinger of good things. Rabbi

Eliezer seems not to know how ill he is, and he questions his visitors in order to find out.

"Why have you come?" he asks them.

"We have come to study Torah," they say.

Study Torah with a banned heretic?

"And why did you not come before now?"

"We had no time," they tell him.

We had no time. The subject of death subtly enters the conversation. Rabbi Eliezer sees through their gentle deceit, however. Death is clearly on his mind.

"I wonder if such as you will die a natural death," he says to them aloud. The occupation under the Romans is worsening. Rabbi Eliezer may be the only one of their small group to die peacefully in bed. Like the patriarch Jacob, lying in his deathbed surrounded by his sons at the end of the Book of Genesis, Rabbi Eliezer seems to have been granted a bit of prophetic vision, and he tells his former companions what they can expect at the end of their days.

"And what kind of death will be mine?" Rabbi Akiva asks.

"Yours will be crueler than theirs," he answers.

Rabbi Eliezer places his arms over his heart, and he wails, "Alas for you, arms of mine, that are like two Torah scrolls about to be rolled up and put away!"

A poignant—and equally odd—deathbed soliloquy follows:

Much Torah have I learned, and much have I taught . . . yet I have not taken from my teachers even as much as the water a dog laps up from the sea . . . and my students have taken from me no more than the paint a paint stick picks up from its tube. Moreover, I have studied three hundred laws on the subject of a bright discoloration on the skin, yet no man has ever asked me about them. Even more, I have studied three hundred rules about planting cucumbers by magic, and no man other than Akiva ben Yosef ever asked me about them. Once, while he and I were walking on a road, he said to me, "My master, teach me the planting of cucumbers by magic." I uttered a single word, and the whole field about us was filled with cucumbers. Then he said, "Master, you just taught me how to plant them. Now teach me how to pluck them." I uttered another word, and all the cucumbers gathered into one place.

As his final separation from his colleagues approaches, his friends keep a vigil by his bedside. They ask him about the laws of ritual cleanliness and uncleanliness, the very subject that led to his banishment, his first separation from them:

Concerning that which was unclean, Rabbi Eliezer kept saying, "Unclean," and concerning that which was clean, he kept saying, "Clean," until his soul departed as he uttered the word *clean*.

Taking this as a sign, a sign that Rabbi Eliezer died in a state of spiritual cleanliness, Rabbi Joshua stands and exclaims, "The ban is lifted, the ban is lifted!"

Rabbi Eliezer dies on the eve of the Sabbath. Unable to travel on the Sabbath, the sages remain overnight in Rabbi Eliezer's town. As he returns from Caesarea to Lydda the following day, Rabbi Akiva, encountering Rabbi Eliezer's bier, rips his garments in grief. This is a conventional sign of mourning, but Rabbi Akiva continues to tear at himself until he has lacerated his flesh, and his blood drips on the ground. Sobbing, he moans, "Woe is me for the loss of you, woe is me for the loss of you, my teacher, for you have left an entire generation fatherless!"

These are odd words for the premiere sage of his age to pronounce over the body of a banned heretic, one suspected of Christian sympathies and ritual sexual depravity. Fatherless at his death, surely the generation was made fatherless from the moment he was banned!

THERE'S MUCH THAT DOESN'T make sense here. Everything in this story is an alabaster pitcher filled with sooty ash: nothing is as it appears on its surface. How, for instance, does the most theologically conservative member of their community, *a man who has never spoken a word he hasn't heard from his teacher*, find himself banned as a heretic?

I'm not a fan of conspiracy theories, and I can't prove, of course, that Rabbi Joshua killed Rabban Gamliel, using Rabbi Eliezer as his weapon, though it has a certain elegance as an explanation. However, many of the things that seem to make no sense in these two stories make better sense if we follow this view. Rabbi Joshua not only had the means, the motive, and the opportunity, he also had a well-documented, long-simmering animus towards the Nasi.

I remind you of the words he mutters to himself upon being humiliated publicly by Rabban Gamliel: *Were I alive and he dead, I could contradict his ruling, for the living are able to contradict the dead.*

The Motive: Though in a few incidences, as we've seen, Rabbi Joshua swallows his pride and gives in to the greater authority of Rabban Gamliel, when the good of the people and the cohesion of their community are not at stake, he appears less amenable, and the gall he feels towards Rabban Gamliel is less concealed.

Once, for instance, at a banquet hosted by Rabban Gamliel's son, Rabbis Eliezer, Joshua, and Zadok all recline on couches while—incongruously—the Nasi serves drinks to them:

> He offered a cup to Rabbi Eliezer, but he would not take it; then he offered a cup to Rabbi Joshua, who did take it. Rabbi Eliezer said to him, "How can we allow this, Joshua? We are seated, while Gamliel, our superior, is standing over us and serving us drinks!" Rabbi Joshua replied, "In Scripture, we find a greater man than he acting as a waiter. Abraham was the greatest man of his generation, and yet of him it is written, 'And he stood over them.'"

As recounted in the eighteenth chapter of the Book of Genesis, though his guests were angels in disguise, the patriarch Abraham, believing them to be Arab traders, runs to serve them a meal. Rabbi Joshua concludes: "Should Rabban Gamliel not stand over us and serve us drinks as well?"

Rabbi Zadok—perhaps still smarting over the loss of his first-born calf?—chimes in:

How long will you disregard the honor due the One who is every-where and concern yourselves with the honor due the Holy One's creatures? The Holy One causes winds to blow, clouds to rise, rain to fall, and the earth to sprout, and yet before each and every one of us he sets a table. Should Rabban Gamliel, even though our superior, not stand and serve us drinks?

Despite the self-serving sophistry of Rabbis Joshua and Zadok, I have to agree with Rabbi Eliezer. Though it may be permissible by some stretch of sacred law for the head of the Sanhedrin to renounce the honor due him, certainly his doing so appears un-seemly. Something is out of whack when neither a son honors his father nor rabbis their Nasi.

A MORE SUBTLE EXAMPLE of Rabbi Joshua's animus towards Rabban Gamliel: Rabban Gamliel has a beloved slave called Toby. (The name means *best* or perhaps *my goodness*.) Though a slave, Toby is a scholar himself; and in fact, when he dies, Rabban Gam-liel, in contravention of the sacred law, mourns him formally, ac-cepting condolence calls on his behalf:

His students said to him, "Our master, did you not teach us that one may not accept condolences for the loss of a slave?" He told them, "My slave Toby is not like the other slaves. He was a virtu-ous man."

It seems to have troubled the gentle-spirited Rabban Gamliel that he could not free Toby without violating a divine command-ment: "These Canaanite slaves shall be your property; you shall keep them as a possession for your children after you." However, according to another commandment, if one accidentally blinds his slave, the slave wins his freedom.

That's exactly what happens. One day, Rabban Gamliel puts out Toby's eye, and he rejoices over this happy accident! Running into Rabbi Joshua, he tells him, "Did you know that my slave Toby is getting his freedom?"

"How?" Rabbi Joshua wonders.

"I accidentally put out his eye," Rabban Gamliel says.

We can hear the excitement, the joy in his voice, just as we can almost hear Rabbi Joshua shaking his head.

"Your admission," he tells Rabban Gamliel, "is legally null and void without witnesses testifying on the slave's behalf."

PERHAPS I'M IMAGINING IT, but I can't help hearing just a soupçon of spiteful glee on Rabbi Joshua's part as he rains on Rabban Gamliel's parade. After all, Rabban Gamliel refuses to accept Rabbi Zadok's testimony in the case of the firstborn calf without witnesses, and it's no different here. Why should the word of a *haver*, insufficient there, be legally sufficient here?

Though Rabban Gamliel might wish to turn a literal blind eye to this legal technicality, Rabbi Joshua, though a master of innovative rulings, feels no such compunction. Instead, Rabban Gamliel is required to pay a fine, and Toby—by all accounts a fine scholar and a virtuous man—is left a half-blind slave, a condition he maintains until his death.

THE MEANS: A large body of trickster literature stars Rabbi Joshua as its protagonist. In it, he is depicted as an astute man, devious and cunning, always getting the better of someone, it seems, whether it's Emperor Hadrian or the people of Alexandria or the sixty sages of Athens. A man of quicksilver intelligence, he appears in these stories to be creative wit personified, a trip master, a schemer with a chess master's unerring ability to anticipate his opponent's moves three, four, sometimes five jumps ahead.

"No one has ever gotten the better of me," he claims, "except a woman, a little boy, and a little girl." In other words, he can be bested only when he lets his guard down by underestimating his opponents.

One story is particularly telling: One morning, a guest arrives, and Rabbi Joshua gives the man food and drink. In the evening, he takes the fellow up to his loft to sleep. Without the man's knowledge, Rabbi Joshua removes the ladder leading to the loft. In the middle of the night, the man rises, collects all the items of value from the house's upper story, and conceals them in his cloak. Thinking the ladder is there, he attempts to abscond. Instead, he falls and breaks his collarbone. The following morning, Rabbi Joshua, rising early, finds him where he lies, surrounded—presumably—by a cloakful of purloined goods.

"You good-for-nothing, empty-headed thief!" Rabbi Joshua cries. "Do all persons like you act like this?"

The thief doesn't seem to understand the question. "Master," he says, "I didn't know you had removed the ladder!"

"Didn't you realize that from the moment you arrived yesterday, we were suspicious of you?"

This incident, we're told, is why Rabbi Joshua always said, "Consider all men as rogues, but honor them as you would Rabban Gamliel."

A curious statement. A moment of unintentional autobiography perhaps? Could one reverse the line and read it: *Though one must honor Rabban Gamliel, he's nothing more than a rogue?*

THE OPPORTUNITY: I'll be honest: to my knowledge, nowhere in the Talmud or the Midrash is it suggested that Rabbi Joshua murdered Rabban Gamliel using Rabbi Eliezer's prayer as his murder weapon. Still, Rabbi Eliezer's excommunication, an event Rabbi Joshua forces to a head, makes very little sense otherwise. Once again, how is it that the most conservative member of a theological circle is banned as a heretic? Not only does a voice from Heaven concur with Rabbi Eliezer's opinion, claiming that he's always in the right, but even the Holy One, in his wrath, nearly drowns Rabban Gamliel over the matter. And what can we make of Rabbi

Joshua's rushing, at the last moment of Rabbi Eliezer's life, to lift the ban and allow his friend to die reconciled to the group? His undiminished affection for Rabbi Eliezer, his great love of him, as well as his desire to restore his colleague's good name: it's all a bit suspicious.

His behavior is telling—does it speak of a bad conscience?—but not as telling as when, in the wake of Rabban Gamliel's death, Rabbi Joshua enters the House of Study with the intention of at last abrogating all the various (and in his mind nonsensical) rulings of Rabban Gamliel.

Once again, I remind you of the words he muttered to himself: *Were I alive and he dead, I could contradict his ruling, for the living are able to contradict the dead.*

And this is what Rabbi Joshua finally attempts to do. However, in the face of his effrontery, Rabbi Yohanan ben Nuri stands and exclaims:

> The body, I declare, must follow the head! Throughout Rabban Gamliel's lifetime, we set the law in agreement with Rabban Gamliel's ruling, and now you seek to abrogate it? Since the law has already been set in agreement with Rabban Gamliel, we shall not listen to you, Joshua!

Dressing him down in the House of Study, Rabbi Yohanan ben Nuri casually and cruelly removes from him the honorific *rabbi*. And the story continues:

> And there was not a single person who raised any objection whatsoever to this statement.

GAMLIEL IS DEAD. Rabbi Eliezer is dead; he died under a ban or very nearly. And now the pillar upon which the last third of the world stands, Rabbi Joshua, is consigned to rabbinic irrelevance. Running across him one day, Caesar asks him why he no longer participates in the spirited debates between the scholars and heretics. (An unintentionally pointed question, perhaps, reminding Rabbi Joshua of Rabbi Eliezer.)

Rabbi Joshua answers the emperor poetically: "The mountain is covered with snow; it is surrounded by ice; its dogs no longer bark; its stones no longer grind; and for that which I have not lost, I am searching."

In other words: my hair is white, my beard is white, my voice is barely audible, my teeth are worn to the gums, and I'm all bent over.

WELL, AS I SAY, I can prove nothing. Nevertheless, this much is true: in the midst of the chaos of the destruction of the Temple, clinging to their master Rabban Yohanan ben Zakkai, Rabban Gamliel, Rabbi Eliezer, and Rabbi Joshua gave birth to a new world, and then, little by little, they destroyed that world and one another.

In the wake of this destruction, it seems, the light of existence itself was dimmed. "According to Rabbi Eliezer ben Hyrcanus, from the day the Holy Temple was destroyed, scholars became like schoolteachers, schoolteachers like synagogue beadles, synagogue beadles like unlearned peasants, and unlearned peasants more and more impoverished."

And as we behold that fallen world from circumstances even further reduced, the series of unanswered questions, asked by George Harrison, linger in our ears:

Isn't it a pity, isn't it a shame
How we break each other's hearts, and cause each other pain
How we take each other's love, without thinking anymore
Forgetting to give back, isn't it a pity?

Rabbi Akiva (flourished 3855–3895/ 95–135 CE), Shimon ben Azzai, Shimon ben Zoma, and Elisha ben Avuyah

OUR MASTERS TAUGHT: FOUR MEN ENTERED THE Orchard: ben Azzai, ben Zoma, Aher, and Rabbi Akiva. Rabbi Akiva said to them, "When you arrive at the slabs of pure transparent marble, do not say, 'Water, water!' For it is said: 'He that speaks falsehood shall not stand before my eyes.'" Ben Azzai cast a look and died; of him, Scripture says, "Precious in the sight of the Lord is the death of his saints." Ben Zoma looked and became demented; of him, Scripture says, "Have you found honey? Eat only what is sufficient for you, lest you be filled up and vomit it." Aher cut the saplings. Rabbi Akiva ascended and descended in peace.

The ministering angels sought to thrust Rabbi Akiva away, but the Holy One said, "Let this venerable elder be! He is worthy of making use of my glory."

BABYLONIAN TALMUD, TRACTATE *CHAGIGAH* 14B–15B.

Chapter 5

Revelation, Retribution,
Perdition, Ecstasy, and Bliss
An Epic Canvas

ONCE WHEN MOSES ASCENDED ON HIGH, HE FOUND the Holy Blessed One sitting and affixing little flourishes to the letters of the holy alphabet.

"Master of the Universe," Moses asks, "who stays your hand?" Meaning: *Why this late addition to the alphabet when you could have presented the Torah in this fashion originally?*

"At the end of many generations," the Holy One tells his prophet, "there will arise a man—Akiva ben Yosef by name—who will infer heaps and heaps of laws from each of these little crowns that I'm adding to the letters."

Moses is impressed. "Master of the Universe, permit me to see such a man!"

"Turn around," the Holy One replies.

Moses turns around, and instantly he is in Rabbi Akiva's class, seated in the eighth row. Now, the eighth row is the last row. In the ancient wisdom schools, the first row is where the sharpest students sit. If you answer a question correctly, you're moved up. If you answer a question incorrectly—or if you even *ask* a question incorrectly—you're moved back. No one—especially a prophet of Moses's stature—wants to find himself sitting in the eighth row. But it's even worse than that: Moses is trying to follow the discussion—the lecture, the questions, the answers—and he finds that he can't make head or tail of it.

This is Moses we're talking about; Moses who stood atop

Mount Sinai, lashed to the mast, as it were, during the lightning and thunderstorm to receive the holy Torah; who was alive to the voice of his Creator while the souls of everyone about him left their bodies; who remained ritually pure, abstaining from all carnal pleasures with his wife for decades, just in case the Holy One wanted to drop by for a chat; Moses who, it seems, can ascend to Heaven to discuss the Divine Typeface with the Master Printer.

This Moses is sitting in the back of Rabbi Akiva's class, not understanding a single word of the lecture, and he starts to get a little dizzy. He feels a little faint.

As they're getting to a really difficult part, one of Rabbi Akiva's students raises his hand. "Master, where did you learn this?" he asks.

Rabbi Akiva replies, "It's a law given to Moses at Sinai."

Moses is reassured. Some sort of evolution is taking place, and Moses, the humblest of men, is content to have played his part in it.

He returns to the Holy One. "Master of the Universe, you have a man such as this Rabbi Akiva," he says, "and yet you choose to give the holy Torah to the world not through him, but through me?"

The Holy One tells Moses to mind his own business, and not too politely either. "Be silent!" the Holy One says. "This is how it arose in my mind."

Moses persists. "You've shown me the man and his Torah, now show me his reward."

"Turn around," the Holy One says.

Moses turns around again and, this time, he's shown a vision of Rabbi Akiva's flesh being weighed out in the Roman meat markets.

He's appalled. "Master of the Universe, *this* is the Torah, and *this* its reward?"

"Be silent!" the Holy One says again. "This is how it arose in my mind."

SOME FRIENDS OF MINE have TiVo, and occasionally they invite me over to see an interesting program I may have missed.

That's how I saw Bruce Springsteen being interviewed. Springsteen was speaking about his Catholic upbringing. He had a lot of harsh memories of Catholicism as a very strict religion, he said, but he admitted it was also an epic canvas filled with a sense of revelation, retribution, perdition, ecstasy, and bliss.

"All of which," he added, "they presented to you as a five-year-old child."

Our story is a bit like that, I'm afraid. It's a troubling story. Though only 150 words in the original, it's an epic canvas, dark and extreme, presenting a world of terrible and terrifying polarities: The lightness of Moses's comic ascent into Heaven juxtaposed with the heaviness of Rabbi Akiva's flesh being sold in the Roman markets, as dog meat, I presume; the comedy of Moses's dunce-like inability to understand Rabbi Akiva's lecture placed side by side with his inability to comprehend the moral arithmetic of Divine Justice (*Why do the good suffer? Why do the best suffer terribly?*); the sweetness of the Holy One's tinkering endlessly with the minor details of Creation contrasted with the bleakness of a deity whose sense of moral proportion is so beyond human comprehension that he won't even attempt explaining it to his holiest prophet.

ONCE AGAIN, the Aggadist—whoever he is, whoever he was—is up to his usual sly tricks. Eighteen centuries or so before Albert Einstein and Marcel Proust, the Aggadist has relativized time. Within the story, an event in the distant future—Rabbi Akiva's death—is described as part of an event occurring in the distant past—Moses's ascent into Heaven. This is an illusion, of course. Although the story takes place before Moses's death (which occurs, according to tradition, in the year 2488/1273 BCE), it was written, clearly, *after* Rabbi Akiva's death (in 3893/133 CE).

In other words, though written *after* the events it foretells, the story persuades us that it is occurring *before* those events.

And with this storyteller's sleight of hand, the Aggadist adds to his epic canvas a chilling sense of foreknowledge and predestination.

ELSEWHERE IN THE Talmud, Rabbi Akiva's death is presented in greater detail: The Romans have issued a decree forbidding the study of Torah and the practice of its precepts, a decree that Rabbi Akiva publicly and recklessly ignores. Soon, he is arrested, thrown into prison, and sentenced to death. His execution at sunrise coincides with the earliest possible moment a person may recite the morning *Sh'ma*, the affirmation of the unity of the Holy One's name: *Hear, Israel, the Lord our God, the Lord is One.*

From a mystic's point of view, the *Sh'ma* is an affirmation of the oneness of all experience and phenomena. How could it be otherwise? In a system of radical monotheism, one may not ascribe evil to an alternate source. According to the prophet Isaiah, the Holy One makes light and creates darkness, makes peace and *creates evil.*

And Rabbi Akiva is nothing if not a mystic. While his executioners are combing his flesh with hot iron combs, Rabbi Akiva is lovingly preparing to accept upon himself the yoke of the kingship of Heaven by reciting the *Sh'ma.*

His students are stunned. "This far, Master? This far?" they cry, meaning: *Will you carry out your spiritual discipline through the excruciating pain of torture right up to the moment of your death?*

Rabbi Akiva answers them from a wide open place.

"All my life," he says, "I have been troubled by the verse following the *Sh'ma* that states, *You shall love the Lord, your God, with all your soul,* which I interpret to mean that *You shall love the Holy One* even if *he TAKES your soul,* and I always wondered if I'd ever have the opportunity to fulfill this divine precept. Now that the occasion has arrived, shall I miss that opportunity?"

His torturers flay him alive while he's reciting the *Sh'ma,* and when the knives cut into the top of his forehead, into the place where, under brighter circumstances, his phylacteries would have rested, he reaches the prayer's concluding word: *One.*

Stretching out his last breath, Rabbi Akiva dies with the word *One* on his lips.

IN HEAVEN, according to the commentaries, the angels are as appalled as Rabbi Akiva's students are on the earth below. Turning to the Holy One, they cry, "This far, Master? This far?" And they repeat Moses's anguished exclamation, "*This* is the Torah, and *this* its reward?"

And the Holy One, perhaps finding the moment too emotionally difficult to bear, silences them, exactly as he silences Moses. "Be quiet!" he says. "Or I'll return the universe to chaos and desolation!"

A WORD ABOUT chaos and desolation.

According to the second verse of the Book of Genesis—"The earth was in chaos and desolation, and darkness lay on the surface of the deep"—chaos, darkness, and desolation, it seems, precede the work of Creation. Chaos, darkness, and desolation, in other words, are the primary matter, the building blocks—the spheres, cubes, and cones—out of which the Holy One fashions the Heavens and the earth.

And, as we all know, try as we might not to, there are times when you can sense it, when you can feel the chaos, the darkness, and the desolation, howling right beneath the surface of things.

AS DIFFICULT AS Rabbi Akiva's martyrdom is to come to terms with, what can we possibly make of the Holy One's silence and of his insistence upon the silence of others in the face of it? There are many voices of protest in this story—Moses's, the students', the angels'—and the Holy One silences them all. As readers, we can, I imagine, only share in their sense of incomprehension and protest.

And yet, it's difficult to argue with the imagery of the story: Moses is presented as a bit of a dunce seated in the back of Rabbi Akiva's class, puzzling over the lesson. Though he understands, from his own experiences, the meaning of a heavenly rebuke—after the Hebrews' forty years of wandering in the desert, Moses is prohibited, by divine fiat, from entering the Promised Land—still, the moral calculus of Rabbi Akiva's death seems beyond his ken.

He is like Springsteen's five-year-old child, opening up his kindergarten catechism and discovering Dante's *Inferno* and the paintings of Hieronymus Bosch howling inside of it.

And not unlike a five-year-old, Moses is appalled by the unfairness of it all: This *is the Torah, and* this *is its reward?* (In Aramaic, the line actually rhymes, underscoring the inadequacy of the moral lessons we learn in our childhood nursery rhymes.) And the Holy One basically replies, *Shut up and mind your own business. It's* my *universe and I'll run it in my own way, if you don't mind!*

But, of course, we do mind. We all mind. Moses's cri de coeur is fundamentally a human cry against the Holy One's incomprehensible project. And it's true: at times, the Holy One asks too much of us; at times, life is too hard, too violent, too crushing, too bruising, too brutal.

"BE SILENT!" the Holy One commands his prophet.

And to the polarities of tragedy and comedy, darkness and light, earth and Heaven found in our story, we may add the polarity of protest and silence. Silence, in the sacred law, signifies a kind of concurrence, a giving in to the point of view of another. When a person meets an accusation with silence, we may assume he is guilty as charged.

But silence represents a deep knowing as well, a knowing beyond, or rather beneath, the surface of words. Silence and mysticism go hand in hand, and the Talmud restricts the teaching of mystical knowledge behind a veil of murmuring quiet.

According to the Talmud, the "Work of Creation," a kind of cosmic-quantum physics, may be taught only to one student at a time, and the "Work of the Chariot," instructions for achieving direct experience of the divine, cannot be taught to even one student, unless that student is a wise scholar with a discerning mind.

The *No Talking!* signs are vibrant and shrill: "Whoever scrutinizes four things—what is above; what is below; what is before; and what is after—it would be better for him had he never been born."

Further, we are warned: "Into that which is removed from you, do not inquire and into that which is shrouded from you, do not probe. That which you have been authorized to contemplate, contemplate; but you have no business with the hidden!"

These are strong words. Strong words indeed. But since the Talmud is meant to be a compendium of all knowledge, human and divine, it's helpless to restrain itself, and it immediately launches into a detailed discussion of precisely what one cannot know, providing, in this way, a generous menu for the hungry mystic.

This jesting sense of paradox seems woven into the fabric of the entire enterprise. Much of what the Talmud knows of the mystical realms it has learned from the visions of Ezekiel and Isaiah, recorded in the prophetic books of the Bible that bear their names. The Talmudic sages all seem to agree that Ezekiel's prolix report of his vision of Heaven—with its stormy winds and its flashing fires; its gleaming wheels; its electric Kool-Aid acid rain clouds; and its chariot with four winged creatures, each with four faces, human, lion, ox, and eagle, surrounded by a flickering penumbra of flame—pales in its gravitas in comparison to Isaiah's terser account, which simply reads: "I saw the Lord sitting on a throne, lofty and exalted, with the train of his robe filling the Temple. Seraphim stood above him."

"To what may Ezekiel be compared?" the sages ask. "To a villager who saw the king. And to what is Isaiah comparable? To a city dweller who saw the king."

A rube from the provinces unused to the splendors of the Divine Boulevards, Ezekiel jots down every glorious and gaudy detail, while Isaiah, a Parisian flâneur strolling the Champs-Élysées, remarks little and describes less.

Having disparaged Ezekiel's inferior account, the sages then devote much heat to an intense study of it. What choice do they have? Despite Isaiah's superior mind, his greater sophistication, and his broader frame of reference, he has left all the *details* out of his account! He may be the superior mystic, a man on a beach with a broom walking backwards and sweeping away his footprints with every step he takes; but as a consequence, his ascent and his vision are of little use to those who follow him.

This is the paradox of mysticism: the deepest truth may only be communicated in silence.

Despite the dire warnings, despite the risk that one might ruin one's life, the temptation to immerse in this murmuring deep is exquisitely and keenly felt. The Talmud itself calls the forbidden Work of the Chariot "the great thing." Its legal discussions, "the inquiries of Abaye and Rava," are, by comparison, "a small thing."

Still, the ascent into the supernal realms is perilous, and one must proceed with great caution.

RABBI AKIVA seems to know something that Moses does not.

Still, as with Moses's ascent, Rabbi Akiva's seems to be a mixture of darkness and light, comedy and tragedy. When he makes the trip into the Orchard of Paradise, he takes three companions with him: Shimon ben Azzai, Shimon ben Zoma, and a fellow known as *Aher*.

This is already problematic. As we learned, the Work of Creation may be taught only to one student at a time, and the Work of the Chariot not even to one, unless that person is a wise scholar with a discerning mind. What is Rabbi Akiva doing, then, traveling into the supernal realms as part of a quartet of mystics?

He knows how dangerous the journey is, and he issues explicit instructions, or even—given the miserable ends his friends meet—a warning: "When you arrive at the slabs of pure transparent marble," he tells them, "do not say, 'Water, water!' For it is said: 'He that speaks falsehood shall not stand before my eyes.'"

Despite these precautions, things go quickly south:

Ben Azzai cast a look and died; of him, Scripture says, *Precious in the sight of the Lord is the death of his saints*. Ben Zoma looked and became demented; of him, Scripture says, *Have you found honey?*

Eat only what is sufficient for you, lest you be filled up and vomit it.
Aher cut the saplings. Rabbi Akiva ascended and descended in
peace.

These are not good odds. Four travelers: one death, one case
of insanity, one case of apostasy (this is the traditional reading of
"cutting the saplings"). Four travelers: three spectacular flame-
outs, three burnt-out cases, three radical self-defeating protests
against the deeper truth, against the murmuring deep. Even
Rabbi Akiva, ascending and descending in one piece, would have
been driven out of the Orchard by the fiery angels had the Holy
One not intervened on his behalf.

"Let this venerable elder be!" the Holy One commands them.
"He is worthy of making use of my glory."

DEATH, MADNESS, APOSTASY? Questions crowd in: Who are
these people? What are these slabs of pure transparent marble?
How can they kill a man or drive him crazy or compel him into unbelief? Why mustn't one characterize them as *Water, water*? What
is this Supernal Orchard? And finally, how could things have gone
so horribly wrong?

These four ascend together, and, in this way, their fates are
bound. Unless we understand the failures of his three companions, we cannot understand Rabbi Akiva's success, and unless we
understand Rabbi Akiva's mystical ascent, it will be impossible to
come to terms with his death.

BEN AZZAI CAST A LOOK AND DIED.

It's only in English, I suppose, where the expression *from A
to Z* signifies a complete spectrum, that Shimon ben Azzai and
Shimon ben Zoma take on the comical air of a vaudeville team.
Though a kind of twinship exists between the two men, there's
nothing Tweedledee-and-Tweedledum-ish about them.

On the contrary, the two are unmatched as scholars. "There was no one in their time as great in Torah," Rashi says. And they function, in fact, as archetypal figures in the minds of scholars who know of them. "Anyone who sees ben Azzai in a dream," we're told, "can hope for saintliness."

Scholars of later generations jostle in comparing themselves to ben Azzai:

Abaye: "I am like ben Azzai in the streets of Tiberias!"

Rava: "I am as keen-witted as ben Azzai in the marketplaces of Tiberias!"

Rav, upon arriving in Babylonia: "I am the ben Azzai of these parts!"

Even ben Azzai is aware he is the ben Azzai of his time. "Compared to me, all the sages in Israel are as thin as a husk of garlic, except for this baldhead," he says, referring to his teacher Rabbi Akiva.

When ben Azzai dies, we're told, scholarly assiduousness leaves the world, and this is fitting. Ben Azzai has dedicated himself, to the exclusion of all other things, to the study of Torah.

"If one is willing to be degraded for the sake of the Torah's words," he says, "if one is willing to eat carobs and lupines and wear filthy clothes in order to sit assiduously at the door of the sages, though every passerby may say, 'That one is an idiot,' in the end, he will become a scribe, and you will find the entire Torah written in him."

Ben Azzai lives in a kind of closed loop of piety: "The fulfillment of one commandment draws another in its train," he counsels, "and the reward for fulfilling a commandment is the opportunity to fulfill another commandment."

As a result, his scholarship is infused with an unworldly power:

Once when ben Azzai was teaching Scripture, fire was flashing all around him. They went and told Rabbi Akiva, "Master, ben Azzai sits and expounds while fire flashes around him!"

This is the *hasmal*—the heavenly fire, surrounded by a flashing radiance and an amber gleaming—that Ezekiel sees in his vision.

In addition to being a safety hazard, it's also perhaps a sign that ben Azzai may have violated the prohibition against teaching the divine mysteries in public.

Rabbi Akiva goes out to investigate. "I hear that while you've been teaching, fire was flashing all around you," he says to ben Azzai. "Were you perhaps discussing the inmost secrets of the Divine Chariot?"

"No," the younger man avers, "I was merely sitting and stringing words of Torah together, the words of Torah with the words of the Prophets, and the words of the Prophets with the words of the Writing"—he was, in other words, reading (or more probably reciting from memory) not the mystical traditions, not even the oral law of the rabbinic tradition, but simply the Bible—"and yet," he tells Rabbi Akiva, "the words were as full of joy as when they were given at Mount Sinai, as sweet as at the time of their first utterance, and were they not," he reminds his teacher, "at their first utterance, uttered in fire?"

Uttered in fire: He means the ecstatic synesthesia experienced by the children of Israel at the foot of Mount Sinai when Moses ascended it to receive the Torah and the entire people *saw* the thunder and the flames and the sound of the ram's horn.

The story ends before Rabbi Akiva can reply, and so we do not know what he says to ben Azzai. Still, as we will see, I think it's safe to assume he finds this preoccupation with mythic beginnings problematic.

THAT ONE IS AN IDIOT.

We all know a ben Azzai, don't we? The sort of person who, long after its expiration date, insists upon retaining a childlike naïveté. Though ben Azzai is betrothed to Rabbi Akiva's daughter, the two don't seem to have ever married or, if they have, to have shared a bed. Chided by his teachers about leaving the commandment to be fruitful and multiply unfulfilled—an omission that, during the conversation, ben Azzai himself likens to both murder and a diminishment of the image of the Holy One—he can only shrug.

"What can I do?" he says, helplessly. "My soul yearns only for the Torah. Let the world continue through other people."

The continuation of the world holds no interest for him. He lives his true life in a moment deep in the mythic past, as though he were always Moses receiving the Torah high on a mountaintop in the thin air of its rarefied elevation, basking in the heat of its first utterance.

No wonder his simple reading of the Bible causes fire to descend from the Heavens. Unlike Moses, who, each time he ascends Sinai, must descend again, responsible for sons and a wife and the welfare of a nation—not to mention two fractious siblings, a couple of troublemaking nephews, and a rabble of rebellious cousins—nothing binds ben Azzai to this world. He has resigned his part in the casual comedy of life. Possessing a boy's consciousness, he has no wife, no child, no worldly possessions, no occupation. Innocent of sexual knowledge, he indulges in no physical pleasures. Subsisting on carobs and lupines, dressing in rags, he is chaste and distant—emotionally as well as physically— from his betrothed. The eternal student, he has no students himself. As he lacks even the title of rabbi, his legal opinions do not possess sufficient weight to engrave themselves upon the Law.

He is too busy receiving the Torah to ever live by its precepts.

We can understand why, ascending into the Orchard of Paradise and casting a look, ben Azzai dies. He's got one foot in the World to Come already. Arriving at the slabs of pure transparent marble, gazing through their invisible watery veils, perhaps into the very face of the murmuring deep, he is like a lover swooning at the sight of his beloved. The sight is enough for him. It completes his life.

Ungrounded, he burns up in the *hasmal*, in the cosmic electricity described by Ezekiel, and we can only assume he immolates happily without a backwards or a downwards glance.

BEN ZOMA LOOKED AND BECAME DEMENTED.

Just as one dreaming of ben Azzai may hope for saintliness, one dreaming of ben Zoma may hope for wisdom. And just as the dark side of saintliness—an inability to root oneself in earthly life—finishes off ben Azzai, the darker side of wisdom—madness—ruins ben Zoma.

Wisdom and madness resemble each other, after all. The mad and the wise both possess a knowledge that cannot be immediately apprehended by others.

Like ben Azzai, ben Zoma is preoccupied with beginnings. Not the innocence of childhood, but the creation of the universe. It's never far from his thoughts. He even thinks of himself as a kind of Adam, understanding his life in the light of the long shadow cast by the first man.

Upon seeing a large crowd on the steps of the Temple Mount, for instance, ben Zoma utters the blessing: *Blessed is he who discerns secrets.* This is meant as a blessing of astonishment at the diversity of Creation, a recognition that the mind of each person is not like the mind of any other. Appended to this blessing, however, ben Zoma adds the following: *And blessed is he who has created all these people to serve me.*

Now, you might assume, especially because the scene is set on the steps of the Temple Mount, that the *me* in ben Zoma's blessing is the Holy One, but in fact, ben Zoma is talking about himself.

He explains:

How many labors did Adam have to engage in before he obtained bread to eat? He plowed, he sowed, he reaped; he stacked the sheaves, threshed the grain, winnowed the chaff, selected the good ears, ground them, sifted flour, kneaded the dough, and baked. Only then did he eat, whereas I get up and find all these things done for me!

How many labors did Adam have to engage in before he obtained a garment to wear? He sheared the sheep, washed the wool, combed it, spun it, wove it, dyed the cloth, and sewed it, and only then did he have a garment to wear, whereas I get up and find all these things done for me. All kinds of craftsmen come early to the door of my house, and when I rise in the morning, I find all these things ready for me!

On the one hand, I suppose, this is a kind of manifesto of gratitude. In what was then the modern age, one needn't live like Robinson Crusoe, alone on his island. Society, in all its diversity, functions as a single man, a thrumming honeycomb of interconnectivity, with everyone providing for everyone else. This reading gently glides over the seeming egoism at the heart of ben Zoma's statement: it's not that he believes the world exists to serve him or to serve him *exclusively*; rather, he understands that a person simply can't apprehend the world *except* through the perceptual filters of his own ego.

As the first part of ben Zoma's blessing indicates — *Blessed is he who discerns secrets* — this is precisely what is remarkable about a crowd: every person in a crowd imagines himself, even experiences himself, as its subjective center.

On the other hand, there's an implicit recognition that this putting of ourselves at the center of the world, this perceptual self-centeredness, is a *distortion* of reality. Though we can't free ourselves from this cage of self-centered perception, the Holy One, it seems, can: the Discerner of Secrets can read each individual mind. More, unlike a human being, he can hear everyone's thoughts simultaneously without being overwhelmed by the cacophony.

AS A NOVELIST, I've often wondered how one might draft a scene that presents the many subjective perspectives of all its characters simultaneously. Take Edward Hopper's *Nighthawks* as an example. The painting depicts four people through the glass windows of an all-night diner, huddled around its counter. One man, with his back to the observer, sits alone. A man and a woman, sitting side by side, stare ahead in postures of quiet intimacy. The counterman, in white smock and cap, works slightly bent behind the counter. Including the unseen observer, watching from the street outside the windows, there are five people in the scene, all experiencing the moment simultaneously from five different perspectives. There are five internal conversations, an unknown number of external conversations, and five filmic pans of the room, each including a different set of four faces. An accurate depiction of this scene in a novel would allow the reader to experience the perspective of each character simultaneously.

It's an impossible task, as far as I can tell. Which means: *it's impossible to depict reality.* Or even, really, to *experience* it. Though we may develop a compassionate sympathy for the subjective lives of other people, we're helpless to liberate ourselves from the cage of our own subjective perceptions, and we're condemned to apprehend the world through the bars of that cage.

It's the attempt to break out of that cage, to experience the world uncolored by his own subjectivity—in order words, to know the mind of the Holy One, to experience life before it is split into the lightness of Heaven and the darkness of earth—that undoes poor ben Zoma's sanity.

"When you arrive at the slabs of pure transparent marble, do not say, 'Water, water!'" Rabbi Akiva tells ben Zoma, but "water, water" is all ben Zoma has on his mind. He's obsessed, in fact, with the First and Second Days of Creation, when the Heavens and the earth were water.

ACCORDING TO THE Book of Genesis, on the First Day of Creation, when the Holy One's spirit hovers over the surface of the water, the higher waters and the lower waters are mixed and indistinguishable. Only on the Second Day does the Holy One place a Sky between these two liquid bodies.

On the First Day, the Holy One *speaks* the universe into being— *The Holy One said, "Let there be light," and there was light*—and this is true for most of the other Days of Creation as well: the Holy One says, *Let there be . . .* ; and, the narrator tells us, *It was so.*

On the Second Day of Creation, however, the Holy One says, *"Let there be a Sky in the middle of the water that it may separate water from water,"* and, the narrator says, *"The Holy One made the Sky"* (italics mine).

"This is a verse whose apparent implication caused ben Zoma

to shake the world," we're told, and if the world isn't shaken, ben Zoma certainly is.

"This is an unbelievable utterance!" he cries. "Did the Sky not come into being by the Holy One's word?"

Ben Zoma knows his psalms, and according to the psalmist: *"By the word of the Holy One were the Heavens made, and all the hosts of them by the breath of his mouth."* In other words: The Heavens were *spoken* into being, not *made* by the Holy One.

Ben Zoma's concerns are twofold. On the one hand, he's troubled lest he's discovered a flaw, a contradiction, in the Torah. For ben Zoma, the Torah is the blueprint of Creation, the genetic code of the universe, perfect and eternal, a record authored by the Holy One himself. It's inconceivable to him that one might find a contradiction a mere seven verses in, a contradiction that— literally—shakes the foundations of the cosmos.

On a deeper level, though, his anxieties are metaphysical. Ben Zoma understands that the Sky—*made* by the Holy One, rather than *spoken* into being—is somehow qualitatively different from the rest of Creation, not eternal perhaps or perhaps constructed with an eye towards a lesser permanence. (Not insignificantly, the work of the Second Day is the only work the Holy One does not pronounce as *Good.*) The Holy One, in fact, divides the primal water twice—on the Second Day by placing a Sky in the middle of it, and on the Third by gathering the lower water so that land appears— and the small patch of dry earth upon which we human beings play out our little lives appears even more conditional, temporary.

A sensitive mystic, ben Zoma feels the pressure of *water, water* everywhere in the cosmos, dammed by God, or by the will of God. Without that will, the entire world might be flooded again, returned to a primal state of chaos and desolation! This is, of course, what the Holy One threatens to do when the angels protest Rabbi Akiva's martyrdom; and this is what the Holy One all but does a mere six chapters into the Book of Genesis, in the story of Noah. Disgusted by the evil of humanity, the Holy One undoes the two divisions he has made in the water: *All the fountains of the great deep burst apart, and the floodgates of the Heavens broke open.*

But it's even more than that. It's as though ben Zoma senses that, beneath the life of these illusory polarities—light/darkness, Heaven/earth, soul/body, comedy/tragedy, silence/speech—there's another, truer, unified world, which we might call the liquid un-world of First Things.

Ben Zoma is the embodiment of wisdom seeking its own source. He ascends to the Supernal Orchard to know the mind of the Holy One, to apprehend reality in its full light, unfiltered, undeformed, so to speak, by his mental retina. An experience of being beyond the mainframe, a knowing beyond the limits of knowledge, his is a self-obliterating quest: *Ben Zoma looked and became demented.*

The mind cannot stand outside itself. As we learn from the story of Noah, one needs an ark—a body, a vessel, a contained sense of self—to stay afloat in the flood of the primary waters. One cannot stand outside the five dimensions of space, time, and self. To do so is tantamount to standing in a large crowd on the Temple Mount and *being* the crowd: the self disappears.

This is what happens to ben Zoma, I'm afraid; and we have a poignant portrait of his final days:

"Once Rabbi Joshua ben Hananiah was standing on the Temple Mount when ben Zoma walked towards him but, after coming close, did not greet him."

Rabbi Joshua is the elder of the two. The teacher of Rabbi Akiva, he is the teacher of ben Zoma's teacher. Not to greet him is a serious breach of etiquette, and Rabbi Joshua is concerned.

"Where are you coming from and where are you going, ben Zoma?" he asks, gently attempting to situate the younger man more firmly within the coordinates of earthly—as opposed to cosmic—time and space. Where were you, ben Zoma, *before* this moment and *before* this place? Where will you be *after* this moment and *after* this place? Not *before* the moment of Creation nor *after* the universe winks out.

But ben Zoma answers him from the watery depths of his unearthly speculations.

"I have been meditating upon the Work of Creation," he tells

Rabbi Joshua, "and I have found that between the upper waters and the lower waters, there is no more space than three finger-breadths, for as it is said, *The breath of the Holy One hovered upon the face of the water*, like a dove hovering over its young, touching them and not touching them."

This is mad, obsessive talk. The Sky ben Zoma has spent his life obsessing over—that empty space in the middle of the cosmos, that empty space separating Heaven and earth—is dissolving. Ben Zoma's sense of self is dissolving as well. This makes sense. If the Sky is an illusion, conditionally *made* by the Holy One, rather than *spoken* into eternal being, how much less real are we? How fragile a structure is human consciousness, that flimsy temporary scaffolding that fills the three fingerbreadths of space between the waters of the soul and the waters of the body, keeping the two simultaneously joined and apart?

His head swimming in the upper waters, ben Zoma is drowning in the lower waters, as he attempts to inhabit a moment of pre-existence, of time before Time, of space outside of Space, of self outside the confines of Self. His mind can no longer withstand the pressure of these two opposing bodies of water. His mental levee breaks, and he is washed away in a flood of madness, reabsorbed into that liquid unworld of First Things.

After their meeting on the Temple Mount, Rabbi Joshua tells his students, "Ben Zoma is already outside."

Outside time and space.

And not many more days after that, we're told, he dies.

"ANYONE WHO SEES AHER IN A DREAM, *let him fear retribution.*"

Beginnings also obsess Elisha ben Avuyah. The third sojourner into the Orchard, the one whose experiences result in his apostasy, Elisha ben Avuyah is called *Aher—Another*—by our narrator, and presumably by his former friends, all of whom refuse to dignify an apostate by referring to him by name.

Unlike ben Azzai, unable to move from mythological into historical life, or ben Zoma, obsessed with cosmological beginnings,

Elisha ben Avuyah is concerned with his own personal beginnings, not the Creation story of his people, nor of the universe, but of himself.

His teachings seem to address this matter of a good foundation almost exclusively:

"To what can one who has many good deeds and much sacred knowledge be compared?" Elisha ben Avuyah asks. "To a man who, in building, lays stones first for a foundation and then bricks over them, so that however much water may collect, the building will not wash away. But he who has no good deeds, even though he has studied much, to whom may he be compared? To a man who, in building, lays bricks first and then heaps stones over them, so that if even a little water collects, the structure is immediately undermined."

In a restatement of this teaching, he compares a person with good deeds and much learning to plaster over stone: "Even after many rains, the stones will not crumble." A person without good deeds, despite his learning, is likened to plaster over bricks: "Even a little rain will cause the bricks to crumble."

Though the metaphors he uses pile up, his point never changes. He speaks only of two conditions, a person with good deeds and much sacred knowledge, and a person without good deeds despite his sacred knowledge. The first is a cup with a flat bottom (it does not spill), the second a cup without a flat bottom (it spills); the first is a horse with a bridle (when one mounts it, one is not thrown), the second a horse without a bridle (one is thrown).

There are two other cases, of course, but we hear nothing of a person with many good deeds and no learning, nor of a person possessing neither.

This is theology as autobiography: because these variations have no personal resonance for Aher, they escape his attention completely. In his inner world, things are either black or white: having turned his back on holiness, he himself is a waterlogged ruin, a crumbling foundation, an overturned vessel, an unbridled beast, while his colleagues—Rabbi Akiva principally among them—are strong structures with good foundations, upright vessels brimming with wine, bridled horses, docile and compliant beneath their masters' gentle hand.

You can dedicate yourself to holiness, you can place yourself in the House of Study, you can sit at the feet of an enlightened teacher, drinking in his knowledge, but according to Aher, one thing—and one thing alone—determines who will stand and who will fall: your childhood.

"If one learns Torah as a child," he used to say, "the words are absorbed in the blood and a person expresses them distinctly."

"One who studies the sacred wisdom as a child," he says elsewhere, "is like ink written on fresh paper. But one who studies as an old man is like ink written on smudged paper."

This is a rather deterministic theology; and what, in one's theology, is deterministic becomes, in one's personal history, absolutely defeatist. There's a seductiveness to this type of thinking (*Oh, if only I'd had a loving father . . . if only I'd gone to Harvard . . . if only I'd cut my hair, as they demanded, in order to run on the track team . . . then I could have done something with my life . . .*); it lets a person off the hook of personal responsibility.

A guilty pleasure, this kind of thinking is contagious, and another sage, Rabbi Yossi bar Judah of Kfar HaBavli, joins in the conversation—this occurs in the pages of a part of the Talmud called *Ethics of the Fathers*—amplifying Aher's statement about youth and old age:

> One who learns Torah from the young is like one who eats unripe grapes or drinks unfermented wine from his vat. But one who learns Torah from the old is like one who eats ripe grapes or drinks aged wine.

This is where Rabbi Meir enters the conversation. He'll have none of this nonsense. Though a student of Aher's, Rabbi Meir sees through his master's self-defeating nostalgia and the self-limiting prejudices of the man from Kfar HaBavli.

"Do not look at the vessel," he contradicts them, "but at what's in it. Here is a new vessel filled with old wine and, here, an old vessel that does not even contain new wine."

Disdaining the black-and-white thinking of his two colleagues, Rabbi Meir is able to think in all the hues of the color wheel. Wisdom is wisdom, wherever one finds it. Rabbi Meir, in fact, uses this formulation to justify his discipleship under his apostate teacher, refusing to abandon him, even though it gets him in trouble with the Holy One:

> Once Rabbah bar Shila came upon Elijah the prophet, and he said, "What is the Holy Blessed One doing?" Elijah told him, "He is repeating teachings from the mouth of all the rabbis, except from the mouth of Rabbi Meir." Rabbah bar Shila: "Why?" Elijah: "Because Rabbi Meir learned his teachings from the mouth of Aher." Rabbah bar Shila said to him, "Rabbi Meir found a pomegranate. He ate the insides and threw away the peel."

Elsewhere we're told that "Rabbi Meir found a date, ate it, and threw away the kernel."

In other words: The Torah is edible fruit, whether it comes in a digestible skin, like a peach, or an inedible peel, like a pomegranate, whether it's taught to you by a heretic or a saint. This exchange is so convincing, the Holy One actually changes his divine mind and begins repeating Rabbi Meir's teachings—not insignificantly on the subject of divine empathy—by name.

RABBI MEIR'S GENTLE CORRECTION of Elisha's thinking, spelled out as an exchange of ideas on the pages of *Ethics of the Fathers*, is translated into dramatic form in the following story, with both figures assuming their entrenched positions:

> Rabbi Meir was seated in the House of Study in Tiberias on the Sabbath, expounding on the Torah, while his teacher Elisha ben Avuyah was passing through the marketplace astride his horse.

Aher could not have made a more dramatic entrance. Sacred law forbids the riding of a horse on the Sabbath, and the image speaks volumes. In addition to the image of a warrior mounted for battle, a sense of personal elevation (or distance) is combined with the nerviness of so flagrant, so public, a desecration of the holy law. In this image, we can hear the opening notes of the motif that haunts Elisha ben Avuyah's life: a frozen in-between-ness. He could be anywhere at the moment, riding his horse among other non-Torah-observant horsemen, among the Roman cavalry perhaps; but having rejected the Torah, he nevertheless chooses to desecrate its laws in the public thoroughfares belonging to its adherents.

Unable to fully abandon the Law, he's helpless to live within its constraints.

The story continues: "People came by and told Rabbi Meir, 'Your teacher Elisha is here, riding through the marketplace.'"

It's difficult not to hear the aggression in these voices, a raspy sarcasm in their identification of Elisha as Rabbi Meir's *teacher.* Nevertheless, interrupting his teaching, Rabbi Meir goes out to greet Elisha. Still astride his horse, Elisha asks him, "What verse have you been expounding today?"

Rabbi Meir tells him, "'So the Holy One blessed the latter end of Job's life more than his beginning.'"

Perhaps it's mere coincidence, or perhaps Rabbi Meir, familiar with the whole of Torah as well as with Elisha's habits of mind, chooses to respond to his question with a verse that not only speaks to his teacher's ruling neurosis, but contradicts it: the idea that our beginnings determine our ends and that we are helpless in the face of karmic determinism.

"What did you say about it?" Elisha asks.

Rabbi Meir answers with another verse from the Book of Job: "'The Lord gave Job twice as much as he had before.' He doubled his possessions."

Elisha is unconvinced. "Alas for those who are gone and are no more," he says. "Your teacher Akiva would not have spoken thus."

Now, it's no small thing here to learn that Rabbi Akiva is *gone and no more*, that this conversation is taking place after his death. The Roman persecutions are at their height, and Aher appears to be the lone survivor of the four who ventured into the Orchard.

Elisha corrects Rabbi Meir's teaching. "Akiva would have construed these words in this way: 'The Lord blessed the latter end of Job's life *because* of the beginning,' because of the observance of commandments and good deeds that had been Job's at the beginning of his life."

We've returned to the stones and the bricks and the cups and the horses. The two men are speaking in code, with Rabbi Meir saying, *I can prove from the Book of Job that the latter part of your life can be more blessed than its beginning*, and Elisha maintaining, as he does in the teachings authored in his name, exactly the opposite: *a good beginning determines a good end.*

Without the former, you cannot have the latter.

"And what other verse did you expound?" he asks.

Rabbi Meir presses his case. "'Better is the end of a thing than the beginning thereof,'" he tells him, quoting now from the Book of Ecclesiastes.

"And what did you say about it?"

"You have a man who acquired merchandise in his youth and sustained a loss, but in his old age, he makes a profit from it. Or . . . "—a subtle psychologist, he moves in more closely to his patient's inner drama—"you have a man who learned Torah in his youth and forgot it, but it comes back to him in his old age."

We can imagine Elisha staring down at Meir from his horse, his position of master reified by the image, with Meir, the student, the child, the smaller one, looking upwards at his errant teacher with a loving, dedicated, ever-hopeful, ever-benevolent regard.

None of which has any effect on Elisha.

"Alas for those who are gone and are no more. Your teacher Akiva would not have spoken thus," he says. "He would have construed it to mean, 'Good is the end of a thing *from* the beginning'—its end is good when it has been good *from* its beginning."

Still, Elisha's psyche seems to have been stirred by the discussion, and as though Rabbi Meir were conducting a classical Freudian analysis, Elisha's primal memories come, bidden by Rabbi Meir, to the surface.

"So it happened with me," he tells Rabbi Meir. "Avuyah, my father, was one of the notables of Jerusalem. When he was arranging for my circumcision, he invited all the notables of Jerusalem, and among them were Rabbi Eliezer and Rabbi Joshua. After everyone had eaten and drunk, they began to clap their hands and dance. Some of the notables sang songs, others composed alphabetical acrostics, and Rabbi Eliezer said to Rabbi Joshua, 'These are occupied with what interests them. Shall we not occupy ourselves with what interests us?'"

The two began sharing words of Torah, and their experience was not unlike ben Azzai's:

"They began with subjects connected with the Five Books of Moses, then with the Prophets, after that with the Writings. Fire came down from Heaven and surrounded them, at which Avuyah, my father, said to them, 'My masters, have you come to set my house afire over me?' They replied, 'God forbid! We were merely sitting and stringing together words of Torah, then from the Torah, we went on to the Prophets, and from the Prophets to the Writings. The words were as joyful as when they were given at Sinai. For, when originally given at Sinai, they were given in the midst of fire, as it says, *The mountain burned with fire unto the heart of Heaven.*' Elated, my father Avuyah remarked, 'My masters, since the power of the Torah is so great, if this child stays alive for me, I will dedicate him to the Torah.'

"But because the intent of my father's resolve was not for the sake of Heaven," Elisha tells Rabbi Meir, "my study of the Torah did not endure with me."

THIS IS ELISHA BEN Avuyah's Creation myth. The story, which was told to him and which he tells himself, seems to explain his entire life: his beginning wasn't good enough, his father's heart wasn't pure enough, and now his own heart, as a consequence, isn't pure, cannot be pure enough. If it's not congenitally crooked, its deficiencies go back to the eighth day of his life, to his *brit*, to the moment he entered the covenant with the Holy Blessed One.

Having revealed so much about himself, Elisha changes the subject, brushing off the story, as though it held no importance to him. "And what other verse did you expound?" he asks.

Rabbi Meir tells him: "'The Holy One made the one corresponding to the other.'" Another verse from the Book of Ecclesiastes.

"And what did you say about it?"

"Whatever the Holy One created in this world, he created an analogue for it: he created mountains, then hills; he created seas, then rivers. So in a time of good fortune, enjoy the good fortune; and in a time of misfortune, reflect: the Holy One created one as well as the other."

Elisha isn't buying it. "Your teacher Akiva would not have spoken thus," he says, and perhaps this time he has a point. Here, Rabbi Meir seems to be gilding the lily. The verse in context reads: *Consider the Holy One's doing! Who can straighten what he has made crooked?*

This isn't a verse Rabbi Meir would be eager to discuss with Elisha, since he has been insisting all along upon its very opposite: that the crooked can be made straight.

Elisha's reading is darker, bleaker, and yet at the same time closer than Rabbi Meir's to the sense of the original. "Your teacher," he says, and perhaps, in not citing Akiva here, he means himself, "would have said, 'The Holy One created the righteous, then the wicked. He created the Garden of Eden, then the purgatory of Gehenna. Thus each person has two portions assigned to him—a portion in the Garden of Eden and a portion in Gehenna."

Again, Elisha's is a world of stark counterpossibilities. "When a man is declared righteous," he tells Rabbi Meir, "he takes his own portion and the portion of another who, by his actions, has forfeited his portion in the Garden of Eden. When a man is declared wicked, he takes his own portion and the unclaimed portion of a righteous man in Gehenna."

And once again, they are speaking clearly, if in code. Elisha believes that he has forfeited his own portion in Paradise and has inherited the portion of Purgatory unused by a righteous person, no doubt by Rabbi Akiva, who is threaded through the subtext of our story and the subtext of their conversation. (Do we have any question concerning whose unused portion of Paradise Elisha imagines Rabbi Akiva has inherited?)

"And what other verse did you expound?" Elisha continues.

So far—if we imagine that his objective has been to get that damned fellow off his horse and into the House of Study—Rabbi Meir has gotten nowhere.

Meir answers him with another verse from the Book of Job: "'Gold and glass cannot equal it; nor vessels of fine gold be exchanged for it.'"

"And what did you say about it?"

Rabbi Meir makes a subtle move. Having thrice challenged Aher's habitual mindset, having contradicted his thinking and been repelled, he now takes Aher's side, like an aikido master using his opponent's efforts against him, forcing him into the opposite position.

"This refers to the words of Torah," Rabbi Meir tells Elisha. "They are as difficult to acquire as vessels of gold or of fine gold and are as readily destroyed as vessels of glass."

Caught off guard, acting unconsciously anyway, Elisha uncharacteristically agrees with his former student. "By God, even as readily as earthenware vessels!" he says. "But your teacher Akiva would not have spoken thus. He would have said, 'As vessels of gold and even vessels of glass can be repaired if broken, so can a disciple of the wise recover his learning if it has disintegrated.'"

If we're listening carefully, as I assume Rabbi Meir is, we catch a glimpse of Aher's unspoken wish. A broken vessel, he would like to have the glass and gold shards of his psyche gathered together, picked up, melted down, and re-formed. The fear, of course, is that he is mere earthenware, and that, once broken, he can only return to dust.

At last, Rabbi Meir has him where he wants him.

"So you, too, must come back," Rabbi Meir says.

It has taken a while, but this barbed exchange has finally opened their hearts, and they're no longer speaking in code.

"I cannot," he tells Rabbi Meir.

"And why not?"

Elisha tells another story: "I was riding a horse behind the House of Study on a Day of Atonement that fell on the Sabbath"—once again, as in the story of the fuller and Rabbi Elazar, this represents an extreme form of sin—"and I heard a divine voice reverberating, 'Return, O backsliding children! Return unto me, and I will return unto you . . . except for Aher, who knew my strength and yet rebelled against me.'"

THE TWO MEN have been walking during this exchange, Rabbi Meir on foot, Elisha on his horse, and when they reach the Sabbath limit—one is permitted to travel only two thousand cubits in any direction on the Sabbath—Elisha says, "Meir, turn back, for I have just measured by the paces of my horse that the Sabbath limit extends only this far."

Aher, who, according to the divine voice, knows the Holy One's strength and yet rebels, has been counting the paces of the Sabbath limit—helpless to do otherwise?—while, for all we know, Rabbi Meir, though firmly planted within the rabbinic system, may be willing to violate the sacred law in order to keep the conversation going, in order to return his teacher to the fold.

Would he have done so? We shall never know—the story will not allow us to peek around that corner—thanks to Elisha, who, despite his outward rejection of the holy law, is living within its limits, if only internally. Here, again, is a beautiful imagistic rendering of his inner life. He could be riding his horse anywhere, but he chooses to ride it in the marketplace of Tiberias on the Sabbath, near where his devoted student Rabbi Meir is expounding upon the holy Torah. And though he does not obey the Sabbath limit, he is fully aware of its constraints. He is a man frozen between two worlds. He cannot live within the community of the righteous nor apart from it.

Having reached the Sabbath limits, counted internally by him, Elisha instructs his student Meir to turn back. Rabbi Meir says, "You, too, go back!" an imploration that reverberates on many levels of meaning.

"Have I not just told you that I already heard from behind the curtain in Heaven, 'Return you backsliding children — all except Aher'?"

Elisha seems to have fought Rabbi Meir to a draw. Did he not hear a voice from Heaven insisting that repentance is impossible for him? A terrible irony: though an apostate, ignoring the will of Heaven in every other instance, he refuses to defy Heaven over the question of his repentance.

But Rabbi Meir will have none of this, either. Ridiculous to have one's fate determined by a verse overheard while passing a synagogue on a holy day! First of all, the day is an emotional one, Elisha was on horseback, there were prayers all day coming from the synagogue, it's more than possible he misheard some garbled piece of liturgy floating through an open window.

Second, it flies in the face of all Rabbi Meir knows to be true.

When it comes to the concept of free will versus predestination, the rabbinic view is complex and paradoxical. "Everything is seen," states Rabbi Akiva, "yet freedom of choice is given." "Everything is in the hands of Heaven," a Rabbi Chanina says, "except for the reverence for Heaven."

As we are simultaneously free and predestined, the wild card in the deck of human life is piety, it seems. According to the rabbinic view, one's love of the Holy One, one's reverence for Heaven, cannot be coerced or imposed by Heaven itself.

And so, it doesn't make sense to Rabbi Meir that Elisha should be prevented from repenting. Surely, the notion that all backsliding children except Aher may return exists only in Elisha's mind. Rabbi Meir conceives of an experiment to demonstrate to Elisha the foolishness of imagining his entire life can be determined by a verse randomly overheard, despite the terrible errors of his ways.

RABBI MEIR TAKES his teacher to a schoolhouse, where Elisha says to the first child he sees, "Recite for me your verse," meaning the verse the child happens at that moment to be studying.

According to Rabbi Meir's thinking, an idea implicit in the story, if Elisha can find a positive verse, serendipitously encountered, it will nullify the effects of the verse Elisha believes he heard on the Day of Atonement that fell on the Sabbath.

But the child answers, quoting from the Book of Isaiah, "'There is no peace, says the Lord, for the wicked.'"

This is not good. Not good at all.

Still, it's a question of percentages, isn't it? Fifty percent of the time, statistically, the verse will be unfavorable and fifty percent of the time favorable. Rabbi Meir is undeterred. He takes Elisha to another schoolhouse, where Elisha says to another child, "Recite for me your verse."

The child answers, this time from the Book of Jeremiah, "'For though you wash yourself with niter and take much soap, yet your iniquity is marked before me, says the Holy One.'"

After the fall of the Temple, according to the rabbinic view, prophecy was given over to children and madmen. Children are innocent vessels of the divine word. Certainly, these two verses are severe, but playing the odds, one would imagine a slight ray of hope, of reconciliation, of divine mercy might be pronounced through at least one of them, if the sample size were large enough.

To this end, Rabbi Meir takes Elisha to yet another school, where yet again, Elisha says to yet another child, "Recite for me your verse."

Quoting from the Book of Jeremiah, this child answers him, "'And you that are rotten, what do you do, that you clothe yourself in scarlet, that you deck yourself with ornaments of gold, that you enlarge your eyes with kohl? In vain do you make yourself beautiful . . . they seek your life.'"

Rabbi Meir takes Aher to thirteen schools, one after the other, in which all the children quote verses boding evil.

The pièce de résistance: the last child to whom Aher says, "Recite for me your verse," has a speech defect—he pronounces his R's as L's—and when he answers, "'But to the wicked'"—in Hebrew: *ve-la-rasha*—"'the Holy One says, Who are you to recite my statutes?'" it sounds as though he says, *ve-l'Elisha*: "'But to Elisha, the Holy One says, Who are you to recite my statutes?'"

Imagine! Elisha undergoes this process twelve times, hearing the voice of the Holy One scorning him twelve times, until, on the thirteenth time, thanks to the speech defect of the final child, Heaven actually addresses him by name! Thirteen times he throws Meir's complicated kindergarten version of the *I Ching*, and thirteen times, Elisha receives an unfavorable hexagram, the thirteenth time delivered to him personally.

How deep-seated must be his hope that somehow his devoted student Meir will intervene successfully on his behalf. But finally, he can take no more of it.

"If I had a knife," he says, "I would have cut that child to pieces."

Again, the image is autobiographical: Elisha himself feels cut to pieces, the child within him torn to shreds and utterly destroyed.

LIKE THE MAN FROM Kfar HaBavli, the story itself is seduced into Aher's way of thinking, into the belief that our beginnings determine our ends. Now the story attempts to discover what in Elisha's beginning made this end unavoidable:

> It's said of him, of Aher, that when he entered a meeting place for scholars and saw youngsters with scrolls in front of them, he would say, "Why do these sit here and occupy themselves in this way? This one's craft should be that of a builder. This one's a carpenter. That one's a painter, that other one a tailor." When the youngsters heard such talk, they left their scrolls and went away.
>
> It is also said of him, of Aher, that Greek song didn't cease from his mouth and that whenever he rose to leave the House of Study, many heretical books would fall out of his lap.

He is a corrupter of youth—this might explain the karmic rightness of the trial by child played out in the thirteen different schoolhouses—or he's a heretic with a Hellenistic bent.

Two additional explanations are given:

> What did Aher see that made him go wrong? It is said that once, while sitting and studying in the valley of Gennesar, he saw a man climb to the top of a palm tree on the Sabbath, take the mother bird with the young, and descend in safety. At the end of the Sab-

bath, he saw another man climb to the top of the same palm tree and take the young, but let the mother go free; as he descended a snake bit him and he died. Elisha exclaimed: "It is written in the Holy Scripture, 'Let the mother go and take only the young, that you may fare well and have a long life.' Where is the well-being of this man, and where is the prolonging of his life?"

In other words: when the wicked prosper and the righteous suffer, who can believe that a just God runs an ordered universe?

On the other hand:

Some say that Elisha became a heretic when he saw a pig dragging along in its mouth Huzpit the Interpreter's tongue. He said then, "The tongue from which pearls of purest rays used to shine forth is to lick the dust?" Immediately, he resolved to commit a sin. He went out and, spying a harlot, beckoned to her. She asked, "Aren't you Elisha ben Avuyah?" It was the Sabbath, and he pulled a radish out of a furrow and gave it to her. So she said, "He is clearly *aher*, another."

The explanations mount up. In addition to the four we have above, we recall that Elisha has his own explanation: his father's wrongheartedness. But perhaps it had nothing to do with his father, the story now suggests, and everything to do with his mother:

There are some who say he became a heretic because, when his mother was pregnant with him, she passed by temples for idolatry and smelled the aroma of their offerings and craved their meat. They gave her some, and she ate it. The meat permeated her innards like the venom of a snake and affected Elisha.

Or perhaps something happened on that trip into the Supernal Orchard:

Some say: He saw the Archangel Metatron, to whom is given permission one hour each day to sit in Heaven so that he might record the merits of the children of Israel. Seeing Metatron, Elisha said to himself, "It is taught that on High there is no sitting and no jealousy and no rivalry and no back and no weariness. Perhaps, Heaven forbid, there are two divine powers!" Immediately, they brought Metatron out and punished him with sixty lashes of fire, and he was given permission to burn the merits of Aher. A heavenly voice went out and said to him, "Return you backsliding children—all except Aher."

His case, as Freud might say, is overdetermined: it has too many causes, proof, it seems, at least as far as our story is concerned, that Elisha's deterministic thinking is unprofitable and self-defeating.

The story adheres closely to the psychology of its characters, though those characters may be in denial. Threaded throughout the story, hidden, for instance, in the images of Huzpit the Interpreter and of the man who fulfilled the commandment of shooing away the mother bird before taking her young, is the death by martyrdom of Rabbi Akiva.

ALAS FOR HE WHO IS GONE AND IS NO MORE.

So terrible is Rabbi Akiva's death that it cannot even be mentioned explicitly. Rather, a similar image, with an emotional charge of slightly less wattage, is substituted. Right and left, Elisha's holiest colleagues are being martyred by the Romans. The image of Huzpit's tongue being dragged along in the mouth of a pig is a chilling image, as much for what it depicts as for what it merely suggests. Someone cut out that tongue, employed formerly in the repetition of the holy law, and threw it to the swine. In other words: someone with a knife cut that child to pieces.

The image is not unrelated to Moses's vision of Akiva's flesh being weighed out in the Roman marketplace. We begin to understand Elisha's frozenness. The world no longer makes sense to him. If there is a just God, why do the wicked prosper? Why do the good suffer? And why do the best suffer so horribly? Is there not an Eye that sees and an Ear that hears? Shall the Judge of All the Earth not act justly? If the Holy One himself will not adhere to the good, why should Elisha? Why not hire a whore with a radish picked on the Sabbath?

Alas for he who is gone and is no more: the child is gone, the innocent, the naïf who believed that there was holiness in the world, who believed that the good would prosper and the wicked suffer, that by cleaving to the holy law one might fare well and live long, who believed what his father told him, that two rabbis, engaged in the study of holiness, might bring the fire of Heaven down to earth, and that one's own life might be forged in that fire, sanctified and made purposeful.

Elisha is no longer that child. He is *Aher*, another, no longer himself. Today, we might say that he is suffering from posttraumatic stress disorder. Or even Stockholm syndrome: he sits atop a horse like a Roman warrior. And we can read his inability to return to the ways of the Holy One as a shrill, even hysterical, protest against the inhuman suffering imposed upon humanity by its Creator.

In many ways, he seems to be asking the same question Moses asks: *This is the Torah and this is its reward?* The only difference between Moses and Aher, on this score, seems to be that while Moses submits to the Divine Will in silence, Aher cannot reconcile himself to the violence the Holy One permits in his world.

NOW, RABBI MEIR is a problematic figure with issues of his own. For a while, as we've seen, even the Holy One had his holy doubts about Rabbi Meir's piety. Even with a questionable master, though, the Rabbi Meir who appears in our story could not have a more sympathetic and stellar character. The soul of his teacher is all that concerns him here. He sees the better angels of Elisha's nature. He never sees him as *another*, only as his master, and he never wavers in his devotion and his kindness and his desire to help his brokenhearted friend.

The story continues: "Sometime later, Elisha ben Avuyah fell ill, and Rabbi Meir was told, 'Your teacher is sick.'"

Meir visits Elisha, and once again he asks Elisha to repent.

"Having gone so far, will I be accepted?" Elisha wonders.

Rabbi Meir replies, "Is it not written, 'You allow a man to turn, up to his being crushed,' meaning: up until the time that life is being crushed out of him?"

"In that instant, Elisha ben Avuyah began to weep," we're told, "and then he died."

Though the moment is ambiguous—what exactly is the meaning of those tears?—Rabbi Meir decides upon a very definite interpretation: "Rabbi Meir rejoiced, saying, 'My master, it would appear, departed in a state of repentance!'"

(After hearing *your master this* and *your master that* in derision from the community, Rabbi Meir at last reclaims and resacralizes the title. Still, Rabbi Meir is a careful man, and even he admits that the case for Elisha's repentance is circumstantial: *it would appear.*)

As it turns out, Meir seems to have jumped the gun: "After he was buried, fire came forth from Heaven to burn Aher's grave."

The derision begins immediately again: "They went and told Rabbi Meir, 'The grave of your master is on fire!'"

> Rabbi Meir went out, spread his cloak over the grave, and said to him, "Tarry this night, and it shall be in the morning, if he who is good will redeem you, let him redeem. But if he is not willing to redeem you, then, as the Holy One lives, I will redeem you. Lie down until morning."

Here, really, is Rabbi Meir's shining moment. This, in my opinion, is one of the most beautiful and heartrending scenes in the entire corpus of Talmudic stories. Rabbi Meir is quoting from the Book of Ruth. There, Boaz, the old landowner, has taken a liking to Ruth, the young widow of his cousin. On her mother-in-law's instructions, Ruth sneaks into Boaz's room at night and lies down at his feet. When Boaz awakens and finds her there, he covers her with a blanket and says more or less the same thing to her that Meir says to Elisha, assuring her that, in the morning, he will inquire into the intentions of the nearer relative who, according to the sacred law, is obligated to marry her or else publicly declare his intention not to. If this relative, discreetly referred to as "Ploni Almoni" (i.e., So-and-So), declines to marry his widowed cousin, then, Boaz assures her, he himself will marry, or "redeem," her.

A midrashic text offers its own gloss on Rabbi Meir's words:

> "Tarry this night"—in this world which is wholly night—"and it shall be in the morning"—in the World to Come, all of which is morning—"if he who is good will redeem you"—that is, the Holy One, who is good, of whom it is said, The Holy One is good to all—"let him redeem. But if he is not willing to redeem you, then, as the Holy One lives, I will redeem you. Lie down until morning."

A tender moment: their roles reversed, the student becomes the master, the younger man places himself in the role of the older, powerful, benevolent Boaz; Rabbi Meir sees his master now as lovely, feminine, bereft, a foreigner in a foreign land, a stranger to the divine law—Ruth is the paradigmatic convert—greatly in need of caring and compassion.

At last, the stony heart of Heaven, which Elisha seems incapable of moving on his own behalf, softens towards him, and we're told: "The fire was then extinguished."

But the story has a denouement:

> Now, according to some, when Aher died, it was said, "Let him not be judged, nor let him enter the World to Come." Let him not be judged, because he engaged in the study of the Torah; nor let him enter the World to Come, because he sinned.

This doesn't sit well with Rabbi Meir. Understanding how Elisha's frozenness, this state of in-between-ness, caused terrible anguish for his teacher while he lived, Rabbi Meir says, "It is better that he should be judged and afterward enter the World to Come; and when I die, I shall cause smoke to rise from his grave," as a sign that he has been judged and punished for his sins.

And when Rabbi Meir dies, smoke indeed rises up from Aher's grave. And here, we may entertain the hope, as I assume Rabbi Meir did, that the fire and the smoke rising from his grave are signals that Elisha's soul, like shattered gold or broken glass, is being melted down and re-formed in the purgatorial crucible of Gehenna. And perhaps this double burning, the fire and the smoke, indicates that Elisha was right after all, that he did possess two portions of Gehenna. (*When a man is declared wicked, he takes his own portion and the unclaimed portion of a righteous man in Gehenna.*)

OUR OLD FRIEND Rabbi Yohanan, however, is unconvinced and equally unimpressed. "What a mighty deed of Rabbi Meir to burn his master with fire!" he scoffs. "Only one such sinner was in our midst, and we could not save him? If Elisha had been in my care," he says, blind to the future and to the fate of Resh Lakish, another such a one, "who would have dared snatch him from me?" (The two cases—Resh Lakish and Elisha ben Avuyah—are not so dissimilar: Rabbi Yohanan and Rabbi Meir each cared, without ceasing, for the state of his beloved friend's soul.) "When I die," Rabbi Yohanan declares, "I shall extinguish the smoke from Elisha's grave," as a sign that he has been completely forgiven.

And when Rabbi Yohanan dies, the smoke indeed ceases from Elisha's grave.

"Thus the public mourner began his oration concerning Rabbi Yohanan, 'Even the gatekeeper of Gehenna couldn't stand up to you, O Master!'"

NOW THAT ELISHA SEEMS TO have returned, let us return, for a moment, to the image of him internally counting those two thousand paces allowed for travel on the Sabbath. Though he's desecrating the Sabbath by riding a horse, at the same time he's counting the number of paces permitted for travel on that day. Living simultaneously in two separate worlds, he inhabits neither world fully.

Though Elisha will certainly ride beyond those two thousand paces, it's not clear what is happening internally to Rabbi Meir at that moment, or what, in these circumstances, he will do. If

Elisha hadn't stopped him, would he walk beyond the Sabbath limit in order to bring Elisha back? (He is, elsewhere in the Talmud, depicted as, if not lawless, then reckless within the limits of the law: he enters a Roman brothel to save his sister-in-law; he induces one of his students to seduce his wife in order to prove a point.)

The irony, though muted, seems clear: in the end, Elisha is *too* respectful of the limitations the Holy One has placed upon him. Divine voices speaking to him from the Heavens or through the synagogue window or through the mouths of children all inform him that he cannot return, and he reacts passively in the face of those imposed limits.

The horse he rides is a symbol of his passivity. His lower self, his emotional self, seems to direct him, carrying him to the marketplace on the Sabbath, carrying him past the House of Study on the Day of Atonement. Wandering, he is always being carried toward the center of his emotional concerns, despite his intellectual resistance to these places and these issues. When he is depicted as active—picking the radish on the Sabbath and offering it to the prostitute—he is seen as *Aher*, as another, not himself. He is *another* to himself, his emotions and his reason out of sync.

On the other hand, Rabbi Meir and Rabbi Yohanan, men firmly planted within the circle of nonapostasy, are daring, active, brave, even brazen when it comes to defying the diktats of Heaven. We've seen how Rabbah bar Shila argued the Holy One out of his hurt feelings concerning Rabbi Meir. And Rabbi Meir has no qualms— he does not hesitate for a moment—when it comes to putting out the fire with which Heaven has scorched Aher's grave. Quoting Scripture back to the Holy One, defying God in the name of God, he declares, *If the Holy One will not redeem you, then, as the Holy One lives, I will redeem you.*

As powerful as Rabbi Meir is in life, his power to challenge the heavenly dictates only grows after his death: God only knows what kind of bargaining and arguing Rabbi Meir is doing in the corridors of the Divine Law Courts following his departure from this world, but, like a good lawyer, as the smoke rising from Aher's grave testifies, he succeeds in reversing the heavenly decree.

Rabbi Yohanan goes even further, normalizing Elisha's status, kicking ass and taking names, though he's dead, at the very gates of Gehenna.

These men do not share Elisha's passivity. They are not too timid to *underthrow* a divine decree. (As we recall: at least according to the prophet Elijah, the Holy One delights in being *underruled* by his children.) Both Rabbi Meir and Rabbi Yohanan feel free to interact with the Holy One in a full and living relationship, even to the point of imposing *their* will upon the Divine Will.

AHER CUT THE SAPLINGS.

It's not insignificant that Aher's apostasy is described in horticultural terms. He mutilates the shoots. His apostasy is a rebellion against newness. The shoots of a plant are its new growth, after all. (And we know how he feels about roots.) Traumatized by Rabbi Akiva's death, unable to discern a moral calculus in the Roman slaughter of his holy friends, he becomes frozen, frozen in time, frozen in his thinking, frozen in his emotions. His emotions confuse his thinking; his thinking paralyzes his emotions.

There's nothing but contradictions here: Insisting upon the divine presence in the world, Elisha is branded a heretic. When Rabbi Meir tries to prove to him that the voices, all insisting that he cannot repent, are random, and they prove to be patterned, he's stymied within the mind-stopping contradictions of it all: the deity Elisha can no longer serve, because he appears indifferent to human sin, holds Elisha's sin of disbelief against him. Elisha's free will—the will to repent—is denied him by a theology that provides him with free will. Like a hero out of Kafka, he's denied justice by a system that he challenges on the grounds that it isn't just. It's as though the Heavenly Court were telling him, *Yes, the system is unjust, but in your case, we're willing to make an exception.*

ALAS FOR THOSE WHO ARE GONE AND ARE NO MORE . . .

At last, we arrive at Rabbi Akiva, whose martyrdom, seemingly sanctioned by the Holy One, or perhaps merely endured by him in silence, rocks the foundation of the cosmos, sending Heaven and earth—the angels above, Rabbi Akiva's students below, and Moses in between—into paroxysms of horrified disbelief.

The work of Rabbi Akiva's life seems to be to take what he has received from the tradition and to move with it into unmapped territories. The lecture he delivers in his class and his execution as well are both incomprehensible to Moses, although, according to Akiva (within the story) and to the Aggadist (through the imagery of the tale), both are evolutionary consequences of Moses's receiving of the Torah on Mount Sinai.

SEATED HIGH UPON HIS HORSE, Elisha ben Avuyah argues with Rabbi Meir over a verse from the Book of Job: "*The Holy One blessed the end of Job's life more than its beginning.*"

"Your teacher Akiva," Elisha tells Rabbi Meir, "would have construed these words in this way: 'The Lord blessed the end of Job's life *because* of its beginning.'"

But this, of course, is the last thing Rabbi Akiva would have taught. The beginning of Rabbi Akiva's life is blessed *only* in light of its end. We need only to look at the facts. Until the age of forty—ancient in the ancient world—Akiva was an illiterate boor. Nor was he a sweet and pious simpleton either. By his own account, he felt an envious hatred for those more learned than he.

"When I was an unlearned ignoramus," he tells his students, "I used to say, 'Oh, if only I had a scholar before me! I would bite him like an ass!'"

"You mean like a dog, Master, don't you?" they say.

"No, I mean an ass. When an ass bites, he breaks bones. When a dog bites, he breaks no bones."

Things begin to change for him, however, when one day, standing by the mouth of a well, he notices water dripping upon a hollowed-out stone. "Who hollowed out this stone?" he thinks to himself or perhaps wonders aloud, since he's answered: "Akiva, haven't you read that 'water wears away stone'?" (Another quotation from the Book of Job.) "It was water from the well falling upon it constantly day after day that wore that stone away."

"Is my mind harder than this stone?" Akiva wonders. If stone is malleable, why not his own obdurate self? He makes a pledge: "I will go and study at least one section of the Torah."

A forty-year-old rustic, he takes himself to the schoolhouse, where he sits with his young son and, together, they begin learning the alphabet on a child's chalk tablet.

A perfect image of tabula rasa: "Akiva took hold of one end of the tablet, his son the other." They begin at the absolute beginning. The teacher writes down an *alef*, the first letter, for him, and then a *bet*, the second letter. Eventually, the old man learns the entire alphabet and then the entire Torah.

"It's never too late to have a happy childhood," Tom Robbins reminds us in his novel *Still Life with Woodpecker*, and the image of Akiva sharing the blank slate with his son is all you know and all you need to know about an open, childlike heart full of inquiry and empty of mind-shuttering preconceptions.

Having mastered the written Torah, Akiva finds his way to our old friends Rabbi Eliezer ben Hyrcanus and Rabbi Joshua ben Hananiah. According to Elisha ben Avuyah's personal mythology, the presence of these two luminaries at his circumcision, bringing fire down from the Heavens, shipwrecked his life, but Akiva, hungry for a new life, seeks them out, and he asks them to reveal to him the inner sense of the Oral Law.

Each time they teach him a new law, Akiva secludes himself. In privacy, he studies each law atomistically, analyzing it down to its very letters. "This *alef*," he asks himself, "why is it shaped like this? This *bet*, why is it shaped like that?" (As you'll recall, the Holy One himself added those serifs to the font specifically for Rabbi Akiva's benefit.) A more sophisticated scholar, having learned the *alef-bet* long ago, would almost certainly blur out these small details. A more insecure person might be embarrassed to ask, at his late age, such simple—and perhaps unanswerable—questions.

Though I suppose you could argue that his early life as an ignoramus prepares him for the Zenlike beginner's mind he now brings to his studies, Akiva, at this stage in his life, is the personified repudiation of Elisha's teachings: *One who studies the sacred wisdom as a child is like ink written on fresh paper. But one who studies as an old man is like ink written on smudged paper.*

Unlike Elisha, Akiva is a teleological thinker. The beginning doesn't determine the end. On the contrary, the end determines the beginning. By changing your future, you can, in essence, re-write your past.

"When you arrive at the slabs of pure transparent marble, do not say, 'Water, water,'" Rabbi Akiva tells his friends. If I may attempt to paraphrase him, I believe in part what Rabbi Akiva is saying is this: When you arrive at the Never-Before-Seen Chimerical Impossible, and you notice that it sort of looks like water, and you try to understand it and take it in, as a human being does, through analogy and metaphor, *do not* resort to analogy or metaphor! You have no references for this. You have never stood in this place. You have never seen this Chimerical Impossible, and if you imagine that you have, if you tell yourself that lie, if you say, "Water, water," turning the Never-Before-Seen Chimerical Impossible into the commonplace and humdrum—something we all do, by the way, on a daily basis, imagining, for instance, that "water" is merely "water," that its presence at the tap in our kitchen or bathrooms or upon 70 percent of the earth's surface isn't a miracle—then you are, through your perceptions, scarring the pristine surface-depth of Creation. (Words must be invented to speak of these things.) To do so is to traffic in graven images and falsehoods, lying, as it were, about the nonstatic, flowing, ever-changing nature of existence and the self.

Understanding this principle, living it, Rabbi Akiva is free to follow his own preoccupations, walking forward into the new self he has embraced, delving into the new serifs the Holy One has added to the holy font for his benefit alone. Unlike with Aher, Rabbi Akiva's past does not imprison him. Instead, the image of his new self pulls him forward, through time, out of his old self and into the future.

RABBI AKIVA IS not a perfect man, nor is his transformation from an ignoramus into a sage without the occasional pitfall. As his colleague Rabbi Yohanan ben Nuri recalls:

> I call Heaven and earth to witness that many times Rabbi Akiva was punished on my account because I used to bring charges against him before Rabban Gamliel in Yavneh, but I know that Rabbi Akiva's love for me grew, nevertheless, in keeping with the verse "Reprove a man of sense and he will love you."

Once again, we see that the end determines the beginning. Here, the unrefined Akiva understands that Rabbi Yohanan ben Nuri's complaints against him are all part of the process of his refinement. And again, unlike Aher, he will not allow a rebuke—heavenly or earthly—to turn him from his path.

Still, the transformation is slow:

> All the twelve years that Rabbi Akiva was with Rabbi Eliezer, Rabbi Eliezer paid little attention to him, so that when Rabbi Akiva offered his first clinching argument to him, Rabbi Joshua quoted the verse "There is the army you paid no attention to; now go out and fight it."

Slowness is part of the process for Akiva. A childish sense of impatience paradoxically retards the childlike process of growth and change:

> Rabbi Shimon ben Eleazar said: "I will tell you a parable to illustrate what Rabbi Akiva did. He was like a stonecutter hacking away at mountains. One time he took his pickax in his hand, went and sat on top of the mountain, and began to chip small stones from it. Some men came by and asked him, 'What are you doing?' 'I mean to uproot the mountain and cast it into the Jordan,' he said. 'Can you possibly do such a thing?' 'Yes,' he said, and he continued hacking away until he came to a big boulder. He placed an iron claw under it, pried it loose, uprooted it, and cast it into the Jordan. Then he espied another, even bigger boulder, placed an iron

claw under it, and cast it into the Jordan, saying, 'Your place is not here, but there.' Rabbi Akiva had to perform such uprooting of 'big boulders' with Rabbi Eliezer and Rabbi Joshua, in keeping with the verse 'He falls to work upon the flinty rocks, he turns mountains up by the roots, he carves out channels through rock, and his eye beholds every precious thing.'"

By keeping the end and not the beginning in sight, a person, it seems, can rearrange the landscape, and a quality of liveliness is present in this boldly stepping forward into the unknown.

Remarking on this, Rabbi Tarfon famously says to Rabbi Akiva, "Akiva, when a man separates from you, he separates from life."

This sense of open possibilities—reinvention, rebirth, renewal— plays out in all aspects of Rabbi Akiva's biography. He's able to ride the roulette wheel of his life's seemingly capricious fortunes. At times poor, at other times rich, he is a man whose wealth often comes to him through magical means, coughed up on more than one occasion literally out of the sea. He has at least two wives, both of whom bring him unexpected wealth and good fortune. The death of his first wife, Rachel, who sacrifices everything so that he might become a scholar, does not wreck or end him. Nor do the deaths of twenty-four thousand of his students, struck down, as a divine punishment, between the holidays of Passover and Shavuot.

(These twenty-four thousand, it seems, did not treat one another with sufficient respect.)

Starting over with only five students, Rabbi Akiva says to them, "See that you do not act like my previous students, begrudging one another's intellectual gifts."

And these five, we're told, rise and fill the land with divine wisdom.

FOR TWENTY-TWO YEARS, Rabbi Akiva was a student of our old friend Nahum ish Gamzu, who, you'll remember, thanks in no small part to his sense of universal goodness, winds up blind and lame. For those long years, the two studied only a single word, the Hebrew morpheme *ET*. *ET*, a grammatical signifier for direct objects, has no meaning of its own. Its presence in a sentence indicates merely which noun is the subject and which the object. For twenty-two years, in other words, Rabbi Akiva and Nahum ish Gamzu studied the empty, nearly invisible quantum that distinguishes activity from passivity.

Rabbi Akiva's belief in a kind of unified field theory of universal beneficence, his ability to reconcile the extremes of life, to harmonize the eternal comedy of Heaven with the earthdowned tragedy of temporal life, derives, no doubt, from these twenty-two years of study. Rabbi Akiva adapts Nahum's *Gam zu l'tova* ("This, too, is for the good") into his own "All that the Merciful One does is for the best":

> Once, when he was traveling, Rabbi Akiva came to a certain place where he looked for lodging but was not given any. He said, "Whatever the Merciful One does is for the best." He went off and spent the night in the open field. He had with him a donkey, a rooster, and a lamp. A lion came and ate the donkey, a weasel came and ate the rooster, and a gust of wind came and blew out the lamp. Again, he said, "Whatever the Merciful One does is for the best." And that same night, troops came and took the people of that city into captivity. Rabbi Akiva said to his students, "Did I not tell you, 'Whatever the Merciful One does is for the best'?"

Now, this is an easy enough sentiment when you're in the field, protected by a wall of miracles, and not among the captives in the city; but, as we bring to mind the scene of Rabbi Akiva's martyrdom, we realize there is nothing glib about his statement.

THE NEVER-BEFORE-SEEN CHIMERICAL IMPOSSIBLE.

Rabbi Akiva is not the only mystic to delve deeply into the structure of the Hebrew alphabet, as we see from his ascent into the Orchard with his three companions when the story is told again in the *Zohar*, the principal book of Kabbalah:

An Old Grandfather stood up and said to Rabbi Shimon bar Yohai, "Rabbi, Rabbi! What is the meaning of what Rabbi Akiva said to his students, 'When you come to the place of pure marble stones, do not say "Water! Water!" lest you place yourselves in danger, for it is said, "He who speaks untruths shall not stand before my eyes."' But it is written, 'There shall be a sky between the waters and it shall separate between water and water.' Since the Torah describes the division of the waters into upper and lower, why should it be problematic to mention this division? Furthermore, since there are upper and lower waters, why did Rabbi Akiva warn them, 'Do not say, "Water! Water!"'"

Rabbi Shimon bar Yohai answers, "Old Grandfather, it is proper that you reveal this secret."

According to the Old Grandfather, those slabs of pure transparent marble are the Hebrew letter *yud*, two of which make up the letter *alef*. "One is the upper *yud* of the *alef*, and one is the lower *yud* of the *alef*."

Just as W is an E lying on its back, and L is an I wearing cowboy boots, and N is a Z bowing, the Hebrew letter *alef* (א) is two *yuds* (י) playing on a seesaw made from a *vav* (ו).

(The wordplay here is complex. According to the *Zohar*, the marble stones, the two *yuds*, represent Wisdom and Sovereignty. The upper *yud* is the first letter in the unpronounceable four-letter name of the Holy One, while the lower *yud* is the last letter in the sometimes-pronounceable name *Adonai*. The first *yud* is the "male waters," the outer aspects of being, the second *yud*, the "female waters," the inner aspects of life. They mirror each other, like twin bodies of water. Wisdom is spelled יש [*yesh*] and Sovereignty שי [*shay*]. Together, they form שיש [*shayish*], meaning "marble.")

Now, according to the Old Grandfather, deep in the Supernal Orchard—if you can picture such a thing—the two marble slabs, the two *yuds*, hover in space, mirror reflections of each other, one pointing up towards Heaven, the other pointing down towards earth, with the negative space, the empty space, in between them seeming to form a *vav*. The two *yuds*, with the implied *vav* between them, create an *alef*.

A silent letter, *alef* is the first letter of the Hebrew alphabet. In the Torah, the account of Creation, as well as, according to the mystics, the Work of Creation itself, begins with the second letter of the alphabet, the *bet* (ב). The *alef*, in other words, is the silence that precedes Creation, the in-draw of breath that precedes speech, the Planck Epoch, the first 10^{-44} seconds of the universe, unaccountable by scientists, before the Big Bang.

"Here there is no spiritual impurity, only pure marble stones," the Old Grandfather continues, "so there is no separation between one water and the other."

We're back to ben Zoma and the Second Day of Creation, when the Holy One placed the empty sky between the waters of Heaven and the waters of earth. And we're back to the motifs in the story of Moses's ascent into Heaven: with the upper waters representing heavenly joy, the comedy of life, and the lower waters, the waters of our poor planet, representing the bitter waters of separation, of earthly darkness, of heavy materiality and distance from the realms of divine joy.

This split, this dichotomy with all its tensions, is embodied in the human being. We see it played out by our quartet of mystics in the stories of ben Azzai and Aher. Ben Azzai, an eternal boy, lives only in the innocent world of the upper waters, in the world of the Soul, while Aher, feeling himself exiled from the world of soulful joy, endures life in the lower waters, in the realm of the Body, in the realm of experience, where ultimately there is nothing but torture, pain, and death.

THE STORY OF Rabbi Akiva's martyrdom is recounted as the climax of the liturgy on the Day of Atonement, the holiest day on the Hebrew calendar. On the Day of Atonement, there's a tradition of wearing white and of fasting. The white garments, on the one hand, are meant to remind a person of his burial shroud, the fasting, to remind him that, one day, he will no longer eat. (How pitiful and fragile we human beings are, when one day of not eating is a kind of death!) On the other hand, there's another explanation for this tradition: one dresses in white to imitate the angels; one refrains from eating because angels do not eat. Spiritual beings, they're above the demands of the material world and the body.

Here's that split again: In the created world, no being is higher than an angel and no being lower than a corpse. A human being, an angel-corpse, embodies the full spectrum, and, oddly enough, between the white garments and the fasting, an angel and a corpse look exactly the same.

According to the mystics, the soul works to elevate the body through reason, through aspect, through apprehension, to holiness; while the body hopes to ground the soul in physical reality, to bring it, quite literally, to its senses.

"Do not say 'Water, water,'" Rabbi Akiva admonishes his companions. Do not perceive a separation between the realm of Heaven and the realm of earth. Yes, it's true, there seems to be a huge gulf between the comic image of the Holy One tinkering with the holy alphabet in his isolated splendor and the hell we human beings make for ourselves and one another on our small planet, everything the image of Rabbi Akiva's flesh being weighed out in the Roman meat markets stands in for: from war and famine and genocide and murder on one extreme to personal unhappiness and failure and hatred and indifference and boredom on the other.

The Talmud warns the mystical aspirant away from inquiring into what is before and what is after, what is above and what is below. At the slabs of pure transparent marble, these dichotomies—between water and water, between Heaven and earth, between above and below, between before and after, between self and other, between angel and corpse—no longer apply.

Confronted by these fearful symmetries of innocence and experience, the Holy One admonishes his angels and his prophet to be silent, to be silent like the *alef*, to hear the silent roar of the murmuring deep, humming behind all the polarities of Creation.

The images in our stories are honest and clear. The sight of Water, Water, of one body of water reflecting the sparkling surfaces of another body of water, can be, for the human being stuck in the middle, a dizzying experience. Standing in that place, you might lose your balance and drown.

This, of course, is what happens to ben Zoma. He wants to experience the *alef* from within the *alef*. He wants to experience pure reality before it is violated by the coordinates of time and space and self, and, of course, in achieving this as a mystic, he disappears.

On the other hand, although Rabbi Akiva sees these polarities—before/after; above/below; light/darkness; tragedy/comedy—as a misrepresentation of reality (*He who speaks falsehood shall not stand before my eyes*), he does so from an entirely human and embodied perspective. Still, the separation is a misrepresentation. According to Rabbi Akiva, the affirmation of unity in the *Sh'ma* is a correction of this misperception. There is no dark and light, no before and after, no above and below. No comedy and tragedy. It's all One, he tells us. Do not say, "Water, water." Don't split everything into twos. Do not perceive a separation between Heaven and earth. Don't imagine you understand where you are because of where you've been. There is a field beyond these distinctions. The slabs of pure transparent marble resemble water reflecting water, but they are not water. In the same way, each moment of our lives is new and unprecedented. By imagining that we know where we are, we miss the experience of being there for the first and only time.

Rabbi Akiva spent twenty-two years studying the *ET*; he knows the difference between a subject and an object. And with this knowledge, he takes control, from the Romans, of his own martyrdom, turning it into the fulfillment of a spiritual act, a spiritual act that, by the way, perfectly honors the full spectrum of being: Heaven, earth, ancestors, descendants, self, and other.

(In this way, he and Rabbi Yohanan's sister become the two *yuds*, creating the *alef* between them, Rabbi Akiva, the "male waters," external, revealed, and Rabbi Yohanan's sister, the "female waters," internal, hidden.)

Still: *How far, Master? How far?* How far can we take the spiritual discipline of Eternal Oneness? As far as Rabbi Akiva, experiencing his martyrdom as an opportunity to cleave to the Holy One? Our voices—along with the voices of Moses and of Rabbi Akiva's students and of the angels—rise in protest: *It's too hard!* we say. *I'm only a five-year-old child! The Holy One asks too much of us!*

And it's true. It is too hard: The Holy One gives us the reach and scope and apprehension of angels, while condemning us to death in vulnerable bodies that age and die and disappear.

How far are we supposed to take this idea, the idea that the world is filled with holiness and blessing and that, because a human being is created in the image of the Holy One, we can be a source of blessing and of holiness as well?

In the face of the Holy One's terrible silence, in the face of terrible human brutality, in the face of our heartbroken anguish, Rabbi Akiva's answer seems to be: *I will affirm the unity of the Holy One's Creation to my last breath.*

An angel, after all, doesn't have a last breath, and a corpse cannot affirm, through word or deed, the goodness, kindness, and mercy that we all know our lives must embody and our names represent.

Only a human being, that utterly insignificant and simultaneously magnificent creature who exists—for only a brief time—between these two extremes, the angel and the corpse, embodying them both, while transcending them both, can affirm the oneness of the entire spectrum of existence.

Though our lives and the world may appear dark and heavy at times, according to Rabbi Akiva, if we only correct our perception and see the holiness shining within everything, then we destroy the illusion of the separation even between ourselves and the holiness we perceive, and we become that holiness and we become that blessing.

ENDNOTES

The main sources I have relied upon for this work are *The Schottenstein Daf Yomi Edition of the Talmud Bavli*; *The Book of Legends Sefer Ha-Aggadah: Legends from the Talmud and Midrash*, edited by Hayim Nahman Bialik and Joshua Hana Ravnitzky and translated by William G. Braude; and *The Legends of the Rabbis*, by Judah Nadich. I have used the English translations from these works interchangeably, sometimes changing and retranslating passages. As far as names and Hebrew and Aramaic transliterations go, I have striven not for consistency but for the easiest comprehension for an English-language reader.

A NOVELIST READS THE TALMUD

xiv   *wage war against them*   Deuteronomy 2:9.

xiv   *would have been spared*   Bava Kamma 38a–b.

xvi   *tragic implications of Ulla's boorishness*   With the exception perhaps of Rav Abraham Isaac Kook, the major commentators of the *Aggadah* seem to me to have two principal agendas: (1) defining obscure tropes and (2) explaining away behaviors by the sages depicted there that seem to fly in the face of religious law.

xvi   *appropriate way of consoling a mourner*   The Rama, Rabbi Moshe Isserles, c. 1530–1572, the author of the *Mapah*, a gloss on the *Shulchan Aruch* that presents the Ashkenazic legal perspective, forbids the saying of "What can be done?" in a house of mourning. The Rosh, Rabbi Asher ben Yechiel, c. 1250–1327, author of one of the earliest codifications of rabbinic law, is silent on the matter. The *Yam Shel Shlomo*, Rabbi Solomon Luria, 1510–1574 (also called the *Maharshal* or the *Rashal*), known for his work on rabbinic law, *Yam Shel Shlomo*, and his Talmudic commentary *Chochmat Shlomo*, gently suggests that Ulla's methods might bring pain to a bereaved person and recommends extolling the virtues of the deceased instead.

xvi   *to him by night*   *Pirke de Rabbi Eliezer*, chapter 46, cited in Howard Schwartz, *Reimagining the Bible* (New York and Oxford: Oxford University Press, 1998).

xvi   *from between 3960 and 4260 (200 and 500 CE)*   There are actually two Talmuds, two versions of commentary, one compiled by scholars living in Babylon—the Babylonian Talmud, or, in Hebrew, the Bavli—the other by scholars living in the Land of Israel. For years, this earlier Talmud was known as the Palestinian Talmud, but for reasons having nothing to do with rabbinic scholarship, it's often now called the Yerushalmi, or the Jerusalem Talmud. Since it wasn't actually produced in Jerusalem, but in the rabbinic academies of the ancient Galilee, it's also known as the Talmud of the Land of Israel.

xviii *who can vouch for the historical man?* See the work of Jacob Neusner cited in Jeffrey L. Rubenstein, *Talmudic Stories: Narrative Art, Composition and Culture* (Baltimore and London: Johns Hopkins University Press, 1999), p. 297. Ulla lived sometime between the years 250 and 300 CE (4010 and 4060 on the Hebrew calendar). He used to travel from his home in the Land of Israel to visit the communities in exile in Babylonia.

xviii *a coherent system of imagery* I am reminded of Georg Büchner, the German novelist and playwright. See chapter 4, this volume.

xviii *midrashic literature* The Midrash is a body of imaginative and homiletic literature, serving as a commentary on the Bible, created by the rabbinic sages of the post-Temple era.

TIMELINE OF RELEVANT EVENTS

Mattis Kantor, *The Jewish Time Line Encyclopedia* (Lanham, MD: Rowman & Littlefield, 1992).

MEMO 1/CHAPTER 1

3   *remnant of that beauty* Bava Metzia 84a.

3   *as learned—as Rabbi Yohanan* Berakhot 20a; *Bava Metzia* 84a. Also see *Iggeret HaKoshesh*, chapter 5.

3   *while thinking of another* Shulchan Aruch (OC 240:2).

4   *with delicate silver sticks* Bava Kamma 117a.

4   *newly baptized lovers of other men* Genesis 39.

4   *like white geese to me* Berakhot 20a.

4   *approximation of Rabbi Yohanan's beauty* Bava Metzia 84a, as well as for the other parts of the story.

5   *Rabbi Yohanan has no beard* Ibid.

5   *or even—some say—a five-kav flask* Ibid. "According to Rabbi Yohanan, Rabbi Ishmael's is the size of a nine-*kav* flask; and according to Rav Pappa, Rabbi Yohanan's is the size of a five-*kav* flask, though some say a three-*kav* flask. As for Rav Pappa, his is the size of a Harpinian basket."

6   *Your beauty belongs to women* Ibid.

6   *Resh Lakish* Resh is an acronym for Rabbi *Shimon*.

7   *According to Rashi* Rashi is an acronym for Rabbi *Shlomo Yizthaki* (1040–

1104), who, having authored a comprehensive commentary on the Bible as well as the Talmud, is the father of all commentators.

7   *his animal aggression*   In the unbearable light of holiness, the things of this world reveal their true weight. Resh Lakish has perhaps not grown weaker; the world simply feels heavier to him. For this insight, I'm indebted to Carolina Ebeid.

8   *purify and make holy*   According to rabbinic law, a *mikvah*, a ritual bath, must contain no fewer than two hundred gallons of rainwater. As rain is water descended from Heaven, a *mikvah* is literally a pool of heavenly water on earth. In adherence to sacred law, a convert immerses in a *mikvah*, as does a bride before her wedding and a married woman at the conclusion of her menses.

8   *a stroke of storytelling genius*   In Aramaic, the first scene of our story comprises fewer than fifty words; and the second, with its quotation from the Mishnah, fewer than seventy. Thanks to his extreme brevity, the Aggadist must rely upon a handful of deft literary tricks, including, here, an astute use of juxtaposition. The two scenes are, in fact, twins. They have identical structures. By mirroring each other so completely, they amplify each other, their similarities and differences creating a field of meaning greater than that contained in each scene alone. In this way, the scenes themselves mirror their protagonists. Also, the identical structures are an oral tradition's memory aid. We can perhaps think of the written versions we have of these stories as analogous to a musician's "Fake Book," a collection of "lead sheets" with the minimum information needed about each song (lyrics, melody, chords). The bare-bones written version serves the same purpose for the storyteller.

8   *whoever he is, whoever he was*   Yes, I realize, he may in fact be no more than the collective handprint of numerous editors.

8   *one day* (yom ehad)   Genesis 1:4–5.

9   *ritual purity and its opposite*   *Taharah* and *tumah* in Hebrew.

9   *a category of their own*   See *Mishnah Kelim* 13:1.

11   *Resh Lakish fell ill*   Though often translated as different phrases—*Rabbi Yohanan was mortified*; *Resh Lakish fell ill*—the Aramaic word describing both men is the same: חלש (chalash). Not insignificantly, their mortifications follow their character type: Rabbi Yohanan's is intellectual, Resh Lakish's physical.

11   *a single passage of doubtful authenticity*   Which, curiously enough, mentions Shimon ben Lakish.

11   *alchemical romance*   Raphael Patai, *The Jewish Alchemists* (Princeton, NJ: Princeton University Press, 1994), p. 44. "It almost appears as if the sages of the Talmud purposefully shut their eyes to this important aspect of Greek and Jewish culture in Hellenistic Egypt. In any case, the talmudic

references that lend themselves to an alchemistic interpretation are few and vague."

11   *intellectual ancestry*   James Hillman, *Alchemical Psychology* (Putnam, CT: Spring Publications, 2010), p. 33.

11   *bar Nappaha*   Or in Hebrew, *ben ha-Nappach.*

12   *holy scholar*   In fact, ancient drawings of an alembic, an alchemical still—two vessels joined by a long tube—almost look like one well-endowed man confronting another (see "Ambix, cucurbit and retort of Zosimos," reproduced in *Collection des anciens alchimistes grecs*, by Marcelin Berthelot [3 vols., Paris, 1887–1888], at http://en.wikipedia.org/wiki/Timeline_of _chemistry).

12   *of stamping, shaping, and forming*   "Annealing (Metallurgy)," Wikipedia.

12   *It can only be pushed*   Jack C. Rich, *The Materials and Methods of Sculpture* (New York: Dover Publications, 1988), p. 129.

13   *le bain marie*   Patai, pp. 60–61. Mary the Jewess lived in the early third century.

13   *the water moderating the heat*   Hillman, p. 41.

13   *all those blades*   Hillman, p. 26.

14   *remind a penitent of his past*   *Shulchan Aruch, Choshen Mishpat* 228:4.

14   *dressed down his teacher in public*   Compare Rabbi Elazar ben Pedat's treatment of Rabbi Yohanan: "Whenever Rabbi Elazar was about to part from Rabbi Yohanan, he would do the following: If Rabbi Yohanan had to leave first, Rabbi Elazar would remain standing, bowed over, until Rabbi Yohanan disappeared from sight. But if Rabbi Elazar had to leave first, he would keep walking backwards until Rabbi Yohanan could no longer be seen" (*Yoma* 53a).

15   *his parents' earthly work is complete*   *Kiddushin* 31b.

15   *her cravings instantly ceased*   *Yoma* 82b.

15   *persists throughout his life*   In winter, for instance, he wears his arm and his head phylacteries all day long. In summer, when his head aches, he still wears his arm phylactery all day, claiming, "In my case, the name of the Holy One is profaned if I walk even four cubits without uttering words of Torah or wearing phylacteries" (JT *Berakhot* 2:3, 4c; *Yoma* 86a).

15   *the earth and the fullness thereof*   Psalms 24:1.

15   *exclusively for the study of Torah*   Once, for instance, he's ascending a staircase, leaning upon Rabbi Ammi and Rabbi Assi, when the stairs beneath them begin to sag. Fearful that the staircase may collapse, against all expectations, Rabbi Yohanan not only dashes to the top of the stairs unsupported, he carries his two aides along with him. When they ask, "Since your strength is so great, why do you require support?" he answers, "Otherwise what strength will I have left for Torah in my old age?" (*Ketubot* 62a).

15   *Tiberias to Sepphoris*   Tiberias and Sepphoris were the most important administrative and rabbinic centers of Roman Galilee. The two cities were both associated with Herod Antipas, who rebuilt Sepphoris sometime after a futile revolt in 4 BCE and still later founded Tiberias. They were connected by the major road built by Hadrian from Acco to the Sea of Galilee. See Stuart S. Miller, "Intercity Relations in Roman Palestine: The Case of Sepphoris and Tiberias," *AJS Review* 12 (1): 1–24.

16   *six days to create the entire world*   Exodus 31:17: "In six days the Holy One made Heaven and earth."

16   *forty days and forty nights*   Exodus 34:28: "And Moses was there with the Holy One forty days and forty nights." The story itself is from *Exodus Rabbah* 47:5 and *Leviticus Rabbah* 30:1.

16   *Rabbi Yohanan's earthly renunciations*   Yevamot 109b.

17   *than the rest of Creation*   The ancient rabbinic math doesn't hold up. (It often doesn't.) Because the Holy One creates the sun only on the fourth day, each of the fabled six days of Creation cannot be understood as a twenty-four-hour solar day, the sort of days and nights, in quality and kind, through which Moses worked as God's amanuensis. Cf. *Ramban (Nachmanides) Writings & Discourses, vol. II*, translated and annotated by Rabbi Dr. Charles B. Chavel (New York: Shilo Publishing House, 1978), pp. 64–65.

17   *in the dry months of summer*   Berakhot 43b.

19   *the two of them weep together*   Berakhot 5b.

20   *no needy among you*   Taanit 21a.

23   *a loan without witnesses*   Yoma 9b.

23   *Can one hand clap by itself?*   JT Sanhedrin 2:1.

23   *one who kills himself for them*   Gittin 57b.

23   *and seeks to slay him*   Sukkah 52b.

23   *one against the other*   Sanhedrin 24a.

24   *into Rabbi Abbahu's mouth*   Song of Songs Rabbah 1:6 #1.

24   *"God hates you!"*   Yoma 9b–10a.

25   *questions they put to him*   Taanit 21a.

25   *Throw ben Lakish into the water!*   Megilla 28b.

25   *sold himself . . . to cannibals*   Or, some say, as an unarmed contestant in the gladiatorial games.

26   *he's hidden a stone*   This is the same sort of "bottle" the sages' male members are compared to, for what it's worth.

26   *And he killed them all*   Gittin 47a.

26   *swathed with bands of fire*   JT, *Shekalim* 6:1, 49d. According to Resh Lakish, while writing the Torah, Moses wipes the reed against his hair—and this fiery ink spill is why his face glows when he comes down from the mountain. See Exodus 34:35.

26 *no water except Torah* Bava Kamma 17a.

26 *neither can he go three days without the Torah* Bava Kamma 82a. Hence, the establishment of the thrice-weekly reading of the Torah.

26 *he would take the pitcher and drink* Ecclesiastes Rabbah 3:9 #1.

27 *to desist from it altogether* Berakhot 5b.

27 *only with the fellows of his craft* Ecclesiastes Rabbah 3:9 #1.

28 *nor big-shot ramblers* Woody Guthrie, "This Train Is Bound for Glory," 1958.

28 *the wood choppers and the* water carriers Deuteronomy 29:9–10.

29 *pierce him with this knowledge* In Adlerian psychotherapy, this analytic method is called "Spitting in the Client's Soup."

30 *central figure* Adin Steinsaltz, *Talmudic Images* (Jerusalem: Koren Publishers, 2010), p. 71.

31 *male and female he created them* Genesis 1:26–27.

32 *they were not ashamed* Genesis 2:21–25.

35 *she passes an idolatrous altar* Genesis Rabbah 63:6.

35 *a rapist of betrothed maidens* Ibid. #12.

35 *sparing his brother Jacob's dignity* Ibid. #8.

35 *he kills his first man* Ibid. #12.

35 *Esau wept aloud* Genesis 27:34–38.

36 *Let your widows rely on me* Jeremiah 49:7–11.

36 *His doom is sealed.* Even if we translate ואיננו not as "He is no more," but as "There will be no one to say, 'Leave your widows and orphans to me . . . ,'" we can understand Rabbi Yohanan as saying, "Look, though coarse and violent, at least your husband isn't an Esau."

36 *garments red* Genesis Rabbah 63:6 #12.

37 *Esau's long-simmering rage against him* Genesis 33:1–3.

37 *what he did to your father* Taanit 9a.

37 *the Jabbok River* Genesis 32:25.

37 *The stranger gives him a new name* Genesis 32:19–32.

38 *Your beauty belongs to women* We can almost hear the Shakespearean echo of this: "Call me but love, and I am newly baptized."

38 *and dissolved into tears* The Hebrew word for mercy—רחמי—is related to רחם, the Hebrew word for womb. In a sense, the sages pray that, in his mercy, the Holy One will send Rabbi Yohanan a womb. Born of a fiery furnace, Rabbi Yohanan dies in that watery womb.

39 *always together, always threatening to part* Samuel Beckett, *Waiting for Godot: A Tragicomedy in Two Acts* (New York: Grove Press, 1954).

39 *against her will, by the way* Pirkei Avot: Ethics of the Fathers, 4:22.

39 *The Hebrew root of the word* Lakish לקש. See Matityahu Clark, *Etmological Dictionary of Biblical Hebrew* (Jerusalem, New York: Feldheim Publishers, 1999).

39 *when life is over* Pirkei Avot: Ethics of the Fathers, 2:5.

41 *they've established bathhouses*   *Shabbat* 33b–34a, and for the rest of the story.

45 *every crumb and scrap*   *Nedarim* 49b–50a; *Taanit* 30a–b.

45 *provided me with a robe*   *Nedarim* 49b.

46 *he constructs a second set*   See Exodus 34:1–4.

46 *the first speaker on every occasion*   *Shabbat* 33b.

48 *the mother of all life*   Genesis 3:20.

49 not *the Elijah in the Bible's Book of Kings*   See Book of Kings.

49 *with utter destruction*   Malachi 3:24–25.

50 *communing with the Holy One*   1 Kings 19:5–10.

51 *immediately consumed by fire*   Compare Elijah's exit from his cave: he too comes upon a man plowing. Upon seeing Elijah, Elisha says, "Let me kiss my father and mother goodbye, and I will follow you," becoming Elijah's attendant (1 Kings 19:19–21).

51 *same anonymous hand*   Both stories juxtapose scenes with identical structures; both feature a female figure with values counter to the protagonists'; both hide the story's themes in scriptural quotations.

52 *for no more than one year*   A sweet gesture: a mourner recites *Kaddish*, the prayer for the dead, no more than eleven months in order not to give the impression that the departed require a full term in purgatory.

52 *I've always been greedy that way*   "The Night Comes On" (Bad Monk Publishing, Sony/ATV Songs LLC, 1984).

53 *the end of the Book of Malachi*   Elsewhere (*Sukkah* 45b): "It is reported that Rabbi Shimon bar Yohai used to say: 'I see those who will behold the Shekinah in the hereafter, and they are few. If there be a thousand, I and my son are among them. If a hundred, I and my son are among them. If only two, I and my son are the ones.'"

53 *must be interpreted*   *Sanhedrin* 97b.

54 *two words with a single breath*   Debbie Lansford Settler, the daughter of my childhood piano teacher Pat O'Shea, claims she heard Janis Joplin sing two notes simultaneously. For what it's worth: the guitarist Pierre Bensusan is able to whistle and hum simultaneously in two parts.

54 *Rabbi Shimon's son-in-law*   Though, in other texts, he is more often identified as Rabbi Shimon's *father*-in-law.

55 *to the resurrection of the dead*   *Song of Songs Rabbah* 1:1; also *Mishnah Sotah* 9:12.

55 *the ability to raise the dead*   See, for example, *Deuteronomy Rabbah* 3:3.

58 *often conflated with Rome*   Not only in rabbinic literature. See Federico Fellini's *La Dolce Vita*.

58 *a simple man of tents*   Genesis 25:27.

58 *at the city of Shechem*   Genesis 33:18.

58 *without defiling themselves* As I understand it, the depressingness of death severs the feeling of connection to the Holy One, and the priests, working in the Temple, in the space between Heaven and earth, avoid the sight of death as a way of keeping themselves joyous.

63 *Woe to me if you didn't* *Taanit* 21a.

64 *the holiness of his person* We will encounter this theme again soon when we examine Rabbi Pinhas ben Yair's life more closely.

64 *no point in moving him out* For this insight, I'm indebted to Peter Bein.

65 *like wind-blown straw* Isaiah 41:2.

65 *Caesar has them executed* *Taanit* 21a; *Sanhedrin* 108b–109a.

67 *dust, maggots, and worms* *Pirkei Avot* 3:1.

68 *the fifth dimension of morality* See Aryeh Kaplan, *Sefer Yetzirah: The Book of Creation* (Northvale, NJ: Jason Aronson, 1995).

68 *who have never been born* Ecclesiastes 4:2–3. Tradition ascribes the authorship of not only Ecclesiastes but also the Book of Proverbs to King Solomon.

68 *words of the living God* *Eruvin* 13b.

68 *before their own* Ibid.

69 *Now, go and learn* *Shabbat* 31a.

69 *but a feast for the senses* Jackson Browne et al., "Looking East" (Swallow Turn Music, 1996).

69 *and a bruising affair* Who, for instance, having been once, would ever choose to return to high school?

70 *let him* examine *his deeds* *Eruvin* 13b.

70 *Noah's world or Lot's Sodom* Genesis, chapters 7 and 19.

70 *binds up their wounds* Psalms 147:3.

71 *time yields to him* *Eruvin* 13b.

71 *Rabban Yohanan ben Zakkai* *Rabbi*, *Rav*, and *Rabban* are all honorifics for teachers of the Torah. *Rabbi* was used in the Land of Israel, *Rav* in Babylonia, and *Rabban* for the *Nasi*, the head of the Sanhedrin.

72 *recognize your strength* JT *Sanhedrin* 1:2, 19a.

72 *the very best of Rabbi Akiva's rules* *Gittin* 67a.

MEMO 3 A, B, C/CHAPTER 3

82 *this was true worldwide* http://www.ted.com/talks/michael_norton_how_to_buy_happiness.html.

87 *carry even his own cloak* *Song of Songs Rabbah* 5:14:3.

87 *the stock of Rabbi Shimon bar Yohai* *Tanhuma* 13 #38.

88 *carry his own cloak* *Pesikta de-Rav Kahana* 11:22.

88 *the next time we see him* This is my construction. There is, of course, no "next time" between stories in the Talmud.

88   *the mulish side of his character remains*   This story, found in the same section of the Talmud as the story of Nahum ish Gamzu, offers a variation on the importance of seeing and being seen clearly.

90   *both are being addressed*   Although in all fairness the "you" in Hebrew, unlike in the English translation, is unambiguously singular and masculine.

91   *Torah scrolls, phylacteries, and mezuzahs*   Taanit 20b.

91   *wild beasts that prowl at night*   Psalms 104:20.

93   *no longer seems quite so innocent*   One thinks of the Soviet poet Osip Mandelstam, sent to the gulag for reading a poem denouncing Stalin to a small group of friends gathered in his apartment. He was incorrect to assume he shared a sympathetic understanding with at least one of the friends gathered there.

95   *is like the person himself*   Kiddushin 41b.

06   *keeps his soul from troubles*   Proverbs 21:23.

98   *Even my flesh rests secure*   Psalms 16:9.

98   *a cow could pass between them*   Bava Metzia 84a.

99   *father's and son's lives repeat*   Jackson Browne, "Lawless Avenues," *Lives in the Balance* (Elektra/Asylum Records, 1986).

102   *food stuffs from afar*   Proverbs 31:14.

103   *his colleagues do not consider him worthy of the honor*   According to the *Ben Yehoyada*.

104   *did not protest as I should have done*   One thinks of Bob Dylan's "Talkin' John Birch Paranoid Blues": "So now I'm sittin' home investigatin' myself! Hope I don't find out anything . . ." (Special Rider Music, 1970, renewed 1998).

105   *they were able to enter*   Bava Metzia 83b–84a.

105   *but just ordinary asses*   Shabbat 112b.

106   *that I may pass through you*   Hullin 7a–b.

107   *is already feeling fairly cross*   The commentators launch into a small discussion about whether Rabbi Pinhas ben Yair could really have split a body of water more times than Moses. One explanation: Rabbi Pinhas ben Yair only split the river once, but in three stages. "Perhaps initially only the upper waters of the river split, allowing Rabbi Pinhas ben Yair to pass through without drowning, but the lower waters continued to flow up to the height of his neck. He then ordered the river to split further, so that the other man could cross without wetting the wheat he was carrying on his shoulder. Nevertheless, the water remained deep enough to ruin the Arab's merchandise until Rabbi Pinhas ben Yair ordered it to split completely, so that even the Arab could cross with his wares. In sum, the river split only once." Cf. *Toras Chaim, Rosh Yosef, Hullin* 7a.

107   *a land he cannot enter*   Deuteronomy 34:4.

108   *his own father's table*   Hullin 7b.

108   *come take your stores*   Deuteronomy Rabbah 3:3; JT Demai 1:3, 22a.

109 *came down and saved her* Ibid.

110 *a stumbling block before the blind* Leviticus 19:14.

112 *how much more so after their deaths* Hullin 7a–b; JT *Demai* 1:3, 22a.

112 *which he did not eat* JT *Kiddushin* 4:12.

113 *how much less if he had two* JT *Berakhot* 1:2.

114 *take leave of him a second time* Moed Katan 9a.

115 *you have to marry another* Moed Katan 9a–b.

MEMO 4/CHAPTER 4

124 *or Side Four in Harrison's case* The album's third disc, Sides Five and Six, is essentially a bonus disc containing improvised instrumentals.

126 *Will innocence be regained?* This is, it seems to me, the only essential question in life. To quote Yeats: "All hatred driven hence, the soul recovers radical innocence and learns at last that it is self-delighting, self-appeasing, self-affrighting, and that its own sweet will is Heaven's will."

127 *According to tradition* Rav Judah, citing an opinion of Samuel's.

128 *outweigh them all in wisdom* Pirkei Avot 2:10.

128 *his not infrequent trips to Heaven* Described not in the Bible, but in the Midrash.

128 *issue from his family line* Numbers Rabbah 19:7.

129 *to the blast of ram's horns* Exodus 19:14–20:18.

130 *Rabbi Jeremiah* Rabbi Joshua and Rabbi Eliezer belong to the second generation of *tannaim*; Rabbi Jeremiah to the third and fourth generation of *amoraim*. There are six generations of *tannaim*, spanning 10 CE to 220 CE, and six generations of *amoraim*, from 219 CE to 500 CE.

130 *One must follow the majority* Exodus 23:2.

132 *dabbling in its secret orgiastic rites* Peter Schäfer, *Jesus in the Talmud* (Princeton, NJ: Princeton University Press, 2007), p. 11.

133 *surrounded by strong women* Genesis Rabbah 17:8.

134 *they'd be even more learned* Taanit 7a–b; Nedarim 50b.

134 *An older sage* Rabbi Dosa ben Harkynos.

134 *the holy words spoken there* JT Yevamot 1:6, 3a.

134 *and all that it holds* Psalms 24:1.

137 *says the Lord of Hosts* Haggai 2:8.

137 *to study his Torah* Pirkei de-Rabbi Eliezer 1; Avot de Rabbi Natan 6; Genesis Rabbah 42:1; Tanhuma; Lekh Lekhah 10: in Sefer Ha-Aggadah.

137 *a penalty for having fasted on Hanukah* JT Nedarim 81 (40d).

138 *not heard from my teacher* Sukkah 28a.

138 *not heard from his teacher* Ibid.

138 *like the Ark of the Covenant* Song of Songs Rabbah 1:3 #1.

139   *this world and the World to Come*   Sanhedrin 101a.

139   *a pen into the ink tube*   Rabbi Akiva, topping the two of them, claims, "It is not possible for me to say as my teachers have, for in fact my teachers did take something from it, while I have taken no more than one who smells a citron: he who smells, enjoys it, while the citron loses nothing" (*Song of Songs Rabbah* 1:3:1).

143   *Yohanan ben Zakkai escaped death*   Sotah 9:14.

145   *when much of England still lay in ruins*   *George Harrison: Living in the Material World*, directed by Martin Scorsese, 2012.

147   *he insults him as well!*   Berakhot 27b.

148   *who hold that it does*   One thinks prospectively of Copernicus and Galileo, each in conflict with the Catholic Church over the earth's place in the cosmos.

149   *I have no festivals but these*   Leviticus 23:4.

149   *those of little distinction*   Rosh Hashana 24b–25a.

149   *rendering it unfit for sacrifice*   Because the Temple had fallen by the time of our story, no sacrifices would be taking place. Still, the calf would have to be redeemed, exchanged for money, with a priest.

150   *Huzpit the Interpreter stops*   Becoros 36a.

150   *from Ezra the Scribe*   According to the Books of Ezra and Nehemiah, Ezra the Scribe, upon returning from the Babylonian exile, founded the Great Assembly of scholars and prophets, and reintroduced the Torah in Jerusalem. He is, in Leonard Cohen's phrase, "the little Jew who wrote the Bible."

152   *marrying a daughter of Israel?*   See Deuteronomy 23:4.

152   *or perhaps a coal maker*   "Or perhaps a coal maker" is from Rashi's note. But I've added the detail into the dialogue. I like how both details contribute to Rabban Gamliel's characterization.

153   *an intellectual challenge was to be expected*   Sifre Deuteronomy #16.

155   *sacrifices on the Temple walls*   Leviticus 1–5.

156   *the remaining three*   Bava Metzia 59b for the entire story.

156   *a colleague he considers his inferior*   See chapter 2.

158   *not proliferate in the House of Israel*   Bava Metzia 59b.

159   *and be instantly shamed*   Hebrew Prayerbook.

160   *a bit of prophetic vision*   Genesis 49.

161   *left an entire generation fatherless*   Sanhedrin 68a; Avot de-Rabbi Natan 25.

162   *our superior*   The term is *Berabbi*, a title of distinction.

162   *And he stood over them*   Genesis 18:8.

162   *stand and serve us drinks*   Kiddushin 32b.

163   *He was a virtuous man*   Berakhot 16b.

163   *your children after you*   Leviticus 25:45–46.

163   *the slave wins his freedom*   See Exodus 21:26.

164   *maintains until his death*   Bava Kamma 74b.

165 *by underestimating his opponents*   Eruvin 53b.

165 *as you would Rabban Gamliel*   Derekh Eretz Rabbah 5.

166 *the honorific rabbi*   The irony here is profound. Rabbi Yohanan ben Nuri is a kind of mirror for Rabbi Joshua: poor like Rabbi Joshua, upon Rabbi Joshua's recommendation, he was elevated by Rabban Gamliel to a position of authority; unlike Rabbi Joshua, Rabbi Yohanan ben Nuri is a truly humble man, who, as we see, doesn't chafe under Rabban Gamliel's authority. See *Horayot* 10a–b.

166 *whatsoever to this statement*   Eruvin 41a.

167 *I am searching*   Shabbat 152a.

167 *more and more impoverished*   Sanhedrin 39b.

167 *isn't it a pity?*   George Harrison, "Isn't It a Pity" (Harrisongs Ltd., 1970).

MEMO 5/CHAPTER 5

171 *the humblest of men*   See Numbers 12:3.

171 *how it arose in my mind*   Menachot 29b.

172 *as a five-year-old child*   Spectacle: Elvis Costello with . . . (Sundance Channel, broadcast January 10, 2010).

173 *presented in greater detail*   Berachot 61b.

173 *makes peace and creates evil*   Isaiah 45:7.

173 *with all your soul*   Deuteronomy 6:5.

174 *and* this *its reward*   See the Yom Kippur Prayer Book.

175 *from entering the Promised Land*   Deuteronomy 34:4.

175 *our childhood nursery rhymes*   For instance, the truth is: Some children cannot grow up to be president.

175 *guilty as charged*   Bava Metzia 37b.

175 *with a discerning mind*   Chagigah 11b.

176 *had he never been born*   Ibid.

176 *no business with the hidden*   Chagigah 13a.

176 *flickering penumbra of flame*   Ezekiel 1.

176 *Seraphim stood above him*   Isaiah 6:1–2.

176 *who saw the king*   Chagigah 13b.

177 *a small thing*   Sukkah 28a.

177 *stand before my eyes*   Psalms 101:7.

177 *the death of his saints*   Psalms 116:15.

178 *and vomit it*   Proverbs 25:16.

178 *descended in peace*   Chagigah 14b, 15b.

178 *is worthy of making use of my glory*   Chagigah 15b.

179 *as great in Torah*   Sanhedrin 17b; Kiddushin 14b.

179 *can hope for saintliness*   Berakhot 57b.

179 *Scholars of later generations*   Including Rabbi Yohanan, Rav, Abaye, and Rava.

179 *I am the ben Azzai of these parts*   JT *Bikkurim* 2:2; *Kiddushin* 20a; *Eruvin* 29a; JT *Peah* 6:3.

179 *referring to his teacher Rabbi Akiva*   *Bekhorot* 58a.

179 *assiduousness leaves the world*   *Sotah* 49a and elsewhere.

179 *the entire Torah written in him*   *Avot de Rabbi Natan* 11; *Yalkut Proverbs* 964.

179 *to fulfill another commandment*   *Pirkei Avot* 4:2.

180 *the sound of the ram's horn*   Exodus 20:15.

180 *have shared a bed*   *Ketubot* 63a; *Sotah* 49a.

180 *and multiply unfulfilled*   Genesis 9:6.

181 *continue through other people*   *Yevamot* 63b. One is reminded of Rabbi Yossi's statement from the same tractate (109b): "He who says he has only Torah doesn't even have Torah."

181 *rabble of rebellious cousins*   For Aaron and Miriam, see Numbers 12:1; for Nadav and Avihu, see Leviticus 10; for Korach and his band, see Numbers 16–17.

181 *even the title of rabbi*   He and ben Zoma are not sufficiently worldly to have their legal decisions affect real life.

181 *engrave themselves upon the Law*   One is reminded of T. S. Eliot's admiring put-down of Henry James: "A mind so fine no idea could violate it."

181 *may hope for wisdom*   *Berakhot* 57b.

182 *is talking about himself*   There are no capital letters in the Hebrew alphabet, and so, unlike in English, there is no tradition of uppercasing pronouns that refer to the Holy One. Also, in the traditional rabbinic formula for a blessing, pronouns tend to shift. One starts a blessing in the second person singular and finishes it in the third: *Blessed are YOU who sanctified us with HIS commandments.*

182 *these things ready for me*   *Berakhot* 58a.

184 *and there was light*   Genesis 1:3.

184 *The Holy One made the Sky*   Genesis 1:6–7.

185 *by the breath of his mouth*   Psalms 33:6; *Genesis Rabbah* 4:6; *Yalkut Bereshis* 6.

185 *a Sky in the middle of it*   Genesis 1:8.

185 *so that land appears*   Genesis 1:9–10.

185 *the Heavens broke open*   Genesis 7:11.

186 *unworld of First Things*   This is what, in *Pirkei Avot* 5:8, is meant by the tongs with which the first tongs were made.

187 *after that, we're told, he dies*   *Chagigah* 15a.

187 *sees Aher in a dream*   Or for that matter, King Ahab, the prophet Jeremiah, the Book of Job, or the Book of Lamentations. *Berakhot* 57b.

188 *without a bridle*   *Avot de Rabbi Natan*, chapter 24.

189   *expresses them distinctly*   Ibid.

189   *written on smudged paper*   Pirkei Avot 4:25.

189   *of Kfar HaBavli*   His name is not enough. We are also given his address.

189   *or drinks aged wine*   Pirkei Avot 4:26.

190   *does not even contain new wine*   Pirkei Avot 4:27.

190   *and threw away the peel*   Chagigah 15a.

190   *and threw away the kernel*   Ibid.

190   *by name*   Ibid.

191   *more than his beginning*   Job 42:12.

191   *twice as much as he had before*   Job 42:10.

192   *from the Book of Ecclesiastes*   Ecclesiastes 7:8.

192   *comes back to him in his old age*   Elisha ben Avuyah used to say: "A man may study Torah for twenty years and forget it in two. . . . Of him, Solomon said, 'I went by the field of the slothful, and by the vineyard of the man void of understanding; and lo, it was all grown over with nettles, and the stone wall thereof was broken down' [Proverbs 24:30–31]. Once the wall collapses, the entire vineyard, all of it, goes to rack and ruin." See *Avot de Rabbi Natan* 24.

193   *unto the heart of Heaven*   Deuteronomy 4:11.

194   *Another verse from the Book of Ecclesiastes*   Ecclesiastes 7:14.

194   *the crooked can be made straight*   Isaiah 45:2.

194   *a righteous man in Gehenna*   Once again, the Aggadist anticipates the work of Samuel Beckett. In *Waiting for Godot*, Pozzo addresses Estragon: "The tears of the world are a constant quantity. For each one who begins to weep somewhere else another stops. The same is true of the laugh."

195   *fine gold be exchanged for it*   Job 28:17.

195   *only return to dust*   For this insight, I'm indebted to Carolina Ebeid and Anat Benzvi.

196   *Return, O backsliding children*   Jeremiah 3:14.

196   *and I will return unto you*   Malachi 3:7.

196   *to return his teacher to the fold*   Resh Lakish, for instance, his mind so preoccupied with Torah, often unintentionally walked beyond the Sabbath limits. JT *Berakhot* 5:1.

196   *expounding upon the holy Torah*   Of all the gin joints in all the cities in all the world . . .

196   *nor apart from it*   I'm reminded of a story I heard about Isaac Bashevis Singer and Chaim Grade, two of the greatest Yiddish writers of the twentieth century. A friend of Grade's told me that Grade despised Singer for his abandonment of Orthodox Jewish practice. "But Grade did the same thing," I said. "Yes," the friend said, "but he didn't suffer any guilt over it, and *that's* what Grade couldn't stand!"

197   *yet freedom of choice is given*   Pirkei Avot 3:19.

197	*except for the reverence for Heaven* Berakhot 33b.
198	*for the wicked* Isaiah 48:22.
198	*your iniquity is marked before me* Jeremiah 2:22.
198	*over to children and madmen* Bava Batra 12b.
198	*they seek your life* Jeremiah 4:30.
198	*Who are you to recite my statutes* Psalms 50:16.
200	*that you may fare well and have a long life* Deuteronomy 22:7.
201	*an Eye that sees and an Ear that hears* Pirkei Avot 2:1.
202	*Judge of All the Earth not act justly?* Genesis 18:25.
202	*like a Roman warrior* In 3826 (66 CE), two thousand Roman horsemen descend on Jerusalem.
202	*doubts about Rabbi Meir's piety* From stories concerning Rabbi Meir's wife and his sister-in-law, a reader could conclude that a woman was sexually safer in a Roman brothel than in Rabbi Meir's house. See *Avodah Zara* 18b; Rashi on *Avodah Zara* 18a.
203	*up to his being crushed* Psalms 90:3.
203	*Lie down until morning* Ruth Rabbah 6:4; see Ruth 3:13.
204	*marry, or "redeem," her* Ibid.
204	*The Holy One is good to all* Psalms 145:9.
205	*couldn't stand up to you, O Master* Chagigah 15a; JT *Chagigah* 2:1, 77a–b; *Ecclesiastes Rabbah* 7:8:1; *Ruth Rabbah* 6:4; *Kiddushin* 39b; in *Sefer-Ha-Aggadah*.
207	*underruled by his children* See chapter 4.
207	*their will upon the Divine Will* "Make his will your will and he will make your will his will." *Pirkei Avot* 2:4.
208	*the end of Job's life more than its beginning* Job 42:12.
208	*Akiva was an illiterate boor* Avot de Rabbi Natan 6.
208	*he breaks no bones* Pesachim 49b.
208	*Another quotation* Job 14:19.
210	*ink written on smudged paper* Pirkei Avot 4:25.
211	*and he will love you* Proverbs 9:8.
211	*now go out and fight it* Judges 9:38.
212	*beholds every precious thing* Job 28:9–10.
212	*he separates from life* Kiddushin 66b.
212	*on more than one occasion literally* See Avodah Zara 10b and 20a; *Nedarim* 50a–b.
212	*fill the land with divine wisdom* Yevamot 62b; Genesis Rabbah 61:3; Ecclesiastes Rabbah 11:6:1.
213	*the Hebrew morpheme ET* Chagigah 12a.
213	*Whatever the Merciful One does is for the best* Berakhot 60b.
214	*between water and water* Genesis 1:6.

214 *Do not say, "Water! Water!"* Zohar I 26b; *Tikunei HaZohar* 40.

214 *is spelled* שי (yesh) *and Sovereignty* שי (shay) At least according to the *Zohar*. In modern Hebrew, *yesh* means *there is*, and *shay* means *a gift*. I prefer this reading: between the upper waters and the lower waters, there is a gift.

GLOSSARY

Abba, Rabbi: moved from the Land of Israel to Babylonia; active between c. 320 and 371 CE.

Abbahu, Rabbi: a student of Rabbi Yohanan and Resh Lakish; active in the Land of Israel sometime between 279 and 320 CE. When he died it was said that even the marble pillars in Caesarea shed tears.

Aggadah: literally "telling," referring to the ethical, legendary, and philosophical part of Talmudic literature, as opposed to the *halakhic*, or legal-ritual, part.

Aggadist: This is my coinage, referring to the Teller of the Tales. In reality, many tongues and hands, mostly anonymous, created and shaped the oral tradition of the *Aggadah*.

Akhbera: a city north of the Sea of Galilee.

Ammonite: a member of the ancient nation of Ammon, located east of the Jordan River in present-day Jordan. According to the Bible, the Ammonites and the Moabites are descended from the sons resulting from the couplings of Lot and his daughters (Genesis 19:31–38). Deuteronomy 23:3 explicitly forbids Ammonites and Moabites from joining the people of Israel.

Antoninus: a Roman emperor, though it's not clear which one. Various scholars identify him with Marcus Aurelius, Septimius Severus, Caracalla, Elagabalus, and Lucius Verus.

Aramaic: the language of the Gemara and of Onklelos, a translation of the Torah, written in Hebrew characters.

Asya: someplace in Asia Minor, though it's unclear exactly where.

Av Bet Din: literally, "the Father of the House of Law"; the most learned member of the seventy-member Sanhedrin, the ancient Rabbinical Court, second-in-command to the Nasi, the court's head.

Babylonia: the ancient cultural region of southeastern Mesopotamia between the Tigris and Euphrates Rivers, settled around 4000 BCE. It is modern southern Iraq from Baghdad to the Persian Gulf. The Babylonian exile is the period during which a number of the ancient Judeans were held captive in Babylonia, roughly between 423 and 348 BCE. Torah scholarship thrived in Babylonia. The community there, established in the wake of the destruction of the first Temple, lasted for almost 1,500 years.

BCE/CE: abbreviations of "Before the Common Era" and "Common Era," traditional Jewish designations for BC and AD.

Ben/bar: *son of* in Hebrew and Aramaic, respectively.

Ben Kalba Savua: along with Ben Zizit Ha-Kaset and Nakdimon ben Guryon, one of the first-century grandees of Jerusalem who periodically show up in these tales, often as a trio. He was Rabbi Akiva's father-in-law. His name literally means "satisfied son of a dog." Whoever entered his house as hungry as a dog, it is said, left satisfied.

Ben Zizit Ha-Kaset: another of the trio of first-century grandees of Jerusalem. His name, which translates as "son of a tasseled pillow," refers to his being invited to Roman banquets.

Bible: called the Tanakh in Hebrew, an acronym for Torah (the Five Books of Moses), Nevi'im (Prophets), and Ketuvim (Writings). Its thirty-nine books are not exactly the same or in the same order as the Christian Bible.

Biri: a town north of Safed in the Upper Galilee.

Canaanite: a resident of the Land of Israel before the conquest, typically used in the Talmud to denote a non-Hebrew resident of the land.

Day of Atonement: *Yom Kippur* in Hebrew; a day of repentance and atonement, observed on the tenth day of the month Tishrei. On Yom Kippur, one refrains from eating and drinking, bathing, the wearing of leather shoes, anointing oneself with perfumes, and marital relations. These five restrictions correspond to the five levels of the soul.

Edom: in the Bible, a kingdom of the first millennium BCE, inhabiting a part of the Negev south of Judea and the Dead Sea, associated with the descendants of Esau. In the rabbinic imagination, Rome is equated with Edom, and the Roman Empire is thought of as embodying the characteristics of its violent progenitor Esau.

Ein Ya'akov (*The Eye of Jacob*): a 1516 compilation of all the Aggadic material in the Babylonian Talmud, edited by Jacob ibn Habib and, after his death, by his son Rabbi Levi ibn Habib.

Gehenna: a fiery, purgatorial place of cleansing for the soul after death, lasting for no more than twelve months, depending upon the wickedness of the soul in question.

Gemara: the commentary on the Mishnah, the Oral Law; together, the two make up the Talmud.

Gidel, Rav: third-century Babylonian rabbi, a student of Rav. He later went to the Land of Israel and studied with Rabbi Yohanan.

Hadrian: Roman emperor from 117 to 138 CE.

Halakhah: literally, "The Way"; the legal-ritual parts of the Talmud; and connotatively the law itself.

Hanina ben Dosa, Rabbi: miracle worker and pupil-colleague of Rabban Yohanan ben Zakkai, active first century CE.

Hanukah: an eight-day holiday commemorating the rededication of the Temple in Jerusalem in the second century BCE.

Haver: literally, "a friend"; in rabbinic parlance the term connotes a sacred companion, a soul brother.

Imi, Rabbi: beyond his having been kidnapped and subsequently rescued by Resh Lakish, no other information pertaining to Rabbi Imi seems to exist in the Talmud.

Israelite: a resident of the ancient Land of Israel. Terminology is difficult here: *Israelite, Hebrew, Judean, child of Israel, child of Jacob,* and *Jew* are only somewhat interchangeable. Each has a different geographical, historical, and sociological connotation.

Jeremiah, Rabbi: more commonly Rabbi Yirmiah, active between 290 and 350 CE. Originally from Babylonia, he moved to the Land of Israel.

Jordan River: in the Bible, the eastern border of the Promised Land; today, the river divides Israel and the Palestinian territories from the Kingdom of Jordan, running from the Hula Valley to the Dead Sea.

Judean Desert: *Midbar Yehuda* in Hebrew; a desert in present-day Israel and the West Bank, east of Jerusalem, extending from the northeastern Negev to the east of Beit El, having terraces with escarpments that descend to the Dead Sea.

Kabbalah: the Jewish mystical tradition.

Kav: a Talmudic unit of measurement equaling roughly two dozen eggs in volume.

Kohanim (kohen, singular): the priestly caste, descendants of Aaron the High Priest, Moses's brother.

Laodicea: an ancient city in what is present-day Turkey.

Matzah: unleavened bread, eaten during the holiday of Passover, in commemoration of the Hebrews' rushed Exodus from Egypt.

Messiah: in Jewish tradition, a nondivine descendant of King David, through whose leadership will come the spiritual and political redemption of the Jewish people in the Land of Israel, ushering in a thousand-year period of universal peace.

Metatron: an archangel charged with, among many other tasks, recording the good deeds of the children of Israel, an activity during which he was originally permitted to sit, until Elisha ben Avuyah, having ascended with Rabbi Akiva to the Supernal Orchard, saw him and mistook his sitting as an expression of divine sovereignty. Various traditions associate him with Enoch from the Book of Genesis. He appears as a character in my novel *A Curable Romantic.*

Midrash: from the root meaning "to seek out" or "inquire," a body of exegetical texts and homiletic stories created by the Talmudic sages that provides an open analysis of the Torah, often filling in the gaps in the biblical narratives. The word refers both to the activity of this kind of analysis and to the texts produced by it.

Migdal Gedor: an imaginary place, the name literally means "an enclosed tower."

Mikvah (pl. mikvot): a ritual bath containing, in accordance with rabbinic law, no fewer than two hundred gallons of rainwater. As rain is water descended from Heaven, a *mikvah* is literally a pool of heavenly water on earth. It is a womblike place of transformation: a convert immerses in a *mikvah,* as does a bride before her wedding and a married woman at the conclusion of her menses.

Mishnah: the Oral Law, given, according to tradition, by the Holy One to Moses on Mount Sinai, as a commentary on the Torah, the Written Law. The Talmud comprises the Mishnah and the Gemara.

Nakdimon ben Guryon: one of the trio of first-century Jerusalem grandees who periodically show up in these tales. Nakdimon's stores of food helped to feed the city during the Roman siege.

Nasi: literally "Prince"; the head of the Sanhedrin, the ancient Supreme Rabbinical Court.

Nathan, Rabbi: It's difficult to know which Rabbi Nathan is meant in the story of Akhnai's oven. I'm assuming it is Rabbi Nathan the Babylonian, a second-century rabbi who moved from Babylonia to the Land of Israel.

New Year: in Hebrew, *Rosh ha-Shana*, literally, *the head of the year*; the first of the High Holy Days, celebrated on the first day of the month of Tishrei, it commemorates the creation of the human race.

Passover: in Hebrew, *Pesakh*; celebrated on the fifteenth day of the month of Nissan, the holiday commemorates the Exodus of the Hebrews from Egypt. Unleavened bread is eaten during Passover, and a ritual dinner, called a Seder, is held, during which a text called the *Hagaddah* is read. Rabbi Elazar ben Azaryah makes an appearance in the *Hagaddah*, as does the question "Why is tonight different from all other nights?"

The Path of the Just: an eighteenth-century how-to manual for sainthood written by poet, playwright, and mystic Rabbi Chaim Moshe Luzatto (1706–1747).

Phylacteries: in Hebrew, *tefillin*; a set of small black leather boxes on straps containing scrolls of parchment inscribed with verses from the Torah, which are traditionally worn on the head and the arm by men during weekday morning prayers.

Rabbah bar Shila: Babylonian rabbi, active between c. 290 and 350 CE.

Rabbi/Rav/Rabban: honorifics for teachers of the Torah. *Rabbi* was used in the Land of Israel, *Rav* in Babylonia, and *Rabban* for the *Nasi*, the head of the Sanhedrin.

Rabbi Jonathan's Mother: Rabbi Jonathan is a Babylonian rabbi living in the Land of Israel during the beginning of the third century CE. I can find no other reference for his mother.

Rav: third-century Babylonian rabbinic leader; a close colleague of Samuel.

Rava bar Zemina: third-century student of Rabbi Zeira; not much more is known about him other than his appearance in our story.

Sabbath: a day of rest commemorating the Seventh Day of Creation, observed from sundown Friday to sundown Saturday.

Sages: *Hazal* in Hebrew, an acronym for *Hakhameynu zikronam liv'raka*, meaning "Our wise men, may their memory be blessed," a general term referring to the rabbis and teachers from the final three hundred years of the Second Temple until the sixth century CE.

Samuel: a close colleague of Rav; the two are third-century Babylonian rabbis.

Samuel bar Nahmani, Rabbi: third-century sage from the Land of Israel, a master of the Aggadic teachings.

Sanhedrin: the ancient Rabbinical Supreme Court, comprising seventy members, administered by the Nasi and headed by the Av Bet Din. The Sanhedrin interpreted the Written and Oral Law, enacting new rabbinical decrees. As the community in Yavneh flourished, after the fall of the Temple, it eventually formed a new Sanhedrin. Due to Roman persecution, the Sanhedrin moved first to the Galilee and then to nine other locations until it settled in Tiberias in 195 CE.

School of Hillel/School of Shammai: schools of opposing thought founded by Hillel and Shammai, prominent sages from the first century BCE. Over three hundred debates between the two schools are recorded in the Talmud. Though, in the main, rabbinic practice follows the rulings of the School of Hillel, the legal opinions of both schools are considered to be the words of the living God.

Sepphoris: a town in the central Galilee of Israel, four miles or so from Nazareth. Today it's called Tzipori.

Shavuot: celebrated on the sixth day of the month Sivan, the holiday commemorates the giving of the Torah on Mount Sinai. It is one of the three biblically mandated pilgrimage festivals.

Shechem: north of Bethel and Shiloh, on the high road from Jerusalem to the north, the town is the location of many biblical scenes, including Abraham's sacrifice in Genesis 12 and the avenging of the rape of Dinah in Genesis 34.

Shekinah: from the Hebrew "to dwell," the word refers to the Divine Presence in the natural world.

Sh'ma: a statement in the liturgy, derived from Deuteronomy 6:4–9, recited twice daily, affirming the oneness of God.

Supernal Orchard: Pardes in Hebrew; in the sort of Joycean pun loved by the sages, Pardes is an acronym for a four-tiered system of biblical analysis: Peshat (the simple meaning), Remez (the hidden or symbolic meaning), Derash (the midrashic meaning), and Sod (the secret or mystical meaning). The word appears three times in the Bible, in Song of Songs (4:13), Ecclesiastes (2:5), and Nehemiah (2:8), where it means "garden" or "park." In English, the word paradise is derived from it. The Talmud associates it with the Garden of Eden, in both its earthly and heavenly forms: hence, a deep understanding of Torah is the mystical doorway into paradise.

Tarfon, Rabbi: a colleague of Rabbi Akiva, a student of Rabban Yohanan ben Zakkai, active in the first and second centuries CE.

Temple: The first Temple, built by King Solomon, was destroyed in 586 BCE. Rebuilt in the sixth century BCE, it stood until 70 CE, when it was destroyed by the Roman army. In the rabbinic mind, the Temple is the place where Heaven and earth meet.

Tiberias: a city on the western shore of the Sea of Galilee, established in 20 CE. Today it's called Tiveriah.

Torah: literally, "the Teaching," the term refers specifically to the Five Books of Moses, but can expand to include the entire Bible with its commentaries, the Talmud, and all of rabbinic literature up to the present moment.

Ulla: fourth-century rabbi who traveled between Babylonia and the Land of Israel. He died unhappily in Babylonia.

Valley of Gennesar: a plain on the western side of the Sea of Galilee.

Vespasian: Roman emperor from 69 to 79 CE. As a legate, or general, in the Roman military, he oversaw the subjugation of Judea during the rebellion of 66 CE.

World to Come: the afterlife. Though a thorough cartography of the Jewish afterlife is available in the mystic literatures, the Bible and the Talmud are, at best, vague on the subject. The rabbinic view is playfully ambivalent: "One hour of repentance and good deeds in this world is better than the entire life of the World to Come; and one hour of bliss in the World to Come is better than the entire life of this world" (*Ethics of the Fathers*, 4:22).

Yavneh: one of the major ancient cities in the southern coastal plain of the Land of Israel, south of Jaffa and north of Ashdod. After the destruction of the Second Temple in 70 CE, Rabban Yohanan ben Zakkai moved the Sanhedrin, the Supreme Rabbinical Court, to Yavneh. As of this writing, the city is a part of modern Israel.

Yossi bar Judah of Kfar HaBavli, Rabbi: dates unknown; the single teaching quoted in his name is all that remains of him.

Zeira, Rabbi: third-century Babylonian rabbi, he later moved to the Land of Israel.

Zohar: literally, *The Book of Splendor*, the principal text of Jewish mysticism. Tradition ascribes its authorship to Rabbi Shimon bar Yohai, modern scholarship to thirteenth-century Spain.